Hezbollah

To Nur, who made this and other adventures possible

Hezbollah

Socialisation and its Tragic Ironies

Adham Saouli

EDINBURGH
University Press

Edinburgh University Press is one of the leading university presses in the UK. We publish academic books and journals in our selected subject areas across the humanities and social sciences, combining cutting-edge scholarship with high editorial and production values to produce academic works of lasting importance. For more information visit our website: edinburghuniversitypress.com

Edinburgh University Press Ltd
The Tun – Holyrood Road
12 (2f) Jackson's Entry
Edinburgh EH8 8PJ

Typeset in 11/15 Adobe Garamond by
Servis Filmsetting Ltd, Stockport, Cheshire,
and printed and bound in Great Britain

A CIP record for this book is available from the British Library

ISBN 978 1 4744 1950 5 (hardback)
ISBN 978 1 4744 1951 2 (paperback)
ISBN 978 1 4744 1952 9 (webready PDF)
ISBN 978 1 4744 1954 3 (epub)

Published with the support of the University of Edinburgh Scholarly Publishing Initiatives Fund.

Contents

Acknowledgements

This book is the culmination of over fifteen years of research on and observations of Hezbollah. The first time I attempted to examine Hezbollah was during my graduate studies at the American University of Beirut. I confidently argued that the Islamist-Lebanese movement is a realist, pragmatist political actor that is in a ceaseless 'quest for survival' (Saouli 2003). Over the years, however, I modestly came to realise that I had merely scratched the surface of Hezbollah. Hezbollah's pragmatism, I gradually came to find, is the tip of an ideological iceberg. Its quest for survival is but one element of an unrelenting strategic vision that has shaped the Islamist movement's development since its secret birth in 1982. I gradually found myself disenchanted with several dichotomies that overshadow studies on Hezbollah, such as: pragmatist versus ideological; context versus ideology; or politics versus violence. Instead, I was drawn to studying *socialisation*: how political actors seek to be part of, alter or preserve socio-political contexts. Socialisation acts as a mechanism to mediate these supposed dichotomies. In this book I examine the origins of Hezbollah's socialisation and the unintended, tragic consequences it has generated.

Writing this book would not have been possible without the contributions of several people. I express my gratitude to Moutaz Alkheder for his diligent and meticulous research assistance. I thank Faye Donnelly, Vassilis Paipais, Bashir Saade and members of the International Relations Research Group at the University of St Andrews for reading and commenting on parts of the book. A special thanks to Bashir Saade, a friend and a fellow student of Hezbollah, for the many stimulating discussions and the frequent disagreements. I am grateful to Vassilis Paipais, a close friend and colleague, for engaging my work; Vas's expansive knowledge on the tragic ironies of politics has provoked hitherto latent ideas in my thinking. I am indebted to Haytham Mouzahem, Rami Siklawi, Talal Atrissi and Rabie Barakat for their friendship, insights and generous support during my fieldwork in Lebanon. I appreciate and thank all the interviewees for the time they offered me. I also want to thank the two anonymous reviewers of this work for their constructive feedback. I thank the Edinburgh University Press team – Nicola Ramsey, Eddie Clark, Rebecca Mackenzie and Kirsty Woods – and value all the hard work they have done to publish this work. Notwithstanding these significant contributions, I am alone responsible for the lines that will follow.

Finally a word of gratitude to my wonderful family of friends in Edinburgh: Alain, Farah, Julie, Mathias, Michelle, Mihaela, Nicola, Ryan and Sossie. And, last but not least, to Sami, whose own beautiful socialisation brings joy to our life.

Adham Saouli
Edinburgh and St Andrews, 2018

Abbreviations

APM	Armed Political Movement
d.	died
FM	Future Movement
FPM	Free Patriotic Movement
HS	Historical Sociology
IDF	Israel Defence Force
IRG	Islamic Revolutionary Guard
IS	Islamic State
LCP	Lebanese Communist Party
LF	Lebanese Forces
lit.	literally
NSC	National Salvation Committee
PLO	Palestine Liberation Organisation
PSP	Progressive Socialist Party
r.	reigned
SLA	South Lebanon Army
SSNP	Syrian Social National Party

Glossary of Arabic Terms

Ahl al-Bayt: clan of the Prophet, Banu Hashim and (according to Shi'a belief) the Twelve Imams that followed

Ashura: tenth day of Muharram; also, the annual commemoration of the martyrdom of Imam Hussein

bala': suffering; also God's testing for His believers

faqih: jurisprudent or juris consult

fatwa (pl. *fatawa*): religious edict

fiqh: Islamic jurisprudence

fitnah: sedition, strife

Ghadir Khumm: the place where Shi'as believe Prophet Muhammad announced Imam Ali as his successor; *Ghadir Day* is commemorated annually

ghaybah: occultation

Hadith: sayings and deeds of Prophet Muhammad

harakiyyah: religio-political activism

hawzah: religious seminaries

Hayhat min al-zillah: Imam Hussein's slogan: 'we reject, or would never accept, humiliation'

Imamah: leadership of Ali and his descendants, the Twelve Shi'a Imams

kufr: rejection of religion

al-Mahdi: the Messiah; the awaited Imam who, according to Shi'a belief, is now in occultation and will return to bring justice to the world

majalis (sing. *majlis*): councils or congregations

al-Mumahhidun: those who pave the way for the return of *al-Mahdi*

Sayyid: a descendent of the Prophet through his daughter Fatimah

shahadah: martyrdom

Shari'ah: Islamic law derived from the Qur'an and *Hadith*
takfiris: Islamic jihadist groups that delineate religious and political opponents as *kafirs* (unbelievers) enabling their persecution
Taklif Shari'i: religious assigning or commissioning (by God or the *faqih*)
tamhid: preparing or paving the way for the return of *al-Mahdi*
'*ulama* (sing. *'alim*): Islamic religious scholars
Ummah: the Islamic community, which transcends territorial and ethnic boundaries
wilayah: religio-political authority and/or leadership
Wilayat al-Faqih: The Guardianship or Governance of the Islamic Jurist

Introduction: Mask or Mirror?

Do you find Hezbollah's behaviour perplexing? If so, you might not be alone. Since announcing itself to the world in 1985, Hezbollah has not fallen short of surprising friends, foes and observers. In 1990 one observer envisaged that the Islamist movement would have 'no place' in post-war Lebanon and that it would not able to 'rid South Lebanon of all Israeli political and military influence' (Kramer 1990: 156). By 2000, however, Hezbollah had completed a decade-long successful integration into Lebanon's multi-sectarian political system. In May of the same year, it claimed victory for driving Israel out of the country.

Hezbollah's integration in Lebanon and adoption of Lebanese symbols and discourse challenged the perceptions of foes who demonised the movement as a 'terrorist' organisation and an 'Iranian puppet'. Many celebrated the Islamist movement's 'Lebanonisation': the transformation of the Islamist movement from a violent, revolutionary organisation to a pragmatist political party. Hezbollah's survival in the July War of 2006 not only surprised Israel, but also earned the Shi'a-Islamist movement unprecedented popularity in the Arab and Muslim worlds. During and after the war, pictures of its charismatic leader, Sayyid Hassan Nasrallah, dominated Arab cities from Rabat to Sana'a. According to polls of this period, Nasrallah was the most popular figure in the Arab world; it was claimed that 124 newborns were named Nasrallah in the Egyptian city of Alexandria ('Arab Neighbours Thinking Ahead' 2006).

But it did not take long before Hezbollah broke the mould. In May 2008, in response to a government decision to dismantle Hezbollah's vital telecommunications network, Hezbollah violently attacked pro-government militias and swiftly gained control of West Beirut. The move disrupted

Hezbollah's self-restrained behaviour in post-war Lebanon and discredited the armed movement's consistent pledge to refrain from employing its weapons domestically. The move aroused sectarian fears in Lebanon's divided society and evoked controversies about Hezbollah's 'true' identity and motives. Critics accused the movement of aiming to seize power to gradually Islamise Lebanon; the intervention, they insisted, refutes the idealisation of Hezbollah as a Lebanonised, pragmatic political actor. Hezbollah, on the other hand, legitimised its 2008 military intervention in Lebanon as a necessary means to protect its military resistance against Israel. But a salient feature of the 2008 episode was Hezbollah's actual abstention from seizing power, despite its military capability. To the chagrin of its passionate allies, Hezbollah then agreed to join its rivals in a national unity government.

Then came the Syrian uprising in 2011. By 2012, the regime of President Bashar Assad was crumbling, leading many to gamble on its demise. Hezbollah disagreed. To the shock of friends and foes, in 2013 Hezbollah announced its military intervention in Syria. As with previous junctures in the movement's life, Hezbollah's crossing of the border to fight in Syria raised many questions and controversies about its political identity, motivations and behaviour.

Hezbollah's critics accused it of hypocrisy, moral bankruptcy and sectarianism. Military intervention in Syria, they maintained, demystified Hezbollah's alleged 'Lebanonisation', affirming the Shi'a movement's loyalty to the Islamic Republic and Assad's Alawite regime. Hezbollah's silence towards and military involvement in Assad's repression of his people refuted the Islamist party's struggle for freedom against occupation and oppression. One observer argued that 'when a so-called resistance movement fails to support a bottom-up popular revolt against a tyrant, its leaders expose themselves as hypocrites' (Sadiki 2011). Sheikh Yousef al-Qaradawi, an influential Sunni preacher and a former advocate of Hezbollah, described it as 'the party of Satan', adding that: 'I defended the so-called Nasrallah and his party, the party of tyranny . . . in front of clerics in Saudi Arabia . . . it seems that the clerics [harsh critics of Hezbollah] of Saudi Arabia were more mature than me' (Allam 2013). The fame and legitimacy Hezbollah garnered in the Arab world after the Israeli withdrawal from Lebanon in 2000 and the 2006 war waned.[1]

But Hezbollah was not apologetic. It was adamant and confident – or so it appeared: 'Everyone who criticized us for participating in the Syrian war will thank us some day', Nasrallah retorted ('Hassan Nasrallah, 25 May 2013' n.d.). He contended that the military intervention was necessary to protect Assad's regime, a pivotal member of the Resistance Alliance, and to safeguard Lebanon from the lethal threat of al-Qaida-inspired Islamist-jihadists, such as the Islamic State (IS) and Jabhat al-Nusra. The threat was 'existential'; the intervention necessary ('Hassan Nasrallah, 25 May 2013' n.d.).

Hezbollah's development since its birth in 1982 has ignited political and scholarly controversies. Not surprisingly, its political trajectory defies dominant explanations. This is not the predictably linear development of a religious movement that surrenders its ideology as it adapts to political realities. Ideology certainly shapes Hezbollah's behaviour. Nor is Hezbollah's trajectory purely shaped by ideology; socio-political contexts have with no doubt left their imprint on the Islamist movement. So, how are we to understand and explain Hezbollah's political trajectory, or what I prefer to treat in this book as *socialisation*: the origins and consequences of social actors' attempts to be part of, alter or preserve socio-political life. Hezbollah's long-term socialisation has inspired me to examine three key questions: What motivates Hezbollah's socialisation? How did Hezbollah socialise in the varying arenas of Lebanon and the Middle East region? And what are the strategic, political and ethical consequences of Hezbollah's socialisation process?

However, as you go through this Introduction you might still want to ask: Why another book on Hezbollah? Are the tens of available books and hundreds of articles not sufficient to address our curiosities about this Islamist movement? Perhaps. But delving into the literature (many of the Arabic and English works that I could put my hands on), I remained curious about the effect religious doctrine has on political behaviour, and vice-versa; about how Hezbollah's socialisations in Lebanon and the Middle East have moulded its social image and political attitudes; and on how political actors, such as Hezbollah, get entrapped in contexts and situations not of their own choosing. The rest of this Introduction and book, I hope, will show why the effort was worthwhile.

One Trajectory, Two Interpretations, Three Gaps

Students of Hezbollah agree on two aspects of the Islamist movement's political trajectory. First, that Hezbollah successfully managed to evolve from a narrow, revolutionary, ideological, violent and Islamist movement in the 1980s to become a moderate and pragmatic political actor in the 1990s. Hezbollah, they observe, successfully adapted to changing domestic and regional conditions in the early 1990s to become a political party, to run for elections, to enter into coalitions, to provision social services and to finally join government in 2005. Second, most scholars accept that this transformation should be juxtaposed against and explained in relation to Hezbollah's inceptive ideal of establishing an Islamic state in Lebanon (Norton 2014; Berti 2013; Qazzi 2013; Abboud and Muller 2012; Wiegand 2010; Alagha 2011; Norton 2007; Alagha 2006; Harik 2005; Hamzeh 2004; Saouli 2003; Saad-Ghorayeb 2002; Jaber 1997; Ranstorp and Waite 2003; Hamzeh 1993; Kramer 1990).

But it is here where the consensus among scholars draws to an end. What then divides scholars relates to the causes and implications of Hezbollah's transformation: Is the transformation a mask that conceals Hezbollah's true political intentions? Or is it a mirror of the changing political conditions that Hezbollah adapts to?

Proponents of the transformation-as-a-mask interpretation argue that regardless of its choices – be they revolutionary or pragmatic, political or violent – Hezbollah's 'ultimate goal is the same: to seize political power and establish an Islamic order' (Hamzeh 2004: 4; Qazzi 2013: 22; Khatib 2011: 63, 67; Badran 2009; Ranstorp and Waite 2003: 52; Sharara 2007). Political integration was 'another step on the path toward realising the movement's long-term goal of ruling Lebanon' (Azani 2011: 75). Hezbollah's strategy is to 'undermine' the state and to weaken, co-opt or isolate Lebanon's Sunnis to ultimately control the country (Khashan 2013; Gleis and Berti 2012: 49; Badran 2009). Hezbollah's military resistance against Israel, the argument goes, conceals the 'parallel state' which Hezbollah has built and is one that it uses to blackmail its opponents (Qazzi 2013: 28). As such, Hezbollah does not want to integrate in Lebanon; rather, it wants to submit others into its 'totalitarian vision of the "Resistant Society"' (Badran 2009: 61–2).

Do not be fooled, one proponent warns, by the so-called 'Lebanonisation' of or 'shifts' in Hezbollah's ideology: Hezbollah is a 'Lebanese mask of an Iranian *wilayah* [religio-political authority]'; its political project transcends the national boundaries of Lebanon (Qazzi 2013).

On the other hand, proponents of the transformation-as-a-mirror argue that Hezbollah has indeed 'shifted' its ideology and 'transformed' its behaviour. In post-war Lebanon, Hezbollah 'had to shelve aspiration for an Islamic Republic ruled by Muslim religious law' and to 'reform' its behaviour by giving up violence (Harik 2005: 47; Berti 2013; Abboud and Muller 2012: vii; Alagha 2011; Wiegand 2010: 113; Alagha 2006: 36–7; Norton 2014: 6; Wiegand 2010: 113; Balkiz 2006: 36; Saad-Ghorayeb 2002: 26–7). A study on Hezbollah's international socialisation observed that the Islamist movement transformed its political identity 'from a fundamentalist emphasis on pan-Islamic conception of Umma . . . to the Lebanese nation' (Dionigi 2014: 169).

But what happened to Hezbollah's ideology in the course of this transformation? For some, despite Hezbollah's adherence to its religious ideology, it 'does not place precedence on theological over the political as do societal/civil groups'. The party has successfully managed to reconcile its religious ideals to Lebanon's political context (Saad-Ghorayeb 2002: 37, 187; Balkiz 2006: 48; Wiegand 2010: 97). For others, Hezbollah's principles have 'shifted'; its 'Open Letter' (Hezbollah's founding manifesto) has become 'obsolete': 'From a Realpolitik perspective, Hezbollah reconstructed its identity, altered its political strategy'. Make no mistake, one scholar asserts, 'Hezbollah changes as circumstances change' (Alagha 2011: 17).[2]

Three gaps

The literature on Hezbollah evokes interesting questions on political and ideological change (or its lack thereof) and, by association, on the power or powerlessness of actors to realise their goals in constraining contexts. But the way the debate has developed obfuscates interesting dimensions about the Islamist movement's motives and, by consequence, its ideology and behaviour.

First, by juxtaposing Hezbollah's transformation against the ideal of seeking an Islamic state in Lebanon, the literature, I find, has diverted our attention from another crucial driving force for Hezbollah: war-making with Israel. Regardless of its stated or, for the sake of argument, hidden politico-religious goals, war-making – the occasional engagement in and constant preparation for war – has driven Hezbollah's behaviour since its birth. In this book I will illustrate how this motive explains better the Islamist movement's socialisation in Lebanon and the region than the speculation about Hezbollah's goals.[3]

Second, the current debate obscures important questions regarding Hezbollah's ideology and political practice. For the proponents of the transformation-as-a-mirror, Hezbollah has moved from an 'exclusivist religious ideology' to a 'political ideology' to a 'down-to-earth political program' (Alagha 2006: 191); 'The political', thus, 'is the master of all concerns for Hezbollah' (Saad-Ghorayeb 2002: 38). On the other hand, for the proponents of the transformation-as-a-mask, Hezbollah's politics directly flow from its ideology: 'Everything for Hezbollah – society, culture, economy, politics, alliances, media – is in the service of the totalitarian vision of the "Resistant Society"', which is directly tied to *Wilayat al-Faqih* (Badran 2009: 62; Qazzi 2013).

Thus, whilst the former place most of the analytical weight on political contexts, the latter focus on religious ideology to explain Hezbollah's political behaviour. But in doing so, both interpretations wrongly assume the existence of two distinct spheres: an 'ideological' and a 'political'; as such, they leave us wondering about the relationship between ideology and political practice and vice-versa (Knio 2013; Harb and Leenders 2005: 185). Such treatments omit interesting empirical questions that may explain Hezbollah's socialisation: What is the *role* of ideology in Hezbollah's political calculations, pragmatism and war-making efforts? On the other hand, how do political contexts *enable* or *constrain* Hezbollah's realisation of its religio-political goals?

It is interesting in this regard that Hezbollah's own narrative about its political trajectory makes the understanding of the relationship between ideology and political practice even more ambiguous (H. Fadlallah 2015: 40; Abu Rida 2012: 346; Qassem 2008a).[4] For example, when asked about Hezbollah's 2009 political manifesto and the lack of reference to religious doctrines (*Wilayat al-Faqih* or Islamic Government), Nasrallah replied that 'the document did not address religious and ideological doctrines because these are not open for debate' (Qazzi 2013: 39).[5] Nasrallah's answer highlights a dichotomy between the political and the ideological, making debates about Hezbollah's 'transformation' even more complex. It is not a coincidence that Hezbollah's observers drew two conflicting conclusions relating to its 2009 political document: whilst some saw it as 'ground-breaking' (Alagha 2011: 31–2), others believed it offered 'nothing' novel (Qazzi 2013: 39). The analytical link between ideology and political behaviour, however, remains to be established.

Third, emanating from the two previous points, is the obscurity on what Hezbollah is and does. In the early stages, in attempts to debunk political arguments, the literature devoted a lot of attention to illustrate whether Hezbollah is a 'terrorist' or 'resistance' movement (for a useful discussion see Harb and Leenders 2005; Harik 2005: Chapter 11).[6] But this political controversy came at the expense of establishing analytical links between politics and violence. As with the ideology/political dichotomy, the literature assumed two distinct spheres: politics and violence. According to one interpretation, Hezbollah is a 'jihadi movement that engages in politics, not a political party that does jihad' (Hamzeh 2004: 44). For another it is a 'pragmatist terrorist organization' (Azani 2011: 246). With its political integration in Lebanon, Hezbollah appears to have 'two contradictory faces' (Wiegand 2010: vii; Badran 2009). By joining the government in 2005, Hezbollah became 'an ordinary political party' (Berti 2013: 65). For a veteran Lebanese writer and politician, Hezbollah's 'ideology descended [when its] armed resistance ascended' (Pakradouni 2015).

But can politics be separated from violence? Is it sufficient to argue that Hezbollah does both – politics and violence – depending on circumstances (Berti 2013: 25; Wiegand 2010: 2; Hamzeh 2004: 80)? As I will illustrate in this book, war-making with Israel, and this factor's implications on Hezbollah's domestic and regional socialisations, makes the separation between politics and violence analytically irrelevant (see also Abboud and Muller 2012; Saouli 2011; Sadiki 2010; Harb and Leenders 2005). As such, Hezbollah's so-called 'hybrid' nature will appear less as Janus-faced and more consistent with the movement's purposeful socialisation.

Socialisation and its Tragic Ironies

In this book I will address these three gaps, but this is not my primary intention. My overarching aim is to present a historical sociology of Hezbollah that traces the movement's socialisation process from its early days up until 2017. This is, however, not a history of the movement. The purpose of this process-tracing, summarised in Figure I.1 below, and explicated theoretically in Chapter 1 (*On Socialisation and its Discontents*), is to examine the origins of Hezbollah, the causes of its socialisation process and the effects this process had on Hezbollah's political goals, its social image and ethical foundations. I draw on International Relations (IR) and Sociological theories to account for this long-term process. To explain Hezbollah's trajectory, I develop the concept of *socialisation* that suits the purpose of this study and which transcends the state-focused treatments in IR (Thies 2012; Flockhart 2006; Alderson 2001; Finnemore and Sikkink 1998) or the individual-focused ones in Political Sociology (Niemi and Hepburn 1995; Long and Hadden 1985).

This study is based on more than fifteen years of observing Hezbollah. I draw most of the empirical material from primary and Arabic sources, which include: semi-structured interviews; speeches, communiqués and writings of Hezbollah leaders; testaments of Hezbollah fighters; and documentaries.[7]

I conceptualise Hezbollah as an Armed Political Movement (APM). I argue that war-making with Israel – not the ideal of establishing an Islamic state – has motivated Hezbollah's socialisation process. War-making with Israel has placed the Islamist movement at the juncture of two interdependent arenas, which I theoretically depict in Chapter 1 as *Anarchical Orders*: Lebanon and the Middle East region. Hezbollah's socialisation in these arenas took varying shapes. After carving for itself a place during Lebanon's civil war, Hezbollah aimed to maintain domestic stability as a strategic necessity in its war with Israel. In Chapter 3 (*Hezbollah Makes War, War Makes Hezbollah*), I show that Hezbollah in 1990–2008 rationalised its behaviour, exercising political prudence and self-restraint, especially in the use of violence. This process also involved *social re-presentation* of its identity: Hezbollah adopted a Lebanese discourse, muting its Islamist ideals, and attempted to blend its political goals with Lebanon's national interests.

But in this process, Hezbollah's ideology, or what I specify in this study as *religio-political doctrine*, did not dissolve. I show in Chapter 2 (*Being Hezbollah*) that Hezbollah's religio-political doctrine is the backbone of the movement's being, offering religious meaning to what it is and does. Whilst the doctrine does not directly determine Hezbollah's short-term political goals, it offers the framework of its strategic goals. Hezbollah's doctrine shapes its organisational structure and directly contributes to its war-making effort, recruitment and indoctrination of fighters, political mobilisation and international alliances. Hezbollah has disseminated its doctrine among Lebanon's Shi'a – an Islamisation from below – creating a social base, as I illustrate in Chapters 2 and 3. This social base offers Hezbollah a socio-political *springboard* to realise its long- and short-term political goals within and outside Lebanon.

Religio-political doctrine and war-making with Israel have also shaped Hezbollah's perception of and socialisation in the international sphere, as I show in Chapter 4 (*War-making as International Socialisation*). A product of war-making with Israel and influenced by the Islamist revolutionary ideals of its predecessors, Hezbollah perceives the international system as an arena of war: one that divides the world between the forces of good and evil. As a member of the Shi'a-Islamist transnational and trans-historical movement, Hezbollah believes that it is preparing the ground for the return of the awaited *al-Mahdi* (the twelfth Shi'a Imam that is now in occultation). Hezbollah, I find, has not departed from the goals and ideals it set in its founding manifesto of 1985. It still hopes to rid Lebanon and the region from Israeli and Western influence. To realise its goals, Hezbollah has maintained an alliance of *interdependence* with Syria's Assad and its religio-political patron, the Islamic Republic of Iran. In the war with Israel (and the US) and its regional rivals, Hezbollah has promoted the culture and discourse of resistance.

Observing Hezbollah's long-term socialisation, I find that the Islamist movement's behaviour is characterised by continuous attempts to, first, *overcome* political constraints and perceived threats and, second, to *capitalise* on emerging opportunities to advance its strategic goals. Chapters 3 and 4 show that Hezbollah has attempted to increase its political influence in domestic and international arenas, by exercising either restraint or violence when needed.

However, Hezbollah's socialisation did not come without its discontents, as I show in Chapter 5 (*Tragic Ironies*). War-making with Israel and Hezbollah's urge to maintain its regional alliance has required constant military preparation and religio-political mobilisation, effectively transforming Hezbollah from a small armed guerrilla movement in the 1980s into a regional force in 2017. This military and political growth, nevertheless, generated tensions in Lebanon's divided society. Discursive and political attempts by Hezbollah's rivals to curb its power within Lebanon and, consequently, its own attempts to defend itself, generated *security paradoxes* since 2005. Despite Hezbollah's best efforts, these developments politically paralysed Lebanon in the period 2005–16 and deepened the sectarian, especially Sunni–Shi'a, divide.

Hezbollah's socialisation, I also find, generated ethical questions for the Islamist movement. To protect its strategic regional interests, Hezbollah intervened militarily in Syria in 2012 in support of Assad's authoritarian regime; but this questioned its belief in the struggle for freedom against oppression. Not without a twist of irony, Hezbollah began to reproduce the discourse its enemies have used to justify their own actions against it. Military interventions in Syria, but also in Iraq and Yemen, became 'pre-emptive' actions to deter 'terrorists'; defending the 'national interest', argued one Hezbollah member, should transcend national boundaries (H. Fadlallah 2015). These outcomes, I argue, amount to a 'tragic irony' (Niebuhr 1952): the *unintended* consequences of social actors' attempts to survive in the political world not of their own choosing. Hezbollah's religio-political doctrine and war-making with Israel, I find, has set it on a path-dependent trajectory that interlocked it with allies (especially Iran and Assad's Syria). By 2017, Hezbollah's socialisation exposed the Islamist movement's incongruous behaviour: for many years Hezbollah perceived itself as the victim of oppression and a liberation movement in search for freedom but had now become a target of its critics as an 'occupying' power in Syria. The book explains this outcome by showing how the international *anarchic* order conforms actors according to its own dictates (Waltz 1979).

I present my findings and interpretation of Hezbollah's socialisation in five chapters that are divided thematically and chronologically. In Chapter 1 (*On Socialisation and its Discontents*), I lay the theoretical foundations of my approach – general readers and theory-sceptics may wish to skip this chapter! In Chapter 2 (*Being Hezbollah*), I focus on Hezbollah's religio-political

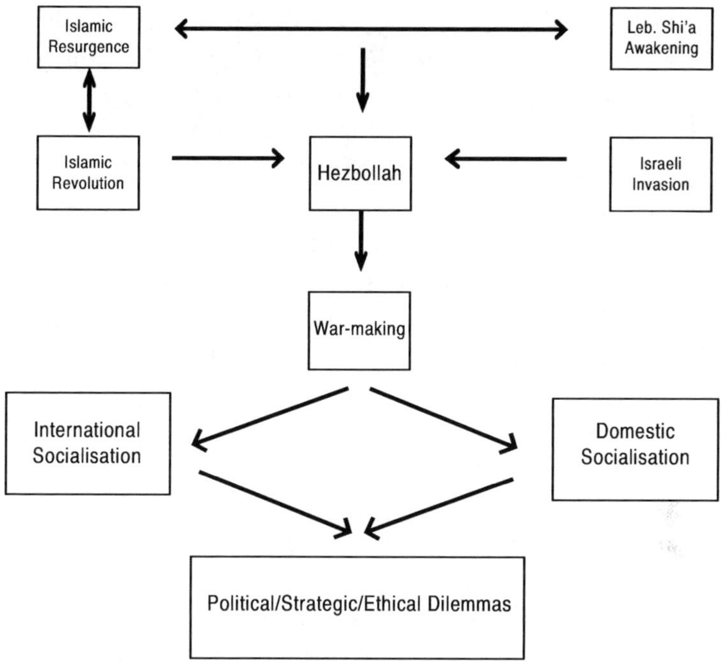

Figure I.1 A historical sociology of Hezbollah

identity, its birth (1978–85) and organisational structure. I also offer an elaborate definition of Hezbollah as an APM. In Chapter 3 (*Hezbollah Makes War, War Makes Hezbollah*), I show how religio-political identity and war-making with Israel have moulded Hezbollah's socialisation in the domestic arena in the period 1985–2005. Chapter 4 (*War-making as International Socialisation*) shifts the analysis to Hezbollah's international socialisation. I examine Hezbollah's perception of the international system, its main wars with Israel and international alliances. In the final chapter (*Tragic Ironies*), I focus on the period 2005–17 and show how domestic-external factors intertwined to generated security paradoxes and ethical quandaries for the Islamist movement.

Notes

1. According to a survey that was published on 7 June 2013 by the Pew Research Centre, a majority in Turkey (73 per cent), Egypt (75 per cent), Jordan (72 per cent) and Lebanon (59 per cent) viewed Hezbollah 'unfavourably'. Results

are found at <http://www.pewresearch.org/fact-tank/2013/06/07/as-it-fights-in-syria-hezbollah-seen-unfavorably-in-region/> (last accessed 15 November 2015).

2. For Saade (2016: 142), since its establishment, Hezbollah's religious beliefs or what he calls 'Islamic practices were subordinate to the cause of armed struggle and not vice versa'.
3. The origins of this idea are found in my article 'Hezbollah in the Civilising Process: Anarchy, Self-Restraint and Violence' (Saouli 2011). Saad-Ghorayeb, whose work sheds important light on Hezbollah's 'political mind' (Saad-Ghorayeb 2002: 3), has shown, citing Hezbollah members, how the movement prioritises military resistance over other concerns (Chapter 6). Gleis and Berti also argue that 'Hezbollah's core raison d'etre lies in its "resistance" agenda with respect to Israel' (Gleis and Berti 2012: 53). But neither of these two works ties war-making to socialisation to explain Hezbollah's political trajectory.
4. Contrast with Harb and Leenders 2005 (186–93).
5. Unless otherwise indicated all translations from Arabic to English are the author's own.
6. Whilst the US considers Hezbollah a 'terrorist' movement, the EU treats Hezbollah's so-called 'military wing' as 'terrorist', but accepts its 'political wing' as legitimate. Hezbollah, however, does not recognise the presence of 'wings' in its organisational structure ('Hassan Nasrallah, Speech 25 July 2015' n.d.).
7. I have conducted seventeen semi-structured interviews in Beirut in the period 2013–15 with Hezbollah members, its allies, rivals and other neutral observers. I have examined a sample of thirty-three testimonies of Hezbollah fighters. See Appendix for the lists of interviewees and names of Hezbollah fighters.

1

On Socialisation and its Discontents

> The more matter-of-fact and calculating politics is, and the freer of passionate feelings, of wrath, and of love it becomes, the more it must appear to an ethic of brotherliness to be estranged from brotherliness.
>
> Max Weber, 'Religious Rejections of the World and their Directions'

'Men make their own history, but they don't make it just as they please', argued an angry Karl Marx, 'they do not make it under circumstances chosen by themselves, but under circumstances found, given and transmitted from the past' (Marx 1963: 15). Marx's observation is key to understand the genesis and socialisation of social actors. Whilst we have no choice about the social world we inherit, as social actors (individuals, groups or states) we have the desire and ambitions to, at least, seek survival in that world; or, for the more adventurous of us, to seek change in that world. As we seek a place in or a change of the social world, we establish relations of interdependencies with others (family, friends, enemies); we also encounter cultural (social, religious, normative), material (financial, coercive) and political contexts not of our own choosing. The interdependencies and the social contexts we find ourselves locked in can constrain or enable our attempts to achieve our goals. This process may generate intended and/or unintended consequences, which affect our social identity, reputation, ideology and behaviour. In this book, I interpret this process as 'socialisation': the causes and consequences of social actors' attempts to be part of, preserve, or alter social life.

This chapter serves as an analytical and conceptual framework for Hezbollah's socialisation and, simultaneously, as a structure for the book's main argument. I prioritise the theoretical over the empirical analysis;

subsequent chapters switch to the empirical analysis. Theoretical frameworks, observed Norbert Elias (Elias 1984: 160), are like maps. They

> show the connections between events which are already known. Like maps of unknown regions, they show blank spaces where the connections are not yet known. Like maps, they can be shown by further investigation to be false, and they can be corrected.

The framework is by necessity and design eclectic: it draws on International Relations (IR) theory, state theory and sociology. My choice is dictated by two considerations: a constraint and an opportunity.

The constraint is the object of this study, Hezbollah, which is at once a Lebanese political party, a member of a religio-political movement and an armed organisation. It is a domestic Lebanese political party and a transnational regional actor with state-like features. Hezbollah's identity, behaviour and socialisation process invite us to transcend the constraining divisions in the social sciences. I have found this indispensable when I examined the various fields to learn about socialisation. Where socialisation is invoked in IR the focus is mostly on states:[1] either on how socialisation in anarchy disciplines states and standardises their behaviour (Waltz 1979); or on how the internalisation of international norms in domestic structures contribute to a state's international socialisation (Thies 2012; Flockhart 2006; Alderson 2001; Finnemore and Sikkink 1998). In Political Sociology – the birthplace of socialisation – the focus is on the other extreme: the socialisation of individuals (Abrantes 2013; Niemi and Hepburn 1995). Despite its rich theoretical and empirical repertoires, the Social Movements literature has not devoted enough attention to the socialisation of social movements (Fillieule 2013: 968). In Political Science, the 'inclusion-moderation' framework explains how ideological parties moderate their behaviour and ideology as they are exposed to competitive and democratic politics (in European cases) or as a response to emerging opportunities in authoritarian systems (the Middle East) (Schwedler 2011; Tezcür 2010; Kalyvas 2000). Whilst useful, this theory is limited on two fronts. First, the focus on domestic politics restricts the understanding of Hezbollah's international socialisation. Second, Lebanon's quasi-democracy and its historically weak and externally penetrated state limit the applicability of the inclusion-moderation theory.

My second consideration, the opportunity, relates to the nature of the topic: socialisation. To examine socialisation, I draw on the rich intellectual tradition of Historical Sociology (HS). HS invites careful attention to historical processes, to contexts that constrain and enable actors' interactions and to the ideational and material factors that motivate actions. It explores the causes of historically grounded socio-political phenomena and events (such as industrialisation, state formation or revolution) and their effects on individuals and societies (Smith 1992; Abrams 1982). This tradition is particularly useful to examine Hezbollah as it 'attend[s] to the interplay of meaningful actions and structural contexts, in order to make sense of the unfolding of unintended as well as intended outcomes in individual lives and social transformations' (Skocpol 1984: 1). In this way HS offers the potential to transcend several dichotomies such as the actor/context, identity/interest or domestic/international that social scientists battle over.

A historical sociology of Hezbollah raises four questions that I will address in separate sections of this chapter. First, under what conditions do actors such as Hezbollah emerge? Second, what is Hezbollah? Both questions are crucial to examine a third one: what is socialisation and what motivated Hezbollah's specific socialisation? Finally, what are the intended and unintended strategic, political and ethical consequences of Hezbollah's socialisation?

Anarchical Orders

The world that gave rise to Hezbollah was far from Max Weber's ideal-type of the state: 'a human community that (successfully) claims the monopoly of the legitimate use of physical force within a given territory' (Weber 1978: 78). That world formed, and still forms, the nexus of two analytically distinguishable but empirically interconnected anarchical orders: Lebanon and the Middle East regional system. No adequate understanding of Hezbollah's socialisation, its identity, ideology, motives and behaviour would be possible without a clear understanding of these two orders. These are the social orders Hezbollah inherited and then sought to inhabit and reshape.

The concept of 'anarchical order' may at first appear as an oxymoron. But anarchical order is, rather, an IR principle on how the political world is arranged. Anarchy does not mean chaos. It refers to a world with no overarching power: no central government to impose rules, to discipline the actions of outlaws or to protect states from potential intruders. But there are various interpretations and types of this anarchical order, two of which will be useful for this study.[2]

The first, the Hobbesian interpretation, refers to a world characterised by 'enmity'. Vying actors do not recognise their mutual rights and fight to dictate their power and world visions over others. Realists, in varying degrees, belong to this category. They argue that states have no other option but to buttress their military and economic power in preparation for war (as the worst-case scenario). After all, they cannot be sure about the intentions of their rivals. The international system is one of self-help, they stress; a state's ultimate aim is to survive (Mearsheimer 2014; Walt 1990; Waltz 1979).

But where is 'order' in this gloomy world of the Realists? As more and more states increase their capabilities, Realists argue, they begin to check, deter, and balance against one another, creating an institution that Realists celebrate as the 'balance-of-power'. This institution might generate stability, despite the absence of an overarching central authority.

The second, a Lockean interpretation, depicts a world characterised by 'rivalry' rather than 'enmity'. Despite their differences, actors recognise the rights (of existence and of values) of their rivals. The idea is one of 'live and let live' (Wendt 1999: 281). Critics of Realism, such as the English School, Constructivism and Liberalism, accept this depiction of political order. They remind their dominant rival that there are other institutions that contribute to world order: international norms and law, such as the respect of territorial sovereignty and human rights, which states must adhere to; or economic integration and interdependencies that increase cooperation among states, regulate their interactions and decrease the likelihood of war. The international realm, thus, becomes more akin to an 'anarchical society' (Bull 2012), than a self-help system of greedy and war-hungry states.

Hezbollah's socialisation can be understood by locating the movement at the juncture of two anarchical orders: Lebanon, which I will depict as a Lockean anarchical order; and war-making with Israel, which pertains to a Hobbesian one. I emphasise, however, that I employ these categories as Weberian 'ideal-types',[3] not as concrete or reified historical realities or as 'cultures of anarchy'.[4] Locating Hezbollah at the crossroads of these two orders offers two advantages. First, it will contribute to understanding how Hezbollah's socialisation in the two orders varies; each order, I will show, constrains/enables Hezbollah's behaviour in specific ways and, thus, shapes it. Second, an analytical division and depiction of these orders will be necessary to show how socialisation in one order shapes socialisation in the other.

Lebanon as a Lockean anarchical order

The making of modern Lebanon was determined by colonial rivals' (France, Britain and Russia) attempts to establish spheres of influence in the post-Ottoman Middle East. This process did not instantly give rise to modern states, but rather it generated 'social fields' where states can form and deform (Saouli 2012: 8–28). These social fields had their boundaries. They included varying ethnic and sectarian compositions: some (such as Tunisia or Egypt) are homogeneous; others (such as Syria or Iraq) are heterogeneous. Some are endowed with natural resources (Saudi Arabia or Kuwait); others are poor (Jordan, Yemen). Some are located in strategic areas (Egypt, Syria, Iraq); others are more peripheral (Morocco, Tunisia). State-formation – the process of creating legitimate governments and institutions with a monopoly over coercion within demarcated and recognised political boundaries – trajectories varied (Saouli 2012: 8–68).

Lebanon had its own trajectory. Not only was the country divided on a religious and sectarian basis, but also its geopolitical location made it vulnerable to external political dynamics. Whilst in many Arab countries state-building involved the monopolisation of coercion and ideology by authoritarian regimes (until this trend was disrupted in the latest political awakening in 2011), in Lebanon the process was more inclusive of the country's various Muslim and Christian sectarian communities. This prevented the emergence of a domestic hegemon, producing a loosely knit consociational democracy: a political cohabitation that reflects Lebanon's divided society and the balance of power among its various communities (Fakhoury 2015). However, sectarian divisions over Lebanon's identity, its foreign policy and its power-sharing arrangements have regularly destabilised Lebanon (1958, 1975–90, 2005–8) (Saouli 2006).

Lebanon's anarchical order is akin to the Lockean variant. Various sectarian communities accept one another as rivals. Regardless of their religious belonging or political colour, they share a common Lebanese identity and institutional bonds. Formally, these bonds include state institutions and the constitution that acknowledges the rights of all sectarian communities.[5] Informally, there is a thick normative fabric that ties together these different communities. Political actors, at least publicly, must adhere to certain norms: that Lebanon is a religiously pluralistic country; that all communities should be represented in the state; that no community should dictate its religious or political vision on others; that political and religious freedoms should be upheld; and, similar to modern societies, that Lebanon should be a sovereign country.

With these institutional bonds, Lebanon settles one step away from the Hobbesian order, but it remains far from Max Weber's ideal-type state. Lebanon's communities are constantly anxious about their security and their share and representation in the state. Belonging to and fear for the community overrides national belonging. To survive, communal leaders penetrate state institutions; through patronage, they install their sectarian and political allies in powerful positions, generally under the pretext of 'equal' distribution of posts among religious communities. State institutions, which in theory should regulate social and political interactions and should be above and independent of various social actors, become private organs for political actors – but this is not very different from other states in their early formation (Saouli 2012: 49–68).

One of the paradoxes of Lebanon's political order is that various communities want to belong to the state, but also strive to maintain their own autonomy. This, as we shall see later, is crucial to understand Hezbollah's position in Lebanon. Through belonging, various communities preserve their own interests and representation in the state. But this is also important to keep the dominance of their rivals in check: namely, to prevent the rise of a hegemon that would otherwise challenge their autonomy. Belonging serves autonomy. But autonomy is reproduced in other ways too. By law religious communities have their councils, courts and charities that deal with personal (marriage, divorce, inheritance, etc.) and social affairs.[6] 'To secure loyalty', observes Brewer (Brewer 1991: 478), 'groups must not only satisfy members' needs for affiliation and belonging within the group, they must also maintain clear boundaries that differentiate them from other groups'.

Lebanon's Lockean anarchy sometimes erodes and gives way to an ugly Hobbesian one. Ties that bind can suddenly break; ties that separate can instantly harden. In the 1975–90 civil war, Lebanon divided territorially amongst its Muslim communities, urging political reform, and the Christian ones. Each community fabricated its own national myth and political vision; each had its various militias, political thugs and external patrons. Lebanon became a battlefield for external powers (Syria, Palestinians, Israel, US, Soviet Union and others). The long Lebanon war caused severe destruction and the loss of more than 200,000 lives (Khalaf 2004; El-Khazen 1997; Fisk 2001) – life seemed short, nasty and brutish!

This anarchical order made possible the secret emergence of Hezbollah in 1982. But it is also this order – in both its normative and institutional facets – that would condition Hezbollah's specific socialisation in Lebanon. Nonetheless, an understanding of this process will be limited if we do not examine Hezbollah's second realm of socialisation.

War-making with Israel as a Hobbesian anarchical order

One of the main arguments of this book is that Hezbollah's driving motive, which had important implications for its socialisation, is war-making with Israel. War-making, the occasional engagement in and constant preparation for war, locates Hezbollah in another anarchical order: the Middle East region.

The Middle East regional system is an extension of the international anarchic order (Saouli 2012; Halliday 2011; Hinnebusch 2015; Brown 1984). Its geopolitical location and natural resources have made it vulnerable to international rivalries. Since the weakening and later collapse of the Ottoman Empire, no state, whether internal or external to the region, has managed to establish hegemony. British and French colonial rivalries, as mentioned above, made possible the emergence of a regional states-system. But then the British-French domination (1920–45) gave way to that of the Soviet Union and the US (1945–90). Regional rivalries between status quo and revisionist regimes have contributed to the reproduction of the anarchical order. The Middle East remains one of the most war-prone regions. The region had one of the longest wars (Iran–Iraq, 1980–88), two international wars in the post-Cold War period (the first and second Gulf wars in 1990 and 2003, respectively) and several internationalised civil wars (North Yemen (1962–68), Lebanon (1975–90) and not least the ones that have erupted as a result of Arab uprisings: Syria (2012–), Libya (2013–) and Yemen (2014–)). However, the most enduring conflict remains the Arab–Israeli one (Schulze 2008). Depending on how you want to count, this conflict has generated over a dozen wars of varying natures and magnitudes: 1948, 1956, 1967, 1973, 1982, 1987, 1993, 1996, 2000, 2006, 2008, 2010/11 and 2014.

It is within the contours of the Middle East anarchical order and the Arab–Israeli conflict that Hezbollah's relationship with Israel can be understood. This relationship is one of enmity, ideological antagonism, uncertainty, self-help and, ultimately, war. It is not a state-to-state relationship; rather, it is between a state (Israel) and an armed political movement (Hezbollah) that operates within another state (Lebanon). The Israeli invasion of Beirut in 1982, which followed its occupation of a so-called 'security zone' in southern Lebanon in 1978, led many Lebanese armed organisations (Syrian Socialist Nationalist Party, Lebanese Communist Party, Amal Movement) to mobilise against the Israeli occupation. Hezbollah, not yet a fully fledged political organisation, was one of them.

Galvanised by the Israeli occupation of Lebanon and inspired by the Islamic Revolution in Iran, Hezbollah was 'born with vengeance' (Jaber 1997). A product of a collapsed state, Hezbollah, like all revolutionary movements, wanted to revise the order it perceived as 'unjust'. As I will show in the following chapters, the Islamist movement's religio-political repertoire converged with its construction of the anarchical order it inherited. In this order there is 'no place for the weak'; 'arrogant powers' (US and other Western powers) through their client regimes (Israel, Saudi Arabia and other Gulf states) intend to subjugate the region; Lebanon and Palestine, Hezbollah believed, cannot be liberated by mere words or through UN resolutions but through armed resistance.

The above two orders are the worlds that gave rise to Hezbollah and are ones that make the understanding of its socialisation intelligible. Before we explore what this socialisation entails, it is first crucial to examine the nature of the socialising actor: what is Hezbollah?

Being Hezbollah

Crucial as it is, this question has not drawn enough scholarly attention, as I complained in the Introduction to this book. Attention was devoted to answer a politically polarising but analytically irrelevant question (Harb and Leenders 2005; Harik 2005: Chapter 11): is Hezbollah a terrorist or resistance movement? This question, however, will not take us far: Hezbollah's supporters will naturally call it a resistance movement; Israel has no choice but to call it a terrorist movement. These political labels are part of the discursive battles associated with political contestations. 'Words' observes Sydney Tarrow 'are polysemic': 'their meaning changes in response to social change, political realignments, and cultural developments [. . .] words diffuse to different locales, where they are adopted by different agents for different purposes' (Tarrow 2012: 160).

Another main problem in conceptualising Hezbollah is that the literature tends to strip Hezbollah of its context and history. A fruitful conceptualisation of Hezbollah, however, is possible by contextualising the movement in its social milieu – the circumstances found, given and transmitted from the past – and by showing how and why its characteristics are similar or different to others.

My starting point is quite straightforward: Hezbollah resembles major political movements in Lebanon, which are products of the country's anarchical order. Hezbollah is an Armed Political Movement (APM). However, due to its war-making with Israel, Hezbollah differs from its Lebanese peers in the degree to which each of these elements constitutes and shapes the organisation's behaviour. Let me elaborate.

Hezbollah is an armed organisation. Armed organisations rise under conditions of state collapse when a ruling regime's legitimacy erodes, when its capacity to police and adjudicate social divisions diminishes and, ultimately, when its monopoly over coercion is challenged by contenders (such as revolutionary committees, courts or militias). The sense of insecurity that revolutionary situations or civil wars generate lead various groups to carry arms: to defend themselves, their communities and their territories; to advance their political programs; to deter their rivals or enemies; and, ultimately, to preserve or alter political regimes (Tilly 2006; Rotberg 2003; Zartman 1995).

In 1985, Hezbollah was one such example. The nascent movement was fighting for a place among Lebanon's warring political factions. The Lebanon war had generated many armed political actors such as the Lebanese Phalange and Lebanese Forces (Christian nationalist parties), the Progressive Socialist Party (PSP, a Druze-led party) and Amal (Hope, a Shi'a movement). Smaller parties such as the Syrian Social Nationalist Party and the Lebanese Communist Party were fighting for both a place in Beirut and, simultaneously, carrying military operations against Israel. All of these actors fought to monopolise coercion in Lebanon and to dictate their political visions. But these attempts failed to materialise until one actor, Syria, managed, thanks to enabling external factors, to impose its control over Lebanon. All Lebanese factions then surrendered some of their weapons and hid others. The Lebanese army and security forces, under Syrian supervision, were rebuilt. The monopolisation of coercion was restored.

However, by virtue of Israel's continued occupation of southern Lebanon and the Syrian–Iranian alliance, which had an interest to maintain pressure on Israel, Hezbollah continued to carry arms. It is here where we can demarcate a difference in degree between Hezbollah and other political factions. Hezbollah's war-making with Israel, as we shall see in later chapters, required constant innovation, growth and development in the armed movement's military capacity. The result was the emergence of a strong, armed political movement with a power surpassing other Lebanese groups and, possibly, the Lebanese National Army (H. Fadlallah 2015: 216) – this as we shall see below is a source of tension in Hezbollah's integration in Lebanon.

Hezbollah is also a political actor. Like all Lebanese political parties, Hezbollah has its political programme and, resembling its peers, it has with time acknowledged the difficulty of realising its political ideals in a divided society. In 1985, at the height of the Lebanon war, Hezbollah announced its political manifesto: it wanted to see Lebanon free from Israeli and Western influence and their domestic allies; it wanted to see an end to the 'abhorred' sectarian system; and, majority of Lebanese permitting, it would like to see an Islamic state. Hezbollah announced its identity: it belongs to a global Islamic movement led by Ayatollah Khomeini; it aspires to liberate Palestine and to support all the downtrodden in the world (for the manifesto see H. Fadlallah 1994).

Hezbollah's ideological connection to the Islamic Republic and its political ideals that transcend Lebanon's national boundaries have led some to treat Hezbollah as an outlier, an anomaly among Lebanon's movements. This is not accurate. We can identify at least three other movements in Lebanon whose political ideology transcends Lebanon's boundaries. Think of the Syrian Social Nationalist Party (SSNP), a political movement that believes in the establishment of greater Syria and has branches in that region (current Syria, Lebanon, Israel/Palestine, Jordan and even Cyprus). Another movement, represented by al-Jama'a al-Islamia (Islamist Association or Group), which is an offshoot the Egyptian Muslim Brotherhood, also believes in the unity of Muslim states. When it emerged in the 1950s, it aspired to see a return of the Caliphate (Elsässer 2007). A third movement is the Arab nationalist movement, which believes in the unity of Arab states and which generated several political organisations, such as the Ba'ath Party in Lebanon, the Nasserite Movement or the Mourabitoun.

But beyond these essentials, Hezbollah is different in important ways. Whilst other political organisations in Lebanon have boiled down to their self-obsessed political leaders, Hezbollah has produced a modern and politically institutionalised movement, with high levels of organisation, discipline and restraint. Despite the charisma and capacity of its leader, Hassan Nasrallah, the party continues to be led by a collective decision-making body, the Shura (Consultative) Council. Hezbollah's specialised units and party organs (military, security, external affairs, social services, research institutes, reconstruction, scouts and music bands) execute the party's political goals efficiently – you should not wonder if Hezbollah scares its rivals as a 'state within a state'!

War-making has also kept alive another feature that is essential to Hezbollah: religio-political doctrine. Whilst many political parties in Lebanon have surrendered their ideology to dusty manifestos, Hezbollah has made its religio-political doctrine the backbone of its war-making with Israel, as we shall see in the following chapters.

Last, but not least, Hezbollah differs in a major way from other Lebanese political parties. Most Lebanese factions focus their strategies on local and domestic issues; they usually adapt their domestic positions to changes at a regional and international levels (Saouli 2014c; Saouli 2006). Hezbollah is different. It is probably the only Lebanese party that acts on a *long-term* political strategy that transcends Lebanon's political borders. This strategy stems from Hezbollah's religio-political doctrine, war-making with Israel, and religio-political ties to the Islamic Republic – elements that are integral to understand Hezbollah's socialisation and ones that will be captured in the empirical analysis in the following chapters.

This brings us to the third element: movement. It is a mistake to conceptualise Hezbollah as a social movement (see for one example Azani 2011). Social movements are a form of collective action that originates outside institutional parameters with the aim of preserving or altering existing political structures or specific laws within them.[7] As an officially recognised Lebanese political party, Hezbollah does not qualify as a social movement that operates outside of state institutions. As an organised and highly structured political organisation, Hezbollah is different from social movements that form and operate with 'some degree of organization' (Snow, Soule, and Kriesi 2004: 11) but usually rely on 'improvisation' (Tilly 2006: 35). But, still, why insert 'movement' in conceptualising Hezbollah as an APM? I have two reasons.

First, whilst Hezbollah is not a social movement, it is a product and member of a broader religious movement. Hezbollah is one political manifestation of a broader (Shi'a) Islamist revivalist movement that emerged in the twentieth century (al-Sayed 2013). The progenitors of Islamist-Shi'a thought – Ayatollahs Khomeini, Mohammad Baqir al-Sadr and Mohammad Hussein Fadlallah – and Hezbollah *believe* that their movement is a *continuation* of a religious mission that starts with Prophet Muhammad, extends to his descendants (the twelve Imams) and one that will culminate with the return of the awaited twelfth Imam (*al-Mahdi*) (Qassem 2010a). This belief lies at the core of Hezbollah's religio-political doctrine, as I will show in Chapter 2, and one that makes Hezbollah a member of a transnational religious movement. The Islamic Revolution activated this mission on social, political and economic levels. Islamic Iran, with the *Wilayat al-Faqih* (Supreme Jurist)[8] at the helm, provided a strategic opportunity for the Lebanese movement. Ideologically, Hezbollah is *organically* connected to the *faqih*, who is perceived as the Deputy of the Hidden Imam, and abides by his religio-political authority. In that sense, Hezbollah is more than a political party, but is less than a religious or social movement.

Second, Hezbollah is also member of the Lebanese-Shi'a social movement (Atrissi 2012). Labelled by its founder, Sayyid Musa al-Sadr, as the 'Movement of the Deprived', this movement aspired for socio-political reforms and (further) Shi'a integration in the Lebanese state. Hezbollah is a product of and vehicle for this movement. Hezbollah's behaviour and worldviews are shaped by the socio-political grievances of Lebanon's Shi'as. Through its own religio-political doctrine, Hezbollah acts as a vehicle to address Shi'a socio-political grievances and to articulate political visions for the community. Hezbollah plays an important role in the political mobilisation of the Shi'a community, which forms the indispensable social base – a springboard – to realise Hezbollah's strategic goals.

Hezbollah's belonging to these two socio-religious movements is constitutive of its religious and social identity, and hence should be integral to any conceptualisation of this social actor as an APM. Put simply, Hezbollah's being is owed to these two movements.

The three elements (armed, political, movement) that make-up Hezbollah interweave; I split them here for purely analytical purposes. As the following chapters will attest, Hezbollah's military activity cannot be understood outside of its political ideals. In turn, these political ideals cannot be isolated from the religio-political beliefs that motivate Hezbollah. Finally, these religio-political beliefs require political actors to articulate and then transform – through organisation and mobilisation – into *political* goals.

However, by attempting to realise its ideals or, as Marx puts it, as it tries to make its own history, Hezbollah does so under conditions not of its own choosing, conditions which I depicted as anarchical orders. It is now the time to bring the actor, Hezbollah, and the anarchical orders together.

War-making as Socialisation

The analytical fusion of the actor and the social orders brings us to the heart of this book's topic: socialisation and (in the following section) its discontents. In IR socialisation focused on states and in Sociology on individuals, as I lamented above, leaving us with a gap when examining the socialisation of APMs, such as Hezbollah. For example, a standard definition of socialisation highlights:

> The ending process of individuals' participation in society and concomitant development of the self, composed by adjusted dispositions, values, ideologies, codes, and information which enables and fosters such participation. (Abrantes 2013: 393)

Political socialisation, specifically, is seen as 'the gradual development of the individual's own particular and idiosyncratic views of the political world, the process by which a given society's norms and behaviors are internalized' (Fillieule 2013: 968).

For the purposes of this study, however, the above definitions are limited. The focus on individuals assumes the presence of a passive social actor: an empty vessel that will participate in society and internalise its values and codes of behaviour.[9] But this contrasts with APMs, or any other type of political organisation, because APMs are not passive assimilators of existing social standards. APMs are carriers of worldviews and political ideals – the desire that transforms worldviews into political action (Gerth and Mills 1974: 280) – which not only make their genesis possible but are also ones that define them as social beings. They are active participants in the production and reproduction of social standards: some spill blood to keep certain socio-political values alive; others struggle to eradicate them from the face of the earth.

These limitations lead me to propose my own definition. Socialisation, I propose, is the purposeful participation of political actors in a society with the aim of integrating in, preserving or reforming existing power structures. The process involves participants' exposure to and interaction with existing political actors, institutions and social norms; this interaction may enable or constrain the realisation of participants' strategies. Socialisation, thus, leads to intended and/or unintended outcomes that shape and affect the participants' self-perceptions, worldviews, reputations and political strategies.

This definition, I hope, is precise enough to describe what the process entails and fairly general to trigger examinations of specific cases. A definition of socialisation, as Long and Hadden (1985: 42) caution, should be distinguished from the theory of its explanation. Hence, you notice that the definition does not tell us what happens to political actors when they participate in society. It alludes to participants' exposure to socio-political structures, but does not determine whether and why they end up internalising or rejecting social norms. These gaps are filled by offering a *theory* of socialisation and by the examination of specific cases.

What happens during socialisation and why? To explain Hezbollah's socialisation process, I build on insights offered in Norbert Elias's theory of The Civilizing Process.[10] The tying knot of Elias's theory is (European) state formation, which made other social mechanisms possible: monopolisation of violence and taxation, pacification and socio-political integration, economic exchange and growth of markets, war-making and the demarcation of political boundaries.

For Elias, socio-political integration (think of the making of modern Lebanon into a political order that ties different communal groups together) creates webs of interdependencies: configurations and patterns of economic, political and emotional bonds formed by interdependent individuals and groups (Elias 2000: 128–44). These webs of interdependencies lock actors (friends, allies or enemies) in relations of power. The power exerted by one actor over the other has a function, and this function is relational:

> When one person (or a group of persons) lacks something which another person or group has the power to withhold, the latter has a function for the former. Thus men have a function for women and women for men, parents for children and children for parents. Enemies have a function for each other, because once they have become interdependent they have the power to withhold from each other such elementary requirements as that of preserving their physical and social integrity, and ultimately survival. (Elias 2000: 78)

These webs of interdependencies do not determine social behaviour; they, rather, form the external normative and material constraints that shape and mould social action. The 'anarchical orders' which I examined above are webs of interdependence that tie Hezbollah to other actors in Lebanon and the region. Hezbollah cannot be understood outside these webs of interdependence. As Elias observes:

> The structure and pattern of which gives a society its specific character, is not a creation of particular individuals; for each individual, even the most

> powerful, even a tribal chief, an absolute monarch or a dictator, is a part of it, the representative of a function which is formed and maintained only in relation to other functions, which can only be understood in terms of the specific structure and the specific tensions of this total context. (Elias 2001: 14–15)

As such, an understanding of a group's, such as Hezbollah, broader strategy or particular moves cannot be comprehended without the examination of the interlocking relations the group has with its friends and enemies (Elias 1984: 75).[11]

Through socialisation and by virtue of social interdependence, actors develop two interrelated skills that are crucial for their social survival and success: self-restraint and rationalisation. These skills, it is important to emphasise here, are present in any web of interdependence, and need not be limited to Elias's cases (European civilising processes); but they vary in degree depending on the level of social integration and differentiation in a society.[12] Social actors become conscious of their interdependence with others and of the social standards that regulate their interactions. This awareness, or 'knowledge of the whole terrain' as Elias puts it, begins to mould behaviour obliging social actors to exercise restraint:

> The social standard to which the individual was first made to conform from outside by external restraint is finally reproduced more or less smoothly within him or her, through self-restraint which operates to a certain degree even against his or her conscious wishes. (Elias 2000: 398)

External social constraints are internalised:[13] maybe by abstaining from the use of violence; changing the way they represent themselves in society; or the speech they use when they interact with others.

Self-restraint is, in many ways, linked to rationalisation. Social actors become more calculable and thoughtful of the consequences of their actions; they curb and control their desires (Elias 2000: 399). Rationalisation, for Elias, does not develop from enlightened ideas, despite the role wise thinkers played in the diffusion of rationalisation (Elias 2000: 403). As van Krieken notes, 'for Elias "rationality" at the most general level refers to the balance struck between short-term desires and emotional needs, and the longer-term consequences of human action' (Krieken 1998: 87). But, crucially for our purposes, this rationality is not divorced from its social context.[14] What changes with rationalisation is the 'way in which people are bonded to each other' and this is 'not something which comes upon men from "outside"' (Elias 2000: 402).

The monopolisation of violence in a social space is an example of such a change: 'once the monopoly of physical power has passed to central authorities, not every strong man can afford the pleasure of physical attack' (Elias 2000: 169). But limitation on the use of violence does not stop people from exerting pressures on others. As Elias notes, 'if the sword no longer plays so great a role as the means of decision, it is replaced by intrigue, conflicts in which careers and social success are contested with words'. Words, persuasion through social conversations and social representation and performance become important vehicles for social survival and success (Elias 2000: 398).

The social webs of interdependence that tie specific societies together, however, can break. 'The long chains of actions with their division of functions can shrink again. The social and psychological control of behaviour can be reduced . . .' (Elias 2001: 134–5). The civilising process is not unilinear. The framework allows for 'reversals' or 'de-civilising processes', but Elias did not examine these in depth (Elias 2001: 134; Fletcher 1997: 82–3). Building on Elias, Fletcher argues that reversals in the civilising process occur when state monopoly over violence weakens and when socio-economic and cognitive interdependencies fragment. This generates 'a contraction in the scope of mutual identification between constituent groups and individuals' and 'erosion of specific social standards', which had previously dominated a social order. In effect, there is a change 'in the balance of social constraints and self-restraint' (Fletcher 1997: 83–5).

These Eliasian insights are crucial to understand Hezbollah's socialisation process. This process is not unilinear. The literature on Hezbollah has favoured a unilinear understanding of Hezbollah's development: one in which Hezbollah evolves from a violent-revolutionary-Islamist organisation into a pragmatist-political one (Qazzi 2013; Azani 2011; Berti 2013; Gleis and Berti 2012; Abboud and Muller 2012; Wiegand 2010; Alagha 2006). I, rather, prefer to treat Hezbollah's socialisation as a continuous attempt to overcome external constraints and to capitalise on opportunities to realise

Hezbollah's goals. War-making drives Hezbollah's behaviour, which dictates varying forms of rationalisation, self-restraint and foresight in each of the two anarchic orders of Lebanon and the region.

War-making and domestic socialisation

Hezbollah's socialisation in Lebanon can be understood as the continuation of war with Israel by socio-political means. The process increases ties between Hezbollah and its society and exposes it to Lebanese socio-political standards of behaviour. Fighting Israel, as I will show in the following chapter, initially involved the establishment of a disciplined and clandestine organisation. But it did not take long for Hezbollah to realise that the military core of this APM required a social safety net: the base on which Hezbollah's ideological, military and political mobilisations could take place. Hezbollah established a programme of social provisions (hospitals, charitable associations, schools, religious centres) to buttress its social base. With this process, whose bonds deepen and culminate in the emergence of the 'Resistance Society' (Qassem 2008a) by 2005, Hezbollah established ties of interdependence with its core Shi'a community.

The second social web is the Lebanese society, which formed a set of external constraints for Hezbollah. To preserve its war-making efforts with Israel and to maintain its legitimacy as an APM, Hezbollah has had to rationalise its behaviour to conform to Lebanon's Lockean anarchical order. Socialisation in Lebanon dictated restraint in the use of violence, political alliances and, concomitantly, social re-presentation of Hezbollah's political image.

The restraint in the use of violence in post-war Lebanon (1990–2008) is dictated by the foresight of preventing socio-political divisions in Lebanon that would weaken Hezbollah and expose it in its war with Israel. As I will illustrate in Chapter 3, Hezbollah does not only restrain itself but, through speech and performance, it attempts to control the anger, passion and pride of its members, supporters and allies (Saouli 2011). Hezbollah was eager to legitimise its armed resistance to Israel, which required political alliances. It joined the parliament in 1992 and initiated a political opening afterwards leading to various political alliances, not least with its Shi'a partner, Amal, and in 2006 with the (predominantly Christian) Free Patriotic Movement

(FMP) (Saouli 2011). These alliances helped to legitimise Hezbollah, but were also crucial to balance against its rivals, the March 14 Alliance.[15]

Hezbollah's socialisation involved social *re-presentation*, including what Social Psychologists Klein, Spears and Reicher call 'identity performance': 'purposeful expression (or suppression) of behaviours relevant to those norms conventionally associated with a salient social identity' (Klein, Spears and Reicher 2007: 29–32; Saouli 2015). Social identity here 'is intended as a concept that mediates between social context and the action of human subjects' (Reicher 2004: 933–8). For example, in the early 1990s, Hezbollah adopted the Lebanese flag; the discourse of the establishment of an Islamic state was muted; the movement's slogan changed from 'The Islamic Revolution in Lebanon' to a more focused 'The Islamic Resistance in Lebanon'; its 2009 manifesto confirmed Lebanon's 'consociational democracy' (Saouli 2011). The aim of this 'identity performance [is] to change the out-group's stereotypes and treatment of the in-group' (Klein, Spears and Reicher 2007: 36). Through the sword of words and performance, especially the speeches of its leader, Nasrallah, Hezbollah aimed to deconstruct its rivals' stereotypes and accusations, which depicted the movement as an 'Iranian proxy', 'state-within-a-state' or 'war-monger'. In doing so, however, Hezbollah was also reconstructing what it means to be Lebanese.[16] This reconstruction of a social identity can be perceived as a 'project' that aims to 'mobilize people to create social reality' (Reicher 2004: 938). Contrary to the pre-war dominant culture, which believed that Lebanon's 'strength is in its weakness', Hezbollah's narrative and discourse provided an alternative: Lebanon's strength lies in the unity of its 'Army, People and Resistance' against Israel.

However, as Alexander observes, the meaning contesting actors aim to show to others 'may or may not be one to which they themselves subjectively adhere; it is the meaning that they, as social actors, consciously or unconsciously, wish to have others believe' (Alexander 2006: 32). So, does Hezbollah adhere to the discourse it uses in Lebanon? This question has generated a divisive debate, as I showed in the Introduction to this book. Some believe that Hezbollah has evolved from an Islamist organisation into a pragmatist, 'Lebanonised' political party; its development mirrors the changing political circumstances (Berti 2013; Abboud and Muller 2012: vii; Alagha 2011; Wiegand 2010: 113; Alagha 2006: 36–7; Norton 2014: 6;

Balkiz 2006; Harik 2005). Others claim that Hezbollah hides behind a mask; it intends to control Lebanon and to Islamise its society (Qazzi 2013: 22; Khatib 2011: 63, 67; Badran 2009; Hamzeh 2004; Sharara 2007; Ranstorp and Waite 2003: 52). The question of ideology and identity during socialisation, however, requires elaborate attention that goes beyond the mask and mirror.

In the following chapter, *Being Hezbollah*, I address this issue in detail. My central argument is that religio-political doctrine is not something that Hezbollah simply uses as an instrument to achieve its goals; rather, religio-political doctrine is constitutive of Hezbollah as a socio-political actor. It might be comforting to argue that religion serves political ends or to argue the reverse, that politics serves religion. But this dichotomy serves to mask rather than mirror Hezbollah's complex relations to ideology or to the political. Hezbollah's adherence to a religio-political doctrine raises two mundane questions that emanate from this interpretation. First, how do religio-political ideas shape Hezbollah's behaviour? And second what functions do they serve for the movement?

Hezbollah's socialisation is generated by both its religio-political ideals and its actual attempts to realise its goals in Lebanon and the region. Let us call this Hezbollah's rationalisation: the ongoing process through which Hezbollah attempts to strike a balance between its short-term goals and long-term mission. This places Hezbollah somewhere between Max Weber's two categories of social action: the 'value-rational' and the 'instrumentally rational'. You will see in the empirical chapters that Hezbollah reflects the 'actions of persons who, regardless of possible cost to themselves, act to put into practice their convictions', what Max Weber defines as a 'value-rational act'. But, they do not do this 'independent of its prospects of its success', as Weber also suggests of this category. This would be costly in the unforgiving world of politics. Here Hezbollah's actions are 'instrumentally rational': 'when the end, the means, and the secondary results are all rationally taken into account and weighted'. Usefully for Weber these categories are not exhaustive. As he argues, 'the choice between alternative and conflicting ends and results may well be determined in a value-rational manner'. 'In that case', he observes, 'action is instrumentally rational only in respect to the choice of means' (Weber 1978: 25–6).

It is important to think of 'rationality' not as a fixed category or a mindset that Hezbollah possesses. Rather, it should be perceived as a rationalisation process that is integral to the movement's overall socialisation. Hezbollah's war-making with Israel and its socialisation in the Lebanese and regional orders have rationalised its behaviour, dictating self-restraint, foresight and social re-presentation as argued above. But this does not mean that in the process religio-political ideals evaporate – far from it. Religio-political doctrine serves at least five functions, which I identify here and elaborate further on in the empirical chapters.

First, Hezbollah's war-making with Israel has reinforced its religio-political doctrine. War-making with Israel and the strategic support (financial, military, political) Iran has made available for Hezbollah constitute the material bases that keep the Islamist movement's *ideals* alive. The material base contributes to the diffusion and consolidation of ideology.

Second, in a reverse direction, religio-political ideals *enhance* the material basis of Hezbollah's war-making effort. They provide Hezbollah with a world-vision: a framework through which Hezbollah perceives the past, present and future (see the following chapter). This contributes to what Lukmann and Berger (Luckmann and Berger 1991: 71) call 'habitualisation', which provides 'a stable background in which human activity may proceed with a minimum decision-making most of the time, it frees energy for such decisions as may be necessary on certain occasions'.

Third, religio-political doctrine fosters certain values – self-sacrifice, martyrdom, modesty, honesty, patience, preservation of 'authentic Islam' – which form a normative web that ties together and sets standards of behaviour for the movement. Understanding these values is crucial to explain Hezbollah's motivations and behaviour.

Fourth, Hezbollah's belief in *Wilayat al-Faqih* has a direct effect on Hezbollah's organisational structure, the discipline of its members and their overall behaviour. As I will show in the following chapter, the *faqih* offers the broad religio-political vision that guides Hezbollah and guarantees a 'disciplined hierarchical order by virtue of making loyalty to the organisation equivalent to the loyalty to God' (Abu Rida 2012: 581; Qassem 2010a: 124).[17]

And fifth, religio-political doctrine serves in political mobilisation and war-making. Mobilisation and the diffusion of religio-political doctrine contribute to the establishment of a social base from which Hezbollah recruits members and through which it bolsters and extends in its power.

Driven by the goal of war-making, Hezbollah's domestic socialisation has, thus, involved both social re-presentation and the preservation of religio-political ideology – two facets which the current literature has treated as contradictory. In this way, Hezbollah has (temporarily) avoided the tension between its Islamist identity and socialisation in Lebanon's divided society.

War-making and international socialisation

War-making with Israel has also shaped Hezbollah's international socialisation, determining its choice of allies, the discourse employed and its foreign policy. It is not an exaggeration to suggest that Hezbollah's strategic priorities have overridden its domestic socialisation. Traditionally, Lebanese actors have tended to exploit regional developments to improve their domestic standing (Saouli 2014b); Hezbollah, however, has capitalised on its domestic influence to maintain strategic power in the region.

Once again, Hezbollah's religio-political doctrine is key in understanding its international socialisation, as I will illustrate in Chapter 4. The doctrine shapes Hezbollah's perception of the international system and determines its choice of allies (Iran, Syria, Hamas and Islamic Jihad), enemies (US, Israel) or rivals (Saudi Arabia). Hezbollah has with time established strategic interdependent alliances with Iran and Syria, the 'Resistance Axis' (Saouli 2013). This alliance is the cornerstone of Hezbollah's war-making with Israel and its foreign policy, including the military intervention in Syria, since 2012.

War-making has also shaped Hezbollah's international socialisation in Arab politics. Here, Hezbollah employed revolutionary discourse, notions such as 'Liberation of Palestine', 'Dignity', and 'Resistance', to challenge alternative dominant discourse that championed negotiations to resolve the Arab–Israeli conflict. Hezbollah sought alliances with Arab nationalists, Islamists and secular forces that share its political goals. The Islamist movement capitalised on every opportunity (the Palestinian intifada of 2000, the Gaza wars and the Lebanon 2006 war) to expose the Arab regimes' incapacity. Its goal has been to delegitimise pro-Western Arab regimes and to promote resistance as an Arab/Islamic political project of liberation.

In doing so, Hezbollah has been also reconstructing what it means to be an 'Arab' (Valbjørn and Bank 2012; Barnett 1998). Hezbollah's discursive battle focused on Muslim/Arab 'unity' and aimed to transcend sectarian divides. In this 'identity performance', sectarian differences were muted; direct intervention – whether through discourse or other forms – in the politics of individual states was avoided. The aim was to prevent rivals (such as Saudi Arabia) or enemies (the US or Israel) from exploiting sectarian divides to delegitimise Hezbollah and Iran. Ultimately, Hezbollah hoped to distinguish non-Arab friends (Iran) from enemies (Israel and its Western backers). Hezbollah's behaviour is a response to its rivals' campaigns that accuse it of being an 'Iranian thorn' in the Arab world, of stimulating sectarian (Sunni–Shi'a) sedition and of war-mongering.

Notwithstanding its rivals' campaigns, Hezbollah's successful military resistance against Israel, which we will explore in detail in Chapter 4, and the revolutionary discourse it promoted, established it as a respectable and determined Arab and Islamic resistance and a model to emulate. But Hezbollah's socialisation did not come without its discontents.

Tragic Ironies

Purposeful socialisation has consequences, both intended and unintended. Hezbollah's socialisation illustrates the limits political actors have over the world they want to inhabit. Socialising in anarchical orders reveals Hezbollah's limited control over how rivals will interpret its actions or how they will reconstruct its identity to suit their interests. Socialisation also reveals that the orders that enabled Hezbollah's rise can also entrap the movement in strategic dilemmas that generate ethical and political tensions. In Chapter 5, *Tragic Ironies*, I identify three interrelated discontents that Hezbollah's socialisation has generated: security paradoxes, conformity and ethical dilemmas.

The 'tragic' and 'ironic' dimensions of political action and processes has haunted Realist political theorists from Reinhold Niebuhr (Niebuhr 1952) through to Hans Morgenthau (Kostagiannis 2014; Paipais 2013), John Mearsheimer (Mearsheimer 2014) and Ned Lebow (Lebow 2003).[18] The tragic irony of political action is lucidly captured by Niebuhr in the opening lines of his *The Irony of American History*:

> If men or nations do evil in a good cause; if they cover themselves with guilt in order to fulfil some high responsibility; or if they sacrifice some high value for the sake of a higher or equal one they make a tragic choice . . . Irony on the other hand consists of apparently fortuitous incongruities . . . If virtue becomes vice through some hidden defect in virtue; if strength becomes weakness because of the vanity to which strength may prompt the mighty man or nation; if security is transmuted into insecurity because too much reliance is placed upon it; if wisdom becomes folly because it does not know its limit – in all such cases the situation is ironic. (Niebuhr 1952: xxiii–xxiv)

Whilst all Realists agree that tragedy is an inevitable outcome of political action, they disagree about its root causes. Some place weight on the agent: his/her pride and blindness to reality (Niebuhr) or his/her urge for power and control of others and his/her destiny (Morgenthau). Other Realists (such as Wolfers, Herz, Waltz and Mearsheimer) tilt the weight towards the (anarchical) contexts that actors find themselves in. A historical sociology approach would trace the process of the interaction of purposeful actors and enabling and constraining contexts to account for the choices actors have to make, some of which are tragic and ironic. In my tracing of Hezbollah's socialisation process, tragic ironies appear to result from: Hezbollah's integration in contexts and situations not of its own choosing and in ones which it has no total control over; from the intended and unintended strategic choices it has to pursue for survival; and from the intended and unintended political and ethical consequences of its actions.

One main reason for this is that Hezbollah's emergence and socialisation has set it on a *path-dependent* trajectory. Path-dependent trajectories are ones that are usually difficult to 'reverse' (Pierson 2004: 21). Margaret Levi compares political trajectories to a tree: 'From the same trunk, there are many different branches and smaller branches. Although it is possible to turn around or to clamber from one to the other . . . the branch on which a climber begins is the one she tends to follow' (Levi 1997: 28). Why is it difficult to reverse? First because path dependency involves 'positive feedback': 'the *relative* benefits of the current activity compared with once-possible options increases over time' (Pierson 2004: 21; emphasis original). Another is that the cost of reversal becomes high. However, path dependence in Hezbollah's case will have to transcend the rationalist assumptions that underpin this approach and integrate identity as an enabling and constraining variable that conditions behaviour.

Hezbollah's Islamist identity and war-making with Israel set it on a path that determined its political trajectory. Hezbollah's Islamist identity and doctrine informed its perception of the political world and, hence, the discerning of friends, allies and enemies. War-making with Israel determined the nature of its socialisation process in Lebanon and the region – as discussed above. On the way, Hezbollah established webs of interdependence with allies (in Lebanon and with Iran and Syria) and enemies (Israel and the US). Its identity and political interests locked the movement in these webs and reinforced the path in two ways that make it costly to reverse. First, the path involved 'positive feedback' – such as Hezbollah's successful campaign to drive Israel out of Lebanon, its ability to mobilise Lebanese support for its war-making efforts and its ability to defend Lebanon against Israel (and later Islamist jihadists) – that reinforced Hezbollah's identity, political strategy and interdependence to allies. But, second, the more Hezbollah pursued the path, the more it became dependent on its allies for survival, making reversal impossible. But it is here where the tensions of socialisation begin to surface.

The deeper Hezbollah's socialisation process was, the more locked in the webs of interdependence it became, and the less control it had over the process. 'Socialization' in anarchical orders, argues Kenneth Waltz, 'reduces variety': 'structures', he observes, 'limit and mould agents and agencies and point them in ways that tend toward a common quality of outcomes even though the efforts and aims of agents and agencies vary' (Waltz 1979: 74–6). Hezbollah's socialisation transformed the Islamist actor in ways that comply with the nature of its social context and the necessities of political and military survival. Hezbollah's conformity with these orders proceeded, as Waltz observed of 'non-conformist' actors, 'at a pace that is set by the *extent* of the involvement with the system' (Waltz 1979: 128; emphasis added).

First, Hezbollah's constant military build-up and socio-political mobilisation within Lebanon, which aimed to deter Israeli threats, raised fears of its rivals in the divided society of Lebanon and generated counter-mobilisations, especially after the Syrian withdrawal in 2005. The result was 'security paradox': 'a situation in which two or more actors, seeking only to improve their own security, provoke through their words or actions an increase in mutual tension, resulting in less security all round' (Booth and Wheeler 2007: 9; Posen 1993). Its rivals (the March 14 Alliance, which accused Syria of murdering former Prime Minister Rafic Hariri) wanted Hezbollah to surrender its weapons to and integrate in the state, but for Hezbollah this amounted to a 'political coup', which would benefit Israel. One direct consequence of the security paradox was its effect on sectarian mobilisation and divisions. Rivalry between Hezbollah and its political foe, Hariri's Future Movement, mobilised sectarian fears and emotions: Lebanon's traditional Christian–Muslim schism began to give way to a Sunni–Shi'a cleavage (Saouli 2006).

These cleavages deepened when in an attempt to curb Hezbollah's military wing, on 5 May 2008, the March 14 government (many months after Hezbollah and its allies resigned from government) tried to outlaw Hezbollah's vital telecommunications network. Hezbollah perceived the decision as a 'declaration of war' (Saouli 2011: 938) and swiftly and violently took control of Beirut, overwhelming pro-government militias. Hezbollah's use of violence in post-war Lebanon marked an important shift in the movement's political history. It managed to transform a potential threat into a strategic opportunity to re-establish itself at the centre of power in Lebanon.

Although Hezbollah did not capitalise on this supposedly defensive military action to impose its own political will on Lebanon (see why in Chapter 5), the move did not prevent questions related to the security paradox from emerging: 'When does "legitimate self-defence" become "predatory behaviour"? When does "enhancing the status quo" slip into being a "revisionist" policy?' (Booth and Wheeler 2007: 2). As I will show in Chapter 5, Hezbollah's use of violence deepened the political and sectarian divide in Lebanon. Framing it as the 'invasion' of (the predominantly Sunni) Beirut, Hezbollah's rivals accentuated their attacks against Hezbollah; their previous accusations of Hezbollah as an outlaw materialised. In effect, Hezbollah's purposeful social re-presentation was challenged. By 2011, Hezbollah's attempts to maintain domestic unity and to prevent a Sunni–Shi'a confrontation had failed.

The 2008 episode generated a shift in the external constraints: the ability of Hezbollah's rivals to withhold its power began to diminish. This increased

Hezbollah's confidence, but it did not secure its total control over the situation. The paradox here is explained by Elias's exposition of group dynamics:

> It is perfectly possible that by their own actions, groups of people consciously oriented towards preserving and maintaining the present figuration in fact strengthen its tendency to change. It is equally possible for groups of people consciously oriented towards change just to strengthen the tendency of their figuration to remain as it is. (Elias 1984: 147)

The unintended consequence of Hezbollah and its rivals' interaction was institutional paralysis (failure to hold parliamentary elections, to elect a president or to issue a national budget), and simultaneously the erosion of the ties and social standards that bind different groups in Lebanon's anarchical order – the reverse of what Hezbollah hoped for.

Second, with Hezbollah's socialisation we observe a gradual transformation of the realist-defensive attitude to one of an unintended conformity. Conformity here is not a choice about accepting common standards and traditions of behaviour. It is rather a consequence dictated by Hezbollah's belief in its limited abilities to generate change in Lebanon. This belief emanates from Hezbollah's perception of the state in Lebanon as 'weak' (H. Fadlallah 2015). Lebanon's state weakness, you could argue, is an 'objective reality' given its divided society and tumultuous political history. However, state weakness in Lebanon is also a socially and politically constructed reality. If all actors *believe* that the state in Lebanon is weak, then they will act on the basis that it is weak by buttressing their own power and, in doing so, they will *reinforce* its weakness. Hezbollah's rise, war-making with Israel and political interactions in Lebanon have entrenched this belief, leading it to build its own social and military capabilities independent of any national goal of state-building. In this way, like its Lebanese peers, Hezbollah is both a victim and a perpetuator of Lebanon's anarchical order. Despite its call for a 'strong and capable state', Hezbollah's behaviour, dictated by the security paradox, edges more to preserving autonomy than to the realisation of a national state-building. To buttress its social basis Hezbollah established a network of social services, which employs, educates and trains tens of thousands of predominantly Shi'a Lebanese. This investment in the socio-economic infrastructure of the Shi'a community promoted political stability and offered Hezbollah a strong social base to buttress its political strategy. However, as an unintended consequence, this has also, at least temporarily, diminished the need for a state, turning this social base into a clientalistic network of another sectarian patron, Hezbollah.

The third discontent generated by Hezbollah's socialisation falls in the realm of ethics. The story, one could argue, starts with Hezbollah's birth. The emergence of political actors frequently disrupts existing power structures and generates resistance from dominant forces. Hezbollah's attempt to establish a place for itself among Lebanon's Shi'a community and later in Lebanon and the region generated resistance from rival powers and caused bloody battles between Hezbollah and Amal in the 1980s (see Chapter 3). However, it was in the Syria war (since 2012) that Hezbollah faced major ethical predicaments. The strategic urge to back Assad in order to maintain the Iran–Syria–Hezbollah alliance and to prevent its own isolation and possible Israeli attack against it, countered the ethic of supporting the oppressed against oppressor. Hezbollah supported the Egyptian and Tunisian revolutions and congratulated their people for succeeding in driving oppressive leaders out of power. To the chagrin of many Gulf states, it supported the Bahraini people's right for freedom and political participation.

Syria was more complex. Syria, Hezbollah claimed, is a member of the Resistance Axis; its regime supported resistance movements, such as Hezbollah, Hamas and al-Jihad; it remains adamantly against the recognition of Israel until the latter withdraws from occupied Arab territories; Syria's military is the Arabs' only army that is still ideologically indoctrinated against Israel; last, but not least, Syria along with Iran continue to resist US hegemony in the region. Whilst Syria needs political reform, Hezbollah acknowledged, the political identity of its regime should be preserved. This principled position ties to Hezbollah's ethical and religio-political foundations that call for national independence, resistance against US hegemony and Israel and the liberation of Palestine.

Hence, Hezbollah's principle of freedom from oppression against imperialism stood against the quest of freedom of many Syrians against their internal oppressor. Hezbollah's rivals accused the movement of 'double standards', questioning its ethical integrity, moral foundations and 'actual' goals in Lebanon and the region. The support Hezbollah has garnered in Arab societies began to erode. Hezbollah's backing of the Bahraini uprising and later of the Ansar Allah (Houthi) movement in Yemen led many to raise questions on Hezbollah's silence over Assad's brutal oppression of his domestic rivals (in the period 2012–17, Al-Manar television, Hezbollah's mouthpiece, was careful to avoid coverage of Assad's violent repression). Hezbollah's support of Assad, the Bahraini uprising and Ansar Allah reinforced perceptions and constructions of many that Hezbollah is a sectarian movement that contributes to increasing Iranian – rivals like to use the label 'Persian' – influence in the Arab world. Hamas's withdrawal from the Resistance Axis (Saouli 2013) contributed to turn the axis into a predominantly Shi'a one, in effect challenging the social image Hezbollah aimed to construct for itself.

Notwithstanding the above criticism, Hezbollah intervened militarily in Syria to support Assad. Yes, the intervention still required justification. As Ned Lebow argues 'It is impossible to formulate interests intelligently outside some language of justice' (Lebow 2003: 16). What is striking in the formulation of Hezbollah's interests is its resort to the discourse used by hegemonic powers, which Hezbollah has for long criticised. Intervention in Syria was a 'defensive' and 'pre-emptive' act aiming to protect Lebanon from the dangers of 'terrorists' (Islamist jihadists) and enemies of the Resistance Axis, who wish to turn Syria into another Western sphere of influence. Pre-emption and fighting on 'any territory' to protect Lebanon, Palestine and the whole alliance became the new language used by Hezbollah. Reflecting Hezbollah's greater influence and capacity at a regional level, its intelligentsia supplied the intellectual package. In what would have appeared several years back as an imperialist (or neo-conservative in the campaign to invade Iraq) discourse, Hassan Fadlallah, Hezbollah's MP and one of its biographers, argued that there is a need to transcend the 'narrow' and 'traditional understanding of international relations and state boundaries', which was dominant in the twentieth century. For national security purposes, states now (should) intervene in other states to protect their interests; this is a sign of a state's capability and an element for its respect. 'In its modern understanding, security', he argues, 'cannot be confined to specific boundaries' (H. Fadlallah 2015: 218–20).

Fadlallah's intellectual adventurism may justify Hezbollah's external interventions in Syria, Iraq or Yemen; ironically, however, this does not only counter all of the ethical foundations Hezbollah stood on, but it also provides the intellectual basis for Hezbollah's rivals to deter threats by intervening in the territories of their enemies (Saudi Arabia in Yemen; Israel in Gaza, the West Bank or Syria; Turkey in Iraq; etc.). Despite Fadlallah's confident tone, Hezbollah's behaviour reflects the state of insecurity that haunts the Islamist movement and its rivals in a changing region. The current situation in the Middle East has dissolved into one of a Hobbesian anarchy. The chains of interdependency that have restrained different political groups are eroding. The Arab uprisings and the consequent state disintegration in Yemen, Iraq, Syria and Lebanon reflect not only the collapse of ruling regimes, but also a set of values that have dominated domestic and regional politics for at least six decades. 'Hypocrisy', observes Ned Lebow, 'is the hallmark of transitions. It is most pronounced when old values have been broken down but are still honored publicly because the new values that guide behaviour have not yet been articulated or legitimated' (Lebow 2003: 17).

Notes

1. One exception is Dionigi (2014), who examines how Hezbollah's incorporation of international norms generated an identity shift for the Islamist movement.
2. The third, which is unfortunately not of use to this study, is the Kantian type. The Kantian category (referring to Immanuel Kant) is neither about enmity nor rivalry, but friendship. In this society, war is considered illegitimate; whilst violence is sometimes used, it is not common. Differences are settled through negotiations and legal frameworks not war. For analysis of the three orders see Wendt 1999 (246–312).
3. An 'ideal-type' is a precise and unambiguous concept of an institution, action or relationship that is 'always constructed with a view to adequacy on the level of meaning' (Weber 1978: 20). The ideal-type 'does not serve as a description of concrete historical reality, but is a construct used to elucidate the features of historical reality' (Morrison 1995: 271).
4. Although I use Wendt's classification of different anarchical orders (Wendt 1999: 246–312), I do not adopt his theoretical framework.
5. For example, major positions in the state are divided among the main sectarian communities: Presidency for the Christians, House Speaker for the Shi'as, and Premiership for the Sunnis; other posts in the state are/should be equally divided between Muslims and Christians. For a thorough discussion of Lebanon's consociational democracy, see Fakhoury 2015.

6. Major councils include: The Shi'a Higher Council, Dar al-Fatwa (Sunni 'House of Religious Edicts') or Maronite (Catholic) Patriarchate.
7. For Charles Tilly (2006: 182) social movements involve 'sustained challenges to power-holders in the name of one or more populations living under the jurisdiction of those power-holders by means of public displays dramatizing those populations' worthiness, unity, numbers, and commitment'.
8. *Wilayat al-Faqih* is the Guardianship or Rule of the Islamic Jurist. The *wali* is the jurist, henceforth, *al-faqih*.
9. As Luckmann and Berger argue of individual socialisation, 'The child does not internalize the world of his significant others as one of many possible worlds. He internalizes it as *the* world, the only existent and only conceivable world, the world *tout court*' (Luckmann and Berger 1991: 154; emphasis original).
10. *The Civilizing Process* is the title of Elias's ground-breaking book which was first published in German in 1939 and later published in English in 1978. One of the greatest social thinkers of the twentieth century (Smith 2001; Krieken 1998; Mennell and Goudsblom 1997), Elias explored the origins and practices of manners and etiquettes (when and why various segments of European societies learned how to behave and appear in public; how to eat at the dining table; how, when and when not to burp, spit or blow one's nose; how to retain wind) and linked this to the process of state formation in Europe in the period thirteenth to nineteenth centuries. *The Civilizing Process* is divided into two volumes: the history of manners and state formation.
11. Elias has examined group dynamics and generated 'game models' (similar to Weber's 'ideal types') to elucidate inter-group relations (Elias 1984).
12. As Elias notes, 'social drive-controls and restrictions are nowhere absent among people, nor is a certain foresight; but these qualities have a form and degree among simple herdsmen or in a warrior class different from those found among courtiers, state officials or members of a mechanized army. *They grow more powerful and more complete the greater is the division of functions, and thus the greater the number of people to whom the individual has to attune his or her actions*' (Elias 2000: 403; emphasis added).
13. Internalisation here refers to 'an understanding of one's fellowmen and, second, for the apprehension of the world as a meaningful and social reality' (Luckmann and Berger 1991: 150).
14. As Elias observes: 'Bourgeois industrial rationality is generated by the compulsion of the economic mesh; by it power-opportunities founded on private or public capital are made calculable. Court rationality is generated by the

compulsion of the elite social mesh; by it people and prestige are made calculable as instruments of power' (quoted in Krieken 1998: 88).

15. 'March 14' is the name of the alliance that emerged after the assassination of PM Rafic Hariri in 2005. It has been Hezbollah's main rival and is anti-Syria and Iran.
16. This process started with Hezbollah's emergence in the early 1980s (Saade 2016), but was stimulated with Hezbollah's further integration in Lebanese politics, especially after 2005.
17. The presence of *al-faqih* solves one key problem for Islamic movements: *Hakimiyya*, or governance within the framework of Sharia law. The identification of the legitimate (i.e. religiously ordained) leader has been a thorny issue for Islamists. But for the followers of Khomeini's theory the answer is simple: it is the *faqih* (the supreme leader) (Saouli 2014: 17–18).
18. For an authoritative discussion of tragedy and politics in Realist IR, see the edited volume by Erskine and Lebow 2012.

2

Being Hezbollah

Not ideas, but material and ideal interests, directly govern men's conduct. Yet very frequently the 'world images' that have been created by 'ideas' have, like switchmen, determined the tracks along which action has been pushed by the dynamic of interest.

Max Weber, 'The Social Psychology of World Religions'

إنّ كلّ ما لدينا هو من عاشوراء

All that we possess comes from *Ashura*.

Ayatollah Khomeini

During the bloody and long 33-day Israel–Lebanon war in 2006, Hezbollah fighters sent a letter to their leader, Hassan Nasrallah. In the letter they expressed their loyalty to Hezbollah's mission, to its founders and martyrs and their passion for Imam Hussein, the Prophet's grandson. They pledged to protect Lebanon and to realise Nasrallah's 'Sincere Promise', code-name of Hezbollah's military operation that led to the abdication of Israeli troops and the one that triggered the war. A day later, Nasrallah broadcast a response (Nasrallah 2006). 'Yes, you are the Sincere Promise' he replied, and added:

My brothers! You are the authentic origin of the history of this *Ummah*;
You are the gem of its soul;
You are its civilisation, culture, values, passion and gratitude [also knowledge];
You are the title of its manhood [or courage];
You are the immortal cedar on our mountains, and the humble spikes of wheat in our homes;

> You are as mighty as Lebanon's mountains, the highest of the high and the strongest among the strong;
> After God, we placed and we will always place our hopes and faith in you;
> I honour you for making us all so proud;
> I kiss your hands, which hold the trigger by which God will destroy the killers of his prophets and servants and those who cause corruption in the land;
> I kiss your feet that are ingrained in this land and do not tremble and do not move away even if the mountains wither;
> My brothers, you have dedicated your souls to God and have reached the unreachable, my answer to you is 'thank you', if you accept me as a brother among you; because you are the [true] leaders, the masters, and the pride of the *Ummah*;
> And you are the men of God, the source of our revival.[1]

Nasrallah's address to his fighters is loaded with emotional, national and religious meanings. The moving address attracted admiration from Hezbollah's supporters and its adversaries. In a region where (authoritarian) leaders are detached from their society, Nasrallah's words reflected his emotional and ideological connection to his fighters. It also showed his humbleness. The address would then be repeatedly played on Al-Manar television. After the war, a respected secular Lebanese singer, Julia Boutrous, transformed parts of the address into a song and a new album called *Ahibba'i* ('My Beloved Ones').[2] The proceeds of the album were allocated to the many Lebanese who were wounded in the war.

Observers of Nasrallah's address focused on his modesty, clarity, emotional ties to his fighters, or leadership skills. Notwithstanding these attributes, the substance of Nasrallah's address was not entirely novel. The address is embedded in a thick religio-political repertoire – the historical, religious, cultural and political stock – from which Nasrallah extracted his words. It was, as this chapter will show, a reproduction of the Islamist movement's religio-political identity that delineates the values and ideals that form Hezbollah's being.

Discussing 'being' means engaging with Hezbollah's genesis, religio-political identity and organisational type. This I will do in two parts. First,

I will examine the Islamic-Shi'a identity and the theory of *Wilayat al-Faqih* which form the basis of Hezbollah's doctrine (what Hezbollah recognises as '*aqida*). Then I will show how these ideational factors and other immediate political circumstances contributed to Hezbollah's emergence in 1978–85. Second, I will examine Hezbollah's organisational type, namely, what I will depict in this book as an Armed Political Movement (APM), which ties directly to Hezbollah's doctrine, war-making with Israel and overall socialisation (see Figure 2.1 below).

Instead of 'ideology',[3] I believe Hezbollah's holds a *religio-political doctrine*: a set of interrelated religious and political beliefs, norms and ideals that shape Hezbollah's behaviour and ones which it carries, disseminates and strives to realise. Hezbollah's religio-political doctrine is not a mere justification that Hezbollah 'uses' or 'invokes' to achieve its political goals (Saade 2016: 14); rather, these set of beliefs constitutes what Hezbollah *is*. By hyphenating 'religio' and 'political', I show that Hezbollah's political ideals cannot be perceived outside of its Islamist-Shi'a identity and belonging. One reason is that Hezbollah's Islamist belonging is in itself political: whether you want to Islamise society from below or above or whether you want to do this peacefully or violently, that mere act is *political*, for it has a direct impact on political power and institutions in a given context. Hence, detaching Islam from politics is a misunderstanding of both spheres. But there is another reason why I want to distinguish the 'religio' from the 'political'. This has to do with the fact that religious beliefs and ideals are open to various (and usually opposing) political *interpretations* within specific contexts. Indeed, examining Hezbollah's purposeful socialisation gives these religious beliefs a socio-political grounding (see previous chapter).

However, arguing that religious or ideological beliefs are open for interpretation by political actors means that these beliefs exist somewhere (in religious texts, memory, traditions or even emotions) and thus they first need to be identified to allow for their interpretation or scholarly examination. I concur with Saade that Hezbollah has no clearly articulated ideology, thus my preference to use 'doctrine'; however, I find that Hezbollah has more than 'a particular treatment of the past that produces ideological coherence' or 'different nationalist imaginaries' (Saade 2016: 24).[4] Hezbollah's perception of the past, which has a direct effect on its present and future vision, I show, is embedded in and is extracted from its Islamic (Shi'a) religio-political doctrine and history. My framework allows for greater autonomy for religio-political beliefs, which enables me to show how these beliefs shape Hezbollah's being and political behaviour and vice-versa.

Genesis

It is common to trace Hezbollah's origins to the Islamic Revolution in Iran (1979) and/or to the second Israeli invasion of Lebanon (1982). Some look further back and link Hezbollah's emergence to a Shi'a political revival in Lebanon. These events and developments certainly form the immediate conditions for Hezbollah's emergence, as I will affirm below. But to understand Hezbollah's doctrine, our point of departure has to be in Islam and in Shi'ism as a rebellious movement and faith within it. The aim of the discussion is neither to draw a history lesson nor to present an accurate historical narrative – that is for the historians to sort out (Cole 2009; Newman 2013; Dabashi 2012; Almuhager 1994). Rather, it is to locate Hezbollah in a broader religious movement that has a history and to show how Hezbollah *interprets* and narrates this history as it grapples with immediate and long-term religio-political goals.

Islam and Shi'ism: the quest for legitimate rule

When Nasrallah described his fighters as the 'authentic origin of the history of this *Ummah*', he was alluding to authentic Islam, which in Shi'a belief and narrative refers to the Islam of the Prophet Muhammad and his family, or *Ahl al-Bayt* (People of the House) of Banu Hashim. The death of the Prophet in AD 632 generated a political crisis of succession. The supporters, or *Shi'as*, of Ali ibn Abi Talib believed that he should be the successor, the Caliph, to the Prophet. Ali was the Prophet's cousin from his Banu Hashim section of Quraysh and the husband of his only daughter, Fatimah.[5]

According to Shi'a tradition, the Prophet designated Ali as his successor at *Ghadir Khumm*, an event that is annually commemorated by Shi'as.[6] However, after the Prophet's death, a consultation (*shura* in Arabic) took place among the Prophet's companions and Abu Bakr (r. 623–4) was chosen as successor, to be followed by Omar (r. 634–44), Osman (r. 644–56), before Ali became the Caliph (r. 656–61). In Sunni interpretation, the first four successors are perceived as *Khulafa'a al-Rashidun* (the Rightly Guided Caliphs).

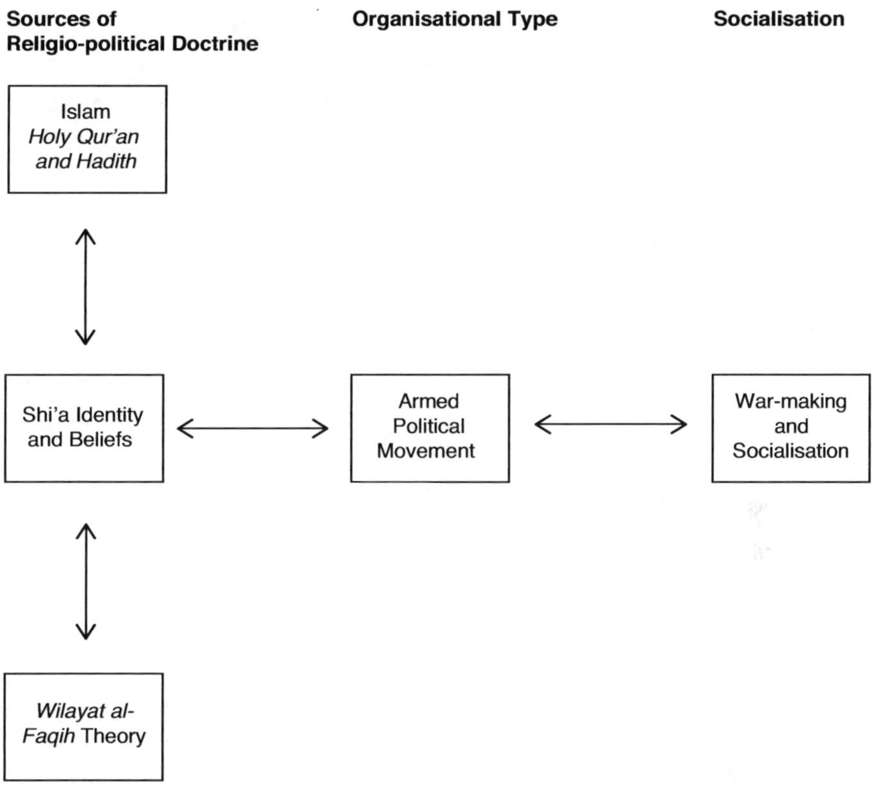

Figure 2.1 Being Hezbollah

But in Shi'a belief, the line of succession is drawn from the Prophet directly to Ali, his sons Hassan and Hussein, and other Imams (See Appendix).

Despite this schism, the demarcation of Sunni–Shi'a identities did not crystallise in the early period of Islam. After Ali's assassination (AD 611), his son, Hassan, became Caliph. However, Hassan would surrender the Caliphate to Mu'awiya, a companion of the Prophet from the rival Banu Umayya section of the Qurayshi tribe. In Shi'a narrative, Hassan faced two irreconcilable choices: either to maintain his rule and risk a great *fitnah* (sedition, civil strife) or give up power and prevent a bloody division among Muslims (al-Sayyid 2008: 15–53).[7] A more difficult dilemma, however, would face Hussein, Hassan's brother and the Prophet's grandson. Before his death (680) Mu'awiya paved the way for his son, Yazid, to succeed him. After Mu'awiya's death, Yazid began to seek pledges of allegiance (*al-bay'ah*) from influential notables, including Hussein, in various cities. As the direct descendent from the Prophet, Hussein garnered respect, support and legitimacy. But Hussein refused to pledge allegiance to Yazid, whom he perceived as corrupt (al-Sayyid 2008: 101).

In Shi'a narrative, Hussein faced a limited choice. A simple pledge of allegiance to Yazid would have saved Hussein's life and the life of his supporters; but that would have threatened the authentic message of Islam. Hussein rather chose martyrdom (*shahada*) over humiliation (*al-zull*). In AD 680, he, his family and supporters left Medina to Kufa in Iraq to prepare the battle against Yazid's forces. Hussein could have refused to pledge allegiance to Yazid in Medina. Rather, the narrative goes, he wanted his martyrdom to expose Yazid's oppression and to establish a paragon for revolution against oppression and self-sacrifice for the preservation of authentic Islam (al-Sayyid 2008; Qassem 2010b).

In Karbala, or *ard al-karb wa al-bala'* (the land of sorrow and calamity),[8] Hussein, and a few remaining supporters, confronted the forces of Yazid in the Battle of Karbala. Shi'as around the world commemorate the event annually during *Ashura* (first ten days of Muharram). The story of Hussein, his sacrifice and courage is narrated to an audience in *majalis Ashura* (*Ashura* congregations) that commemorate the battle by weeping, tapping on their breasts and, in extreme cases, striking heads with a blade causing blood to flow. The story conveys how Hussein was killed; how his head was chopped before passing it through various towns to deter people against rebellion; how other members of the Prophet's family were brutally killed; how the young Ali, Hussein's son, was hit by an arrow; how the tents of Hussein's family were plundered and then burned; how women, including Sayyidah Zaynab, Hussein's sister, are taken to Damascus (capital of the Ummayad state) as *sabaya* (slave women) by Yazid's forces.

However, why did Hussein choose to take his family, including women and the elderly, to a battle that he believed he would lose? According to Shi'a interpretations – narrated in books, *majalis Ashura* and speeches – Hussein was realising God's will. For Sayyid Ibrahim Amin al-Sayyid, of Hezbollah's Shura Council, the only 'capabilities' Imam Hussein possessed were his willingness to sacrifice himself and his family in defence of true Islam. The Battle of Karbala was a testing – *bala'* – in times of calamity, which Hussein endorsed. In Shi'a belief, Hussein's martyrdom constituted a *Taklif Ilahi*, commissioning or order by God for Hussein to be martyred with his family and companions to protect Islam (al-Sayyid 2008: 42–50). He is celebrated as the 'Doyen of the Martyrs'.

Historical accuracy and objectivity aside, the Battle of Karbala has had its lasting impact on Shi'a-Islamic identity and doctrine. In *Ashura* commemorations, Khomeini's slogan of 'Everything that we possess is from *Ashura*' is always salient. 'Everything' being the culture of sacrifice, revolution and dignity, and 'we' referring to Shi'as. Whilst for Sunni-Muslims the martyrdom of Hussein is a tragic event in the history of Islam, for Shi'as it constituted a formative moment. The Battle of Karbala formed the beginning of a new culture, ingraining a melange of feelings and beliefs in Shi'a collective consciousness: grievances and anger for the failure Muslims to protect and support the Prophet's grandson's legitimate movement; love and passion for Hussein and his family; revolution against and freedom from injustice and oppression; dignity against humiliation; and patience and restraint in the face of hardships. These values, as we shall see below, constitute an important part of Hezbollah's belief system.

With time, the Battle of Karbala and its annual commemoration, *Ashura*, deepened the political Shi'a–Sunni schism. It brought to an end the phase of rivalry among Muslims over succession and initiated a phase of rivalry over what constitutes legitimate rule in Islam. The martyrdom of Hussein rendered political rulers in the eyes of many Shi'as illegitimate. The locus of legitimacy after Hussein centred on his nine descendants (see the Appendix). In Shi'a-Islamic belief, the Twelve Imams form the immaculate and infallible decedents of the Prophet, hence the vast majority of Shi'a-Muslims belong to the Twelver Shi'ism school of Islamic jurisprudence.[9] They are the legitimate rulers after the death of the Prophet, starting with Ali and ending with Imam Muhammad, the Twelfth Imam (al-Sayyid 2008; Qassem 2010b, 2010a).

Whilst Sunnis, out of conviction or fear of oppression and *fitnah*, recognised incumbent political rules, Shi'a doctrine perceived rulers as illegitimate (Rose 1983: 170–6). Many Shi'as, thus, turned to the *wilayah* (religio-political authority) of the Imams, as the rightful successors of the Prophet. In so doing, they established a parallel, usually concealed, locus of authority. The Imams are venerated as the grandsons of Hussein and the Prophet who possess the knowledge to interpret the Holy Qur'an and the *Hadith* (sayings and traditions of the Prophet) and have the right to collect zakat (religious tax) from their followers (Newman 2013: 47).[10]

Parallel religio-political authorities, nevertheless, disrupt political power, for they offer opportunities for religio-political mobilisation and change. The Imams' parallel authority, with its various sources of legitimacy, threatened incumbent rulers under various Islamic dynasties, starting with the Umayyads (661–750) (Newman 2013: 16–31).[11] Rulers perceived Shi'as with suspicion: either as a sect that has diverted from mainstream Islam or, more fatally, as an internal enemy seeking to ingrain *fitnah*. Thus, according to Shi'a sources, most Imams were killed by incumbent Caliphs. One exception was the last (Twelfth) Imam, Muhammad al-Mahdi. According to Shi'a doctrine, the Twelfth Imam went into *ghaybah*, or occultation, in AD 940 and will return to the world to end oppression and bring justice (Qassem 2010a). [12] This belief lies at the heart of Shi'a religious doctrine and, as we shall see, is one that shapes Hezbollah's identity and worldview.

Shi'as, Shi'ism and political order

Shi'a doctrine, however, cannot be separated from the history of the Shi'as. Shi'as treat Shi'ism as a coherent set of beliefs, despite the somewhat varying interpretations they hold. But historically Shi'ism developed only gradually. But it is logical to argue that during the Greater Occultation a more coherent narrative of Shi'a religious doctrine begins to crystallise: 'there could not be an Imami or "Twelver" form of Shi'ism before the death of the Eleventh Imam and the disappearance of the Twelfth' (Watt, 1983: 21), despite, one should add, the prevalence of *Hadith*s attributed to the Prophet in relation to the forthcoming occultation of an Imam of his family. What emerges with time, however, is a triangle of three social spheres: the Shi'as as a communal group (*ta'ifah*) in various contexts; Shi'ism as a religious doctrine that is separate from other Sunni schools of jurisprudence; and political orders (empires or states) which Shi'a communities had to coexist with. The interaction of these three spheres over time defines Shi'a history from Karbala to Hezbollah.

Consider the Shi'as as a community, or what Newman depicts as 'pockets of the faithful scattered across the region' (Newman 2013: 36; Almuhager 1994: 8). This community shared an identity – a religio-political claim and common understanding of the past – that transcended the political boundaries of the day, be they empires or modern states, and maintained relations, even if 'distant' (Chehabi 2006b) until this day. Shaped by the Battle of Karbala, Shi'a identity inculcated two seemingly conflicting attributes: self-preservation, including the exercise of *taqiyyah* (prudential dissimulation of one's beliefs) in the face of violent oppression *and* revolution against injustice. Thus, in Shi'a consciousness, it is in *Ashura* where 'blood triumphed over the sword'. This religio-cultural repertoire offered Shi'a leaders with a spectrum of political choices ranging from the exercise of restraint to revolution, depending on political circumstances (Saouli 2011: 930; Qassem 2010b: 25–6).

During the occultation of the Imam, the Shi'a locus of legitimate authority, or *wilayah*, turns to Shi'a religious scholars in the form of an Islamic-Shi'a *faqih* (jurisprudent who is knowledgeable in the principles and ordinances of Islam) or *marja'* (religious source of emulation). By articulating and transmitting Shi'a religio-political beliefs, these men (they were only men) have historically played a crucial role in keeping Shi'a beliefs coherent and communities intact. They have also acted as the unofficial arbitrators among various social and political forces within their communities (Newman 2013: 78–97; Almuhager 1992: 304).

But the political activism of religious scholars was constrained by Shi'a doctrine. Understanding these constraints is key to explaining Hezbollah's adoption of *Wilayat al-Faqih* in the twentieth century. During the Greater Occultation, the question of the *wilayah* formed a cornerstone of Shi'a doctrine, debate and confusion. Particularly contentious was the degree of authority the *faqih* should hold. Shi'a jurists generally agree that in the absence of the awaited *al-Mahdi*, the *wilayah* should focus on socio-religious matters.[13] But disagreements have, nevertheless, centred, even until this day, on whether the *wilayah* should involve the jurisprudents' direct exercise of political authority.[14] The various doctrinal attempts to extend the role of the *faqih* to the political realm failed to materialise until an angry Islamic-Shi'a jurist called Ayatollah Ruhollah Khomeini (1902–89) advanced his own revolutionary interpretations.[15]

In a series of lectures given in 1970 during his exile in Najaf,[16] Khomeini laid the theoretical foundations for the 'Islamic Government' (*al-Hukuma al-Islamiyya*) or *Wilayat al-Faqih* (Khomeini n.d.), which would later materialise in the Islamic Republic of Iran. His treatise involves doctrinal and circumstantial elements, both of which are useful to understand Hezbollah's origins and being. Khomeini's thesis is straightforward. The opening lines of his treatise express his shock that Islamic scholars have not yet seen the obvious:

> The governance of the fakih is a subject that has . . . little need of demonstration, for anyone who has some general awareness of the beliefs and ordinances of Islam will unhesitatingly give his assent to the principle of the governance of the fakih as soon as he encounters it. (Khomeini n.d.: 7)

Islam, he prompted, is a 'comprehensive' faith that offers solutions and ordinances to all economic, social and political spheres of life, which are found in shariah (comprehensive law of Islam originating in the Qur'an and *Hadith*) (9). Shariah, urged Khomeini, requires institutions to realise its goals (15, 18, 37); its natural home is in government. Islam is, thus, a religion and a state. The Prophet, Khomeini reminded, established a state, waged wars, collected taxes and entered into treatises: 'The Messenger(s) of God was an executor of the Law' and that is why he designated successors (16, 18, 29).

But who has the authority or *wilayah* over the Islamic government? Who leads the *Ummah* during the occultation of the *Mahdi*? The *faqih*s, Khomeini unequivocally answered. They are the most knowledgeable people in shariah and, thus, the natural successors of the Prophet until the return of the awaited *Mahdi* (38–46).[17] For Khomeini, it is 'the [religious] duty of the Imams and the just fuqaha [pl. of *faqih*] to use government institutions to execute divine law' to preserve Islam (37). The *faqih* 'is the leader of the Muslims' (50); 'obedience to them [the fuqaha] is a [religious] duty' (64).

In this way, Khomeini laid the religio-political foundations for *Wilayat al-Faqih*, the theory on which the Islamic Republic of Iran stands and the one which Hezbollah adopted in the 1980s. Despite the reservations and refusal of the theory by many Shi'a scholars, it is not an exaggeration to argue that Shi'i doctrine and world vision would for ever change after Khomeini's intellectual revolt. However, what gave the theory its real-world basis is the circumstances under which it was produced, namely: the religious, social and political orders which Khomeini revolted against. This is the second element of his treatise.

In many ways, Khomeini was a product of the twentieth century. Like other Islamist (and secular) revolutionaries, he deplored the political division of Muslim territories by colonial powers, especially the Ottoman Empire. He condemned Western control of Muslim countries and resources and the 'puppet regimes' they have empowered. He attributed Muslim decline to an imperialist conspiracy that has aimed to keep Muslims subservient. This diagnosis led Khomeini to prompt his followers – especially religious scholars – to revolt. *Wilayat al-Faqih* is, thus, not a mere theory or reinterpretation of religious texts: it is a political manifesto. It offers an answer to Lenin's 'What is to be done?' question. Khomeini urged followers to:

> [G]enerate a wave of intellectual awakening, to emerge as a current throughout society, and gradually, to take shape as organized Islamic movement . . . to pave the way in society for the implementation of Islamic law and the establishment of Islamic institutions . . . (78) Make Islam known to the people, then, and in so doing, create something akin to Ashura. Give the people Islam . . . for Islam is the school of jihad (82). Whatever is needed to preserve national independence and liberty is, again, precisely what the faqih has to offer . . . for [he] refuses to submit to others . . . the faqih does not deviate either to the left or to the right. (85)

It is common to think of Khomeini as a rebellious jurist who disrupted the so-called Shi'a 'political quietism'. But Shi'a history is replete with revolts by Shi'a religious leaders (Almuhager 1992, 1994). The nineteenth and twentieth centuries were not short of Shi'a revolt. *Faqihs* like M. H. Shirazi (1892) or M. T. Shirazi, which Khomeini mentions in his treatise, played crucial roles against British control of Iran and Iraq. In the twentieth century, scholars like[18] Muhammad Baqir al-Sadr, Mohammad Hussein Fadlallah and Mohammad Mehdi Shammesddine challenged the political orders of Lebanon and Iraq. Seeking to curtail the influence of the secular political trends (Arab nationalism, socialism and communism), they mixed religious learning with political activism (or *harakiyyah*) to relocate Islam to the heart of the political world. Al-Sadr contributed to the formation of the Islamic Dawa Party in Iraq (Jabar 2003). Fadlallah (1935–2010) played a key role in the education and mobilisation of what would later be called *al-jil al-Muslim* (the Muslim generation), several of which would become Hezbollah leaders. Fadlallah believed in the empowerment of the Islamist movement and in enhancing its confidence. His writings echoed Khomeini's: 'the true Islamic position', he noted, 'is rebellion [against] and movement to change the reality of oppression and injustice' (M. H. Fadlallah 2003: 61; Saouli 2014a). Like Khomeini, these scholars have shaped Hezbollah's identity, perceptions and behaviour.

Whilst Islamist-Shi'a thinkers have lamented the colonial division of the region into territorial states, this actual division has, ironically, offered opportunities that empowered the Shi'as as a community, Shi'ism as a doctrine and Islamist-Shi'ism as a political movement. The observation of a so-called 'Shi'a Revival' in the Middle East is the result of long processes of Shi'a appropriation of intellectual and political spheres in Iran, Lebanon, Iraq, Bahrain and Yemen, which was enabled by the emergence of the state-system. Hezbollah's emergence in Lebanon is one consequence of these historical processes.

Lebanon and the making of Hezbollah

In many ways Hezbollah is a product of the historical and transnational religious movement described above. Islam, Shi'ism and *Wilayat al-Faqih* are all key pillars of Hezbollah's being as I will demonstrate below. But before doing so it is important to explore the context, the fertile ground of Lebanon, that made Hezbollah's emergence and later socialisation possible. The making of Lebanon in 1920, a culmination of overlapping indigenous wishes of the Christian-Maronite community and the French colonial interest, constituted a major turning point in the history of the Shi'as of Greater Syria. Many attribute Lebanon's Shi'a political awakening to Imam Musa al-Sadr. Whilst this is largely accurate, it fails to appreciate the variety of approaches through which the Shi'a encountered the modern state: initial resistance to the idea of Lebanon; adaptation to and appropriation of the opportunities offered in the nascent state; and later, only later, a political awakening associated with the aim of gaining an effective share in Lebanon's confessional system.

French control of the Levant invited resistance from Arab forces refusing the division of the Arab world. Two examples are Sayyid Abd al-Hussein Sharafeddine (1872–1957) and Sayyid Muhsin al-Amin (1867–1952), both influential religious scholars and leaders from Jabal Amel (southern Lebanon), who refused colonial divisions of the region and along with other Shi'a notables pledged allegiance to Prince Faisal's government in Damascus.

Coinciding with the Arab revolts in Iraq and Syria in 1920, some Ameli Shi'as, such Adham Khanjar and Sadek Hamza, resorted to violent resistance against French forces and allied Christian villages in south Lebanon (Kourani 2012).

The failure of indigenous forces to disrupt colonial designs brought to an end the Arab resistance. However, the making of Lebanon, the establishment of a new bureaucracy and, importantly, the official recognition of the Shi'a community offered significant opportunities for Shi'a development and gradual integration in the state. Politically, the Shi'as earned the Speaker of the House position in the National Pact, an unwritten agreement that apportioned state positions to major sectarian groups in 1943 (the Maronites reserved the presidency and the Sunnis the premiership). However, there were two trends that contributed to Shi'a politicisation in Lebanon. First, beside the mainstream feudal families (such as the Asa'ads, Hamadis, Ouseirans), who had a conservative outlook and ruled over a largely illiterate community living in the socio-political peripheries of the country (namely, in the south of Lebanon and Beqaa regions), stood the traditional voice of religious scholars. The behaviour of these forces, such as Sharafeddine, fluctuated between political adaptation and dissent, depending on the issue.[19] Perceived socio-economic marginalisation and vulnerability to Israeli infiltrations constituted two areas that would shape Shi'a relations to the Lebanese state, from Sharafeddine to Nasrallah.

Second were the more radical Shi'a middle-class forces who, in search for a political voice, began to be drawn into secular (communist, socialist, Arab nationalist) political movements. This trend reflected major socio-economic transformations within the Shi'a community – increasing education, economic migration to Beirut and abroad and political mobilisation – which disrupted the social base on which Shi'a feudal families stood, creating political opportunities for change (Kourani 2012; Mustafa 2003; Siklawi 2014).

However, Shi'a political development in Lebanon began to take a different turn in the early 1960s. In 1957, the frail and ailing Sharafeddine invited his relative, the young Sayyid Musa al-Sadr, to come back to his homeland to play a leading role in the affairs of the Shi'a community in Lebanon. Al-Sadr, who had completed his studies in Najaf and Qum, accepted the invitation. By the early 1960s he was set on politically mobilising Lebanon's

Shi'as. Lebanon's consociational democracy, based on the country's multiconfessional Lebanon, offered many avenues to promote Shi'a interest. Notwithstanding his religious education and knowledge, al-Sadr was inclined to activism. He first sought to organise the Shi'as, both at home and in the diaspora, and to establish a core of educated cadres to lead the movement. The goals of his social movement, *Harakat al-Mahrumin Amal* (Amal: Movement of the Deprived) aimed to deepen Shi'a integration and representation in the state and to alleviate their poverty in peripheral regions. His charisma, status as an 'Imam' and 'Sayyid' (descendent of the Prophet), and moderate and prudent but politically powerful message appealed to many Shi'as and other Lebanese. By establishing a movement and by engaging in the day-to-day political management, al-Sadr departed from the traditional role played by Shi'a religious figures.

By the late 1960s, al-Sadr managed to mobilise a Shi'a social base, challenging secular parties that accommodated many Shi'as (Chehabi 2006b: 209).[20] In 1969, he established and gained legal recognition for the Shi'a Higher Council. In the early 1970s, despite his urge for calm in the boiling political circumstances that preceded the eruption of the civil war (1975), he, with help from the Palestinian Fateh movement, secretly established an armed wing for his movement, *Afwaj al-Muqawama al-Lubnaniyya* (Lebanese Resistance Brigades) (Chehabi 2006b). The Brigades, he claimed, aimed to resist Israeli incursions into Lebanon; but carrying arms certainly had its domestic rationale related to Shi'a self-defence in the ongoing civil war.

Al-Sadr's movement paved the way for Shi'a political awakening and organisation. There are three interrelated events, however, that deepened this awakening and directly contributed to Hezbollah's emergence in the early 1980s. First, al-Sadr's disappearance in a trip to Libya – a tragic event whose circumstances are to still to be disclosed – which ushered a new phase in Shi'a political development. Al-Sadr's leadership of Amal had contained the various factions within it – Islamist and non-Islamist alike. His disappearance, however, exposed Amal's divisions. Initially, Amal's leaders managed to mitigate the emerging political fissures by electing Nabih Berri, a pragmatist, as president and Hussein Mousawi, of the Islamist faction, as vice-president (H. Fadlallah 2009: 69).

Second, the 1979 revolution in Iran and Khomeini's revolutionary discourse emboldened Lebanon's Shi'a Islamists. The ongoing civil war since 1975 and Fadlallah, Shamseddine and the Dawa Party's (Lebanon branch) political activism made Lebanon a conducive arena to accommodate Islamist revolutionary ideals. The revolution, observes Hassan Fadlallah, a Hezbollah biographer and MP, 'generated . . . a melange of moral revival, which had a historical dimension, and a material power that could contribute to Islamist struggles' (H. Fadlallah 2009: 52). Supported by the Islamic Revolutionary Guards (IRG) – which emerged in Iran in the wake of the 1979 revolution to protect the new regime and which supported armed groups fighting Israel in the Middle East – Lebanese Islamists were eager to establish their own political organisation (Qassem 2008a: 25).[21] Nasrallah recalls that a 'major faction within Amal wanted the movement to commit to the theory of *Wilayat al-Faqih'* (quoted in Mustafa 2003: 427–30). But Amal was more akin to a national-communitarian party. It never identified with 'the movements of political Islam'. Although it requires its members to be religious, Amal has no religious goals and did not adopt Khomeini's *Wilayat al-Faqih* (Aballan 2015).[22] By 1982, the ideological divide within Amal was deepening.

Third, the Israeli invasion of Beirut in 1982 hastened the Islamists' need to establish an independent, armed movement. Relieved by the withdrawal of armed Palestinian organisations from their areas, some Shi'as, including Shammesdine and Amal, opted for the so-called 'total civil resistance' to the Israeli occupation. On the other hand, revolutionary Islamists, including M. H. Fadlallah, called for armed resistance (H. Fadlallah 2009: 58–9; Mustafa 2003: 401). In 1982, Amal joined the National Salvation Committee (NSC), which was tasked to negotiate with the US and Israel to end the occupation and to resolve Lebanon's war.[23] Opponents, including Iran, perceived the NSC as a forum to legitimate the Israeli invasion of, and the Western-backed Christian regime in, Lebanon (H. Fadlallah 2009: 68).

Amal's choice to join the NSC led to the defection of Islamist figures (Chehabi 2006b: 217).[24] For the Islamists, the Islamic Republic offered 'hope' and 'practical backing' (Qassem 2008a: 350), a strategic opportunity to realise political goals. Secretly, various groups of the Islamic movement, including the newly formed Islamic Amal, members of Lebanon's Dawa Party[25] and *Tajammu' al-'Ulama' al-Muslimun* (The Association of Islamic Scholars) in Beqaa, began to lay the basis for a new, Islamist movement.

Despite their differences, these factions agreed on three foundational religio-political norms that would have a lasting impact on what would later become Hezbollah (Nasrallah cited in Mustafa 2003: 343; H. Fadlallah 2009: 61–2):

1. that Islam, as a comprehensive set of beliefs and religious laws and rulings, would govern the movement's 'doctrine, practices, stands, and political and theoretical orientations'. The main religious sources that Hezbollah draws from are: The Holy Qur'an, *Hadith*s, Shi'a *madhhab* (or school of jurisprudence), and the biographies and sayings of *Ahl al-Bayt*;
2. that they commit to the theory of *Wilayat al-Faqih* and that the decisions of the *wilayah*, which in 1982 was represented by Imam Khomeini, are 'binding for the movement';
3. on embracing armed resistance against Israel and fighting against its invasion and occupation of Lebanon.

Notice that two of the three pillars emanate directly from the Shi'a-Islamic religio-political repertoire, discussed above. The third relates to immediate political circumstances: ideological divisions within Amal and the response to the Israeli occupation. These foundational pillars will, as I will shortly discuss, form Hezbollah as an APM.

But first it is useful to emphasise that the making of Hezbollah was not a purely Lebanese affair. The strategic alliance that Islamic Iran and Ba'athist Syria had struck since 1979 played a direct role in establishing Hezbollah. The Israeli invasion of Lebanon in 1982 deepened the alliance between the two actors. In the wake of the Israeli invasion, Lebanese Islamists, meeting in a conference in Tehran, asked for Khomeini's assistance (Mustafa 2003: 432). Khomeini, who had cut Iran's relations with Israel and established a Palestinian embassy in Tehran, was ready to come to Syria's and Lebanon's help. Iran feared that the Israeli invasion of Lebanon could potentially isolate Syria and lead it to sign an armistice with Israel. Fearing direct embroilment in the Levant and mitigating Damascus' nervousness of such involvement, Iran, with Syrian blessing, dispatched members of the IRG to train and indoctrinate Lebanese fighters in the Beqaa. Ali-Akbar Mohtashami, Iran's ambassador to Damascus, who played a key role in the making of Hezbollah, supervised the 1,500 fighters (Chehabi 2006b: 213–16; Ehteshami and

Hinnebusch 2002: 122–5). These early developments ingrained the seeds for a strategic interdependence that involves Hezbollah, Syria and Iran, which we will explore in Chapter 4.

Thus, with the presence of a dedicated Islamist movement, Iranian military and ideological aid and Syrian political, albeit contentious, acquiescence, the conditions for Hezbollah's emergence materialised. Initially, Beqaa, where the reach of the Lebanese state was (and still is) short, offered a strategic sanctuary for the nascent movement. The predominantly Shi'a region constituted a reservoir of and a passage for an Islamic 'cultural revolution' imported from Iran to Lebanon (Chehabi 2006b: 218; H. Fadlallah 1994: 14). Moreover, several Hezbollah founding members (Hussein al-Musawi, Subhi al-Tufayli, Hezbollah's first Secretary General and Abbas al-Musawi, Hezbollah' second Secretary General) came from Beqaa (Hassan Nasrallah, originally from south Lebanon, was Amal's representative in the region). Finally, the Israeli invasion and occupation of southern Lebanon, most of Beirut and Mount Lebanon and Amal's control of the southern suburbs of Beirut limited the expansion of the nascent armed group to these areas (H. Fadlallah 2009: 92–6).

Armed Political Movement

By 1985, the rudimentary organisational pillars of Hezbollah were established. In this section we will explore how religio-political doctrine (Islam and *Wilayat al-Faqih*) and political circumstances (war-making with Israel) came to shape what Hezbollah is. This will bring the discussion of this chapter to its home: Hezbollah's being. In the previous chapter, I conceptualised Hezbollah as an APM; here I offer the illustration. I treat each element of this concept (armed, political and movement) separately for analytical purposes; but, needless to say, in reality these three elements interrelate. For the flow of the argument I start with the element of 'movement'.

Hezbollah as a member of religio-political movement

Hezbollah, you will so far have noticed, is one product and manifestation of the Shi'a-Islamist history and movements. It conceives itself to be a member of this historical (transnational) movement. Sheikh Shafik Jaradi[26] observes that Hezbollah's identity and behaviour are conditioned by three religio-political beliefs (he uses the term *'aqidah*, or religious doctrine). The first relates to the *past*: belonging to the Islamic traditions and experience, with particular focus on Imam Ali – his courage, wisdom, planning and pragmatism – and the martyrdom of Imam Hussein. Second, is the *present*, and relates to Imam Khomeini's religio-political revolution. Before Khomeini, he asserts, Shi'as hoped that the return of *al-Mahdi* would 'liberate them'; however, the post-Khomeini ethos is that: 'we are oppressed, but we are also capable of realising our rights/freedoms'. The third factor, developed in post-revolutionary 'epoch of *Wilayat al-Faqih*', relates to the *future*: the preparation for the return of Imam al-Mahdi. The liberation of the community from oppression (whatever its sources are) has now come to have a *raison d'être* for the future, one that falls within Shi'a religio-political doctrine. For Jaradi, 'Hezbollah is a product of a continuous historical tradition and is moving in the direction of the future; it is certain that it will achieve victory' (Jaradi 2015).

You might argue that this perception of a 'continuous' Shi'a-Islamist history is constructed, imagined or inaccurate. You could be right. But what matters for our purposes is not whether the narrative is historically accurate, but, rather, how Hezbollah imagines the past to be, and, ultimately, how this imagination conditions its present behaviour and future planning. These perceptions are salient in Hezbollah's being and behaviour. On 16 February 1985, Hezbollah presented itself to the world with the publication of its founding manifesto, entitled 'The Open Letter to the Downtrodden in the World' (henceforth, 'Open Letter').[27] This formed the first conscious attempt to publicise a cohesive set of beliefs, motives and goals that demarcated Hezbollah as a separate (religio-) political actor. As is common in these occasions, the actor diagnosed a political situation, delegitimised an enemy, prescribed a solution, presented itself as a saviour and called for mobilisation (Tilly 2006; Schwedler 2011).

For many observers Hezbollah's Open Letter is a thing from the past: one that reflected Hezbollah's beginnings before the movement learned the wisdom of moderation and pragmatism during the so-called 'Lebanonisation'. These observers point out to Hezbollah's 'new' 2009 'Political Document', to argue that Hezbollah has 'shifted its ideology' (see Introduction). But this is inaccurate. A close look at the main premises of the Open Letter and Hezbollah's beliefs will show that these have not actually changed. I will further argue that the Open Letter lay bare Hezbollah's strategic goals.

At a doctrinal level, the Open Letter offers an answer to the key question of 'Who are we and what is our identity?':

> We are the sons of Ummat Hezbollah in Lebanon. We consider ourselves as members of the world Islamic *Ummah* . . . to whose vanguards God has given victory in Iran and who established the basis of the central Islamic state in the world . . .
>
> [We] abide by the orders of the single, wise and just authority that is embodied in the *Wilayat al-Faqih*, which possesses the right qualities, and which is now represented in Supreme Ayatollah Ruhollah Musavi Khomeini . . .
>
> We are neither a closed nor a narrow political formation. Rather, we are an *Ummah* that is tied to Muslims throughout the world by a strong religious and political bond that is Islam . . . As such what befalls the Muslims – in Afghanistan or Iraq or the Philippines or others – befalls the body of our Islamic *Ummah*, of which we are an invisible part, and we will act to confront it out of a religious duty and in light of a political vision decided by the leadership of *Wilayat al-Faqih*.
>
> As for our culture, its origins are found in the Holy Qur'an, infallible Sunnah, and the religious edicts and *fatawa* pronounced by the *faqih*, our source of [religious] emulation.

The idea of 'Ummat' Hezbollah ties the founders' religio-political goals to a global, transnational movement (H. Fadlallah 1994: 37–8). *Wilayat al-Faqih*, manifested in Khomeini in the 1980s, forms the religio-political authority of this *Ummah* and one which Hezbollah abides by. Expressive of Hezbollah's transnational identity is its flag (Figure 2.2). Initially, Hezbollah adopted the Islamic Republic's flag; however, by the late 1980s it composed its own.

The centre of the flag is a drawing of the earth symbolising Hezbollah's universal, Islamic religio-political identity that is founded on a book-like sketch representing the Holy Qur'an. The book is attached to the earth by an olive tree branch, which is perceived as holy in the Qur'an. The Kalashnikov symbolises jihad (holy war and/or personal struggle), and on top of it is the verse from the Qur'an: '[T]he Party of God is victorious' (5: 56). All this is integrated in the Arabic word of *Hizb Allah* (The party of God) (Abu Rida 2012: 361–2). In the 1980s the slogan in the bottom of the flag was:

Figure 2.2 Hezbollah's flag

'The Islamic Revolution in Lebanon'; but this was amended to the more realistic ideal in the 1990s: 'The Islamic Resistance in Lebanon' (Saouli 2003). Hezbollah's flag has very similar features to the IRG's flag and other IRG-affiliated movements in Iraq and Syria, which we will come across in Chapter 5.

In their writings and lectures, Hezbollah leaders treat the religio-political beliefs in the Open Letter as 'fixed, unchangeable'.[28] Hezbollah is committed to a 'comprehensive' Islamic vision, which lies at the heart of all facets of the movement's identity and behaviour (Qassem 2008a: 29; Saffieddine 2007: 45). Does this commit Hezbollah to the establishment of an Islamic state? The answer to this question, which has confused observers and shaped the way we examine Hezbollah, is two-pronged. Theoretically, Hezbollah's ideal is to achieve an Islamic state. Any 'committed Islamist', argues Naim Qassem, will aspire to establish such a state (Qassem 2008a: 40). But practically Hezbollah is also conscious of the socio-political impediments, particularly of Lebanon's multiconfessional society and the regional states-system, to the establishment of an Islamic state (Jaradi 2015; Qassem 2008a: 40). Shaped by M. H. Fadlallah's political thought, Hezbollah limits its aim in Lebanon to *da'wah* (call for), but does not 'impose' Islam, violently or otherwise, on others (Saouli 2014a: 13–17; Qassem 2008a: 40). The Open Letter called 'for the establishment of an Islamic system', but added that this has to be 'on the basis of free and direct choice by the people'. Given its religio-political doctrine and the socio-political constraints its faces, Hezbollah has thus opted to Islamise its social base from below. This, as we shall see in the following chapter, was crucial for *war-making* with Israel and socialisation in Lebanon. Hezbollah connects the establishment of a (global) Islamic state to the principal of preparing the ground for and return of the *Mahdi* (Abu Rida 2012: 581), which, as we shall see shortly, shapes the movement's doctrine and organisation.

But dropping the goal of establishing an Islamic state in Lebanon does not make Hezbollah less Islamic. Take Hezbollah's adoption of the theory of *Wilayat*. Whilst this theory lies at the heart of Iran's Islamic system,[29] for Hezbollah it offers a framework of a religio-political *authority*. Hezbollah leaders emphasise that the religio-political edicts (or *fatawa*) of the *faqih* are binding for the movement; they offer 'religious legitimacy' to Hezbollah's actions (Saffieddine 2007: 48; A. H. Fadlallah 2015). In a series of seven articles published in *Al-Ahed* newspaper in 1986, Hezbollah offered an elaboration of its commitment to *Wilayat al-Faqih*: 'We are followers of the *Wilayat al-Faqih*. . . for his *wilayah* resembles the *wilayah* of the Prophet and the infallible Imam, and it is a [religious] duty' (quoted in Abu Rida 2012: 347–8). *Wilayat al-Faqih*, Qassem believes, 'is the deputy of the [hidden] Imam' who is responsible for leading the *Ummah* (Qassem 2008a: 72–3). In the Imam's absence (during the Greater Occultation), he argues, believers (individuals or organisations) need to know what their *Taklif Shari'i* (religious and/or political responsibility or duty) is. As a leader of the *Ummah*, *al-Faqih*, after a thorough 'diagnosis' of social, religious and political conditions, 'identifies the broader strategies in the life of the *Ummah* and the practical role of the *mukallafin* [those who are given a responsibility] in the application of the holy shariah' (Qassem 2008a: 77). Commitment to the rulings of the *faqih* 'is one of the practical foundations in Hezbollah's culture', notes Saffieddine, Head of Hezbollah's Executive Council (Saffieddine 2007: 50). Hezbollah's members, thus, emphasise the 'organic' ties that bind their movement to the *faqih* (H. Fadlallah 1994: 43; Abu Rida 2012: 346). In Hezbollah's discourse, the *faqih*, now Imam Khamenei, is the *Sayyid Qa'id*, or supreme leader.

But does Hezbollah's commitment to the religio-political rulings of the *faqih*, who could belong to another country, contradict its Lebanese belonging? Qassem asserts that in diagnosing a situation and identifying a *Taklif Shari'i*, the *faqih* 'takes into consideration the objective and particular conditions of every group or country' that abides by his *wilayah* (Qassem 2008a: 78). In a defensive stance targeting critics who doubted Hezbollah's loyalty to Lebanon, Nasrallah emphasised that 'Wilayat al-faqih tells us [i.e. Hezbollah] that Lebanon is a multiconfessional, multi-religious (mutanawwi', muta'adid) country that you have to preserve and uphold' (quoted in Alagha 2010: 39). This is reiterated by Sheikh Jaradi who argues that Imam Khamenei has developed the concept of '*al-Tanawwu' al-Thaqafi'* (or Cultural Pluralism) to account for the different socio-political contexts his followers find themselves in. This has theoretically helped Hezbollah 'reconcile its Islamist commitment and its Lebanese belonging' (Qassem 2008a: 79).

Notwithstanding these reconciliations, it needs to be established that doctrinally and practically Hezbollah's commitment to *Wilayat al-Faqih* is paramount and may override the interests of Lebanon as a national state. To simply consider Hezbollah as a Lebanese, nationalist movement misses the deep religio-political identity that forms it. Hezbollah, first and foremost, abides by a religio-political authority that falls outside the constitutional, institutional and power balances within Lebanon. In that sense, Hezbollah is also a member of a *transnational movement*. By taking Lebanon's socio-political conditions into consideration as he issues his religio-political edicts, the *faqih affirms* Hezbollah's commitment to a transnational authority; he simply does not want a religio-political edict, which for Hezbollah is binding, to have a negative impact on the Islamist movement's standing in its own national context.

But such an interpretation need not strip Hezbollah from its Lebanese and Arab belongings and identities. Hezbollah was born in Lebanon and is a product of the country's socio-political fabric and its Shi'a social movement, as mentioned above. But, like other Islamist movements, and indeed some secular organisations (Arab nationalism, Syrian nationalism), as discussed in the previous chapter, Hezbollah has constantly attempted to reconcile its ideological beliefs to its actual presence in the national state called Lebanon. War-making with Israel and its consequences on Hezbollah's socialisation in Lebanon and the region, as we shall see in this book, attest to these attempts.

Nevertheless, commitment to the *faqih*, which Hezbollah announced in the Open Letter, is one of the 'constants' in Hezbollah's religio-political doctrine (Kanso 2013). The theory has had an impact on Hezbollah's organisation on three levels: decision-making, ideological cohesion and discipline. At the top of Hezbollah's structure stands the Shura (or Consultation) Council.[30] Composed of eight members, five of which preside over various *majalis* (or councils), the Shura Council is Hezbollah's governing body (Figure 2.3).[31] Hezbollah has no party boss; it has a General Secretary who supervises all the party's units. Shura's decisions are collectively made and are considered to be a form of *Taklif Shari'i* that binds all members (Qassem 2008b: 80; Abu Rida 2012: 463).

The various Shura councils connect to other units that are diffused geographically and vertically into: sectors (*qit'ah*), sections (*shu'bah*), factions (*fasilah*) and groups (*majmu'ah*) (Abu Rida 2012: 470–82). Through this highly and tightly centralised structure, Hezbollah has the capacity to swiftly execute visions and policies decided by the Shura and to sustain links with its social base.

Where does the *faqih* – now, Khamenei – fall in this hierarchical structure? The *faqih* does not intervene in the management of day-to-day affairs, but, as mentioned above, he is the ultimate authority on major strategic and religio-political affairs (Qassem 2008b: 87–9; Abu Rida 2012: 351). The *faqih* is represented in Lebanon through a *wakil shari'i* (lit. religious representative or agent). For many years, Nasrallah was the representative; now, it is Sheikh Mohammad Yezbek. Among other things, this role forms an important channel to receive religio-political *taklif* and to send back input and feedback associated with Lebanese and regional politics and Hezbollah's role therein. In that sense Hezbollah as a whole plays an important role in advising the *faqih*, which is crucial in the latter's 'diagnosis' of religio-political situations before he issues his *taklif* (Atrissi 2013).

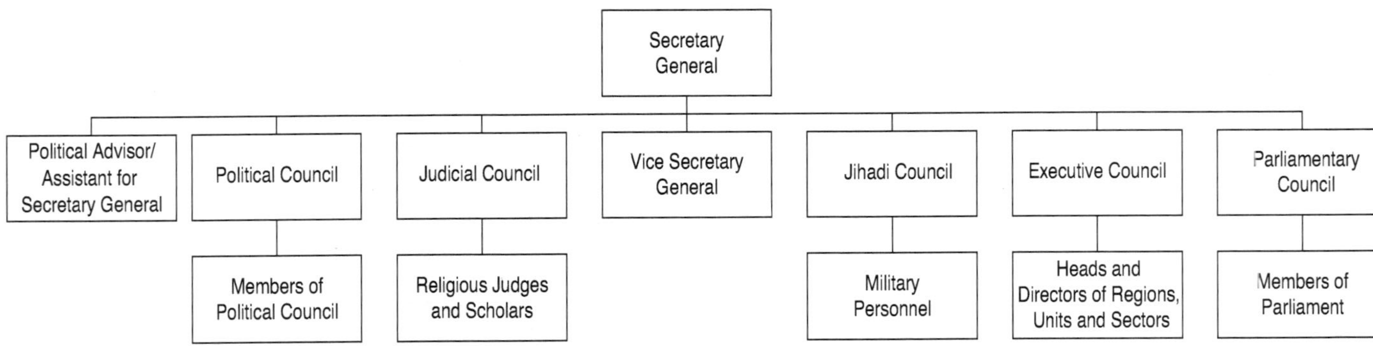

Sources: Figure based on Qassem (2008) and Abu Rida (2012)

Figure 2.3 Hezbollah's Shura Council

What practical impact has Hezbollah's ties to the *faqih* had on Hezbollah? In Nasrallah's own assessment:

> The basis of all of Hezbollah's success goes back to the role of the leader [the *faqih*]. These are the victories of the leader; I was [have been] a mere formal spokesman . . . If Hezbollah was found, if it survived, strengthened and won, it is because of the *Wilayat al-Faqih* . . . [T]he *wilayah* guarantees against deviation; for the *wilayah* has a clear vision and *taklif.* The [Hezbollah] leadership's belief in *Wilayat al-Faqih* unified Hezbollah, making it stronger and more secure, and later Hezbollah managed to unify the [Lebanese] Shi'as around it. (quoted in Abu Rida 2012: 557)

Other Hezbollah leaders add that members' obedience to the Shura orders and through it to the *faqih* has contributed to maintaining 'internal cohesion' and 'discipline' in the party (Qassem 2008b: 80–1; Saffieddine 2007: 50; Abu Rida 2012: 582–3). This organisational structure and discipline connect directly to Hezbollah's doctrinal belief in the Imamate. Hezbollah members believe themselves to be part of a tight hierarchical structure that connects a member in its lowest ranks to leaders in the higher echelons of the party and through them to the *faqih* as the 'deputy' of the hidden Imam, who is realising God's shariah (Abu Rida 2012: 352). This 'doctrinal-organisational principle' equates obedience to the party and the *faqih* to obedience to the infallible Imams, and thus the Prophet and God; this belief, argues Hussein Abu Rida, a Hezbolllah member, is a party 'doctrinal-organisational principle', which Hezbollah prefers to keep out of public discussions (Abu Rida 2012: 581–2).

This doctrinal-organisational framework offers religious legitimation and meaning to Hezbollah's actions. Hezbollah fosters the belief and acts on the basis that it is 'preparing the ground for the return of the *Mahdi*'. Its members are perceived as the *muhayyi'un* (ones who prepare the ground for) or *mumahhidun* (ones who pave the way) for the return of the awaited Messiah. Within its cultural units and fora, Hezbollah invests greatly in the promotion of the 'culture of *tamhid* (paving the way)'. Leaders regularly discuss perceived 'signs' of the return of the Twelfth Imam (al-Sayyid 2008: 78–9) and tie these to religio-political and 'jihadi concerns and goals' (Abu Rida 2012: 581; Jaradi 2015). In his book, *al-Mahdi al-Mukhallis* (The Mahdi, the Saviour), Qassem portrays contemporary regional and international political crises – corruption, oppression, poverty and aggression – as 'possible signs' for the return of the *Mahdi* (Qassem 2010a: 112, 153). Jihad 'against the Zionist occupation', he urges, 'is part of the practical and realistic operation of *tamhid* [paving the way]' (103). Hezbollah's members, thus, become the 'soldiers of the *Mahdi*' (124) or the 'Party of God' (*Hizb Allah*) as opposed to the 'Party of Satan' (*Hizb al-Shaytan*) (109, 124). In a lecture given during *Ashura* in 2006, Sayyid Ibrahim Amin al-Sayyid, one of Hezbollah's founders and head of its Political Council, argued that Hezbollah's resistance located on 'Palestine's borders' is not only a Lebanese resistance: 'they [Hezbollah fighters] are divinely soldiers in the support of the awaited *Mahdi*'. They are struggling against a global 'oppressive' system (al-Sayyid 2008: 81). These beliefs, I will show in Chapter 4, also shape Hezbollah's perception of the international system.

This religio-political doctrine is key in the education of members and fighters who undergo various religio-political, educational and administrative courses, each depending on his or her position and duties in the organisation. 'Cultural courses', for one example, offer material on Islamic and Shi'a doctrine (Qur'an and *Hadith*), the biography of *Ahl al-Bayt*, the Battle of Karbala, Khomeini's religio-political thought and current affairs. These courses come in various levels and their titles reflect the overarching doctrine. For example, it is compulsory for all Hezbollah members to take the first level, '*Junud*' (Soldiers, and refers to the 'Soldiers of the *Mahdi*'). Heads of lower units of the party have to take the second level, *Ansar* (Supporters of the *Mahdi*). The third, more advanced level, which is obligatory for medium and high-ranking members, is called *al-Mumahhidun* (Qassem 2008b: 82–3; Abu Rida 2012: 496–7). Participants, notes Qassem, are spiritually and culturally taught to 'connect to the movement of the Imam al-Mahdi when he appears', when 'Imam Khamenei would deliver the *rayah* (flag or leadership) to the awaited *Mahdi*' (Qassem 2008b: 82–3).

The impact of this religio-political doctrine can be observed by the testaments Hezbollah's fighters leave before heading to the battle.[32] For example, in one representative testament, a Hezbollah fighter (Ali Jamal Jishi) reiterates Islamic-Shi'a identity and commitment to the *wilayah*. He starts by:

> Peace be upon God's Caliph on earth, Prophet Muhammad for consolidating the pillars of Islam . . .

> Peace be upon the carrier of the Prophet's message (Ali) . . .
> Peace be upon doyens of heaven, Hassan and Hussein;
> Peace be upon the nine infallible Imams;
> Peace be upon my leader the Awaited Imam and on your followers; may God Almighty hasten his appearance and make us your followers and those who are martyred under your leadership;
> Peace be upon the Imam Khomeini, instigator of the Islamic Revolution;
> And peace be upon his rightful successor Imam Khamenei, may God preserve his presence;
> Peace be upon my leader, Sayyid Hassan Nasrallah.

He then asks his comrades, *brothers* in Islamic parlance, to preserve the jihadi path and 'to remain committed to the *taklif*, for it is the path [method] that leads to God's grace and the grace of the Awaited *Mahdi*'.

These and other testaments, as we shall further see, reflect the depth to which Hezbollah's religio-political doctrine permeates different levels of the organisation. In the following chapter, we will also see how religio-political doctrine is disseminated in society through social and cultural units of Hezbollah. We will also see in Chapter 4, how these religio-political commitments shape Hezbollah's relations to Iran.

So far we have seen how Hezbollah's religio-political doctrine makes it a member of a transnational movement. Now we turn to another element of Hezbollah's being: war-making.

War-making: Hezbollah as an armed organisation

Hezbollah identifies resistance to Israel, what I describe here as war-making, as one of its main goals. For many of its rivals, and some of its own members (H. Fadlallah 2009: 84), Hezbollah is essentially an armed organisation that has a political 'face'. One Lebanese Shi'a rival of Hezbollah argues that at its core the movement is an Iranian-led 'military group' (or *firqah 'askariyyah*) (A. Amin 2013). These readings, however, require a qualification, for they reduce Hezbollah to a military core and thus strip war-making from its religio-political and social meaning. By carrying arms to fight Israel, Hezbollah has made, as the above analysis has so far shown, a *political* stand. And this political stand cannot be divorced from Hezbollah's religio-political doctrine and the immediate conditions (state collapse in Lebanon and Israeli invasion) the nascent movement faced. Once again, the Open Letter provided a lasting rationale: 'We have no option but to fight', it pointed out, and added that Western and Israeli 'aggression can be confronted by sacrificing blood and souls'.

It is not an exaggeration to argue that since its birth, war-making with Israel has been Hezbollah's principal priority and the cornerstone to understand its socialisation process (Saouli 2011). War-making is so central that as a condition to join the party, all potential members have to undergo military training (Abu Rida 2012: 484–5; H. Fadlallah 1994: 37). Whilst the 'Jihadi Council' and the man representing it on the Shura Council are influential, military decisions are determined by Hezbollah's overall strategy and goals. The party's social, religious and political units are all geared to serve war-making. As such, it is not possible to distinguish the armed units within Hezbollah from other branches in the movement (H. Fadlallah 1994: 37).

Hezbollah's war-making with Israel, as we shall see in some detail in Chapter 4, has involved a combination of guerrilla and conventional warfare including: martyrdom operations (or suicide bombings), hostage-taking, hit-and-run guerrilla tactics, psychological warfare and rocket firing. According to several observers these military tactics have proven 'effective' (DeVore and Stähli 2015; Gabrielsen 2014; Mustafa 2003). However, there is more than the material factors (weapons, training, innovation) to Hezbollah's effectiveness. Religio-political doctrine, which we are focusing on here, is also a crucial – for Hezbollah members *the* crucial – factor in war-making efforts. This takes us to another pillar in Hezbollah's religio-political doctrine: jihad.

Jihad, which is a 'holy war' against oppressors and aggressors or a struggle to overcome one's internal ego or demons, is a main pillar of Islam. Hezbollah places important focus on jihad, which is seen as a religious duty that the *faqih* might order committed believers to pursue. Qassem argues that jihad offers the spiritual basis for the Muslim, who forsakes the indulgences of life, to preserve his belief and defend his orientation. Drawing on Islamist, especially Imam Ali's values, Hezbollah educates its members to perceive life as *Dar al-Fana'a* (lit. Abode of Demise), a passage or transitional phase to *Dar al-Baqa'a* (Abode of Eternity). Life is one of *bala'* (suffering) – a notion we came across when we looked at Imam Hussein's martyrdom – which can only be overcome by patience and belief in the afterlife. In his long will to his son Imam Hassan, Imam Ali urged his son to 'develop the habit of patience against' hardships:

> Remember my son that before you is a long and arduous journey [life] . . . do not be carried away and be allured by the infatuations of the worldly people, in the vicious life and its pleasures . . . by the sight of their [peoples'] acute struggle to possess and own this world . . . [the world] is mortal.
>
> Remember that these worldly-minded people are like barking dogs and hungry and ferocious beasts . . . the mighty lords kill and massacre the poor and the weak.[33]

Hezbollah takes these values to the realm of jihad, and life in general. Jihad is the passage to eternal life. It is not death as such that motivates the fighter, but *shahada fi sabil Allah* (martyrdom in the right path of God). A jihadist 'attains individual fulfilment', explains Saffieddine, Head of the Executive Council, when they 'meet God after he has struggled for his religion, home and humanity'. One Hezbollah fighter (Muhammad Gaafar Dagher), who was killed in Syria in 2013, echoes these beliefs: 'I write these words as my heart beats with love/passion for God and as it is craving for jihad to cleanse itself of this corrupt [lowly] life and its embellishments and indulgences'. Another fighter (Hassan Ahmad Nasser) cautions his brothers 'not to love this life for loving this life is the mother of all sins'.

For the jihadist, notes Qassem, the 'basis is a predilection for martyrdom': 'What the enemy can do', he contends, 'is to scare us of death, but when we debilitate this fear we progress in the direction of enhancing confidence and achieving victory' (Qassem 2008a: 60–6). According to the testament of Ali Jamal Jishi, 'jihad is a door that God has opened for his true believers'. In Hezbollah's doctrine and jihadi culture, 'there is no room for defeat: it is either victory or martyrdom'.

In a rare voice recording,[34] Imad Mughnieh – who was known to most of the world as a notorious terrorist but acknowledged by his enemies and allies alike as a leading Hezbollah strategist – instructs his fighters on the 'essence of spirituality':

> [Spirituality] is the basis [of jihad]; the essence of this foundation is the spirit: religious spirituality and jihadi spirituality . . . When we fight it is

> not our physical abilities that are responsible, it is our spirituality; this is the spirituality that is connected to the infinite: God, the omnipresent.

Supplementing Hezbollah's belief in jihad is the Battle of Karbala and Imam Hussein's martyrdom. Keeping with Shi'a tradition, Hezbollah has invested deeply in the annual commemoration of *Ashura*, as we shall see in the following chapter. But the reinvention of *Ashura* serves as a mobilisation tool for both the movement and its supporters. In their lectures, writings or party courses, Hezbollah leaders reiterate the story of Hussein's martyrdom to distil and disseminate values of: revolt against oppression; patience in the face of calamities; and sacrifice of the self to preserve one's and religion's dignity (Qassem 2010b; al-Sayyid 2008; Jaradi 2014). In their discourse, Hezbollah portrays its enemies – US, Israel or, lately, the so-called Islamic State – as the 'Yazids' of the modern times; Hezbollah fighters are the *Husayniyyun* (Husseinists) (Saffieddine 2007: 52). For Ibrahim Amin al-Sayyid (al-Sayyid 2008: 56), Hezbollah's struggle is 'a Husseini one'. Here there is no place for the 'lovers of [this] life'. One fighter (Adnan Musa Rida) calls upon his brothers to 'rise' against the 'oppressive Great Satan (US)' and asks them not to forget Imam Hussein's slogan: *Hayhat min al-zillah* (we reject, or would never accept, humiliation). As in Karbala, life's hardships are seen as a form of *ibtila'a*, a condition that God orders on the believer to test his or her belief, patience and restraint (Jaradi 2014: 76; H. Fadlallah 1994: 37). One fighter (Hassan Ahmad Akil) asks his mother to be patient after his death and take 'Sayyidah Zaynab as your paragon'.

These values have formed the ideational, spiritual and practical bases for Hezbollah's war-making against Israel (Saffieddine 2007: 50). But what does war-making serve? The strategic Open Letter called for the liberation of Lebanon in the way towards the 'elimination of Israel', contending that the 'historical and political facts clearly indicate there is no salvation for our *Ummah* except by pursuing this path [armed jihad against Israel]'. For Hezbollah, the liberation of Jerusalem is not a mere a political goal, but is a religio-political one. But as we shall see in later chapters, this religio-political doctrine came to serve other military and political goals, such as the military intervention in Syria and the fight against ISIS and other Syrian oppositional groups.

Unlike that of other Islamist movements Hezbollah's jihad is 'defensive':[35] that is, Muslims' right and duty to defend themselves, territories and property against aggression or occupation. The decision to engage in defensive jihad falls within the *faqih*'s remit who carefully assesses the politico-military and economic situation before committing Muslims to bloody wars (Qassem 2008a: 51–3). But, as ever in international relations, war-making and Hezbollah's military intervention in more than one arena in the region will challenge this notion of defensive, pre-emptive wars, blurring the lines between offensive and defensive, as we will explore in the last chapter (*Tragic Ironies*).

Hezbollah as a political party

This brings us to the last component of the APM conception: Hezbollah as a political party. We have come across the arguments that stress Hezbollah's 'transformation' into a political party. But the analysis of this chapter has shown that these interpretations are problematic: religio-political doctrine and war-making are integral in Hezbollah's political trajectory. However, in what ways is Hezbollah political? If religio-political doctrine offers Hezbollah with meaning and religious legitimation and if war-making gives this meaning a practical application, politics, I contend here, offers Hezbollah with other crucial advantages. Interrelatedly, these include: the means to *communicate* its message to friends and enemies; the opportunity to *legitimise* its action in the public sphere; and the avenue to establish *networks* of domestic and international alliances. Again, I isolate the element of politics only for analytical purposes.

The announcement of the Open Letter in 1985 gave Hezbollah a *public* face. By communicating a set of religio-political choices, Hezbollah demarcated its socio-political identity and boundaries (different, say, from Amal or other political organisations). Like Weber's switchmen, these choices conditioned Hezbollah's vision of the world, its public personality and political trajectory. These choices also conditioned how others perceive Hezbollah. The Open Letter distinguished enemies from allies, actual or potential. It identified the 'arrogant world', represented by the US ('The cause of all our troubles'), France and the Zionist entity (Israel), as 'its main enemies'. Domestically it branded the Phalange Party as its domestic enemy: '100,000 innocent deaths is the approximate number of the crimes the US, Israel and the Phalange committed against us'. Drawn from Hezbollah's religio-political doctrine and the political conditions of the early 1980s, which we have examined above, the Open Letter identified Hezbollah's *strategic* political goals. The nascent movement wanted to liberate Lebanon from Israeli occupation and Western influence, seek a resolution to the Lebanese war and to liberate Palestine from Zionism:

> We declare that our ambition is to make Lebanon an invisible part of the geopolitical landscape that is ruled by Islam and its just leadership [Khomeini] and that is in opposition to the US, the arrogant world and world Zionism.

This has placed Hezbollah as a rival to the pro-Western Arab regimes, which the Open Letter described as 'incapacitated . . . defeated regimes'.

This strategic vision determined the Islamist movement's choice of allies: 'Hezbollah builds its friendships and alliances based on whether others are close or distant to the goals of resistance' (A. H. Fadlallah 2015). Whereas Hezbollah presents its religio-political doctrine as coherent and fixed, in the realm of politics, Hezbollah is pragmatic. This pragmatism finds its intellectual roots in Khomeini's and M. H. Fadlallah's political thought. When Hezbollah founders met Khomeini to seek his recognition and support of their new movement, he reportedly told them: 'what matters is action [or practice]' (Nasrallah quoted in Mustafa 2003: 417). In his books, M. H. Fadlallah, who had a strong influence on the young Hezbollah founders, asked the Islamist to be proactive, but also realistic, not to seek 'fictional goals'. Acquiring power, he cautioned, necessitates a 'piecemeal approach and prudent planning', which starts by understanding one's 'spiritual and material strength' and the *context* one finds oneself in (M. H. Fadlallah 2003: 335–7). Hezbollah's behaviour – pragmatist or otherwise – reflects these perceptions.[36] Abd al-Halim Fadlallah, a Hezbollah member, reveals the delicate balance that Hezbollah strikes between political realism and its religio-political identity: 'Political realism contributes to the survival and sustainability [of Hezbollah]. However, if we go to the extreme in our political realism, we threaten our [religio-] political identity' (A. H. Fadlallah 2015).

It is no coincidence that many scholars focus, mostly, on this sphere to depict Hezbollah as a 'realist actor'. But it is more accurate to suggest that Hezbollah's pragmatism is not an end in itself or a 'phase' that Hezbollah has just leaped into; it is, rather, an avenue to realise religio-political goals, not least those associated with war-making with Israel and survival of Hezbollah and its allies (for the theoretical premise of this point, see Chapter 2). As such, Hezbollah did not let its religio-political doctrine come in the way of its political interactions. It did not transform its doctrine into an ideology to govern the Lebanese state (A. H. Fadlallah 2015). Ideological divisions with allies, argues Qassem (2008a: 42–3), should not divert energies from war-making: we need 'not be drawn into a discussion about the sex of angels when our land is occupied; we should buttress our common goals [or capacities] at a practical level'.

Hezbollah's pragmatism has contextual origins too. Its emergence came after the failure of both Arab regimes and organisations (such as the PLO or other secular organisations) to achieve any concrete results in the Arab–Israeli conflict. Fear of embroilment in domestic divides, as we shall see in the following chapter, led Hezbollah to prioritise war-making with Israel over other political differences: it is not important to 'perform military parades', the Open Letter cautioned, 'what is important is to increase [military] operations against Israel'.

Related to pragmatism and context is Hezbollah's endless quest to secure legitimacy: the justification through word and deed rationales to gain socio-political support and recognition. The Open Letter triggered this process when it justified Hezbollah's emergence and the reasons it wanted to carry arms: 'The arrogant world is in agreement to fight us'; 'we have no choice but to confront [it]'. Through discourse – particularly Nasrallah's speeches – Hezbollah has aimed to legitimise its actions to and mobilise the public for war-making efforts in Lebanon and the region. In Lebanon, Hezbollah formalised itself into a political party after the war. With a religio-political *fatwa* in hand, it joined Lebanon's parliament and began a gradual process of socialisation in Lebanon, as we shall see in detail in the following chapter. In 1992, it won seats in the parliament and formed the 'Loyalty to the Resistance' bloc, the head (MP Mohammad Raad) of which is represented in the Shura Council. In 2005, it joined the government for the first time. These actions have contributed to legitimise and to legalise its status as an armed movement in Lebanon.

War-making has pushed Hezbollah to establish its own socio-political base in Lebanon. The Shi'a community was the natural base to build on. Hezbollah established its own social welfare programmes with primary focus given to fighters and their families. This social support, which supplements integration in formal institutions, has offered Hezbollah with social roots and, hence, legitimacy. To consolidate its social base, Hezbollah had to unite the Shi'as around its political goals, tying its fate to the community. Through religious, national and political mobilisation and by the dissemination of religio-political doctrine, Hezbollah has aimed to promote the 'culture' and 'values' of resistance. In doing so, it hoped to establish the basis for *Mujtama' al-Muqawamah* (Resistance Society) (Qassem 2008b), which resonates with al-Sadr's *Mujtama'at al-Harb* (War Society).[37] In his book, Hussein Abu Rida, a Hezbollah member and researcher, discloses that:

> Hezbollah has aimed to reunite the Shi'a community in the context of a comprehensive strategy, making it [the Shi'a community] the spearhead in the universal Islamic strategy according to *Wilayat al-Faqih*'s vision. Hence, the ideology of 'resistance' seemed in the discourse of Hezbollah as both an end and means in one mobilisational framework. (Abu Rida 2012: 582)

Abu Rida's admission is not one that Hezbollah likes to propagate in public; but, ironically, it is one that dovetails with Hezbollah's critics who accuse the movement of 'dragging' Lebanon's Shi'as into regional wars (Fatfat 2015; Costanian 2015).

Through these political acts, Hezbollah aimed to legitimise itself and thus enabled the formation of alliances domestically and regionally. As we shall see in the following chapters, Hezbollah formed strategic alliances in Lebanon (most important of which was the FMP) and the region (Syria, Iran, Islamic Jihad, Iraqi Shi'as) that contributed to its survival and realisation of strategic goals.

In 2009, Hezbollah presented its 'Political Document' (hereafter the 'Document') (*Hizb Allah: al-wathiqah al-siyasiyyah* [Hezbollah: political document] 2009). Many have interpreted the Document as the last nail in the coffin of Hezbollah's 'ideology'. But this is inaccurate. The Document came after more than a quarter of a century of Hezbollah's socialisation processes. It constituted an assessment of Hezbollah's integration in and vision of Lebanon. It emphasised Hezbollah's commitment to Lebanon, *al-watan* (the homeland) (*Hizb Allah* 2009: 30), the country that requires a 'strong state' and a 'national defence strategy' to protect it from Israel. The Document emphasises Hezbollah's commitment to the national state, muting its universalist worldview. It acknowledges Lebanon's 'consociational system' as the most realistic system. It does not mention any internal enemies, but continued to treat the US and Israel as menacing enemies to Lebanon, the Arabo-Islamic world and the world as a whole. The Document recognises European countries as rivals, but not enemies (which is probably due to the recognition of Hezbollah by many European states as a resistance movement). It reiterates the right of armed struggle against Israel.

The Document is a testament to Hezbollah's socialisation in and political adaptation to Lebanon's divided society. It resembles the political 'programmes' of other Lebanese political parties – ones that rarely trigger attention or, let alone, debate. When Nasrallah presented the Document in a conference, Talal Salman, the editor-in-chief of *As-Safir* newspaper, who attended the conference, greeted Nasrallah with the words: 'Welcome to the Lebanese Political Club'. Notwithstanding these remarks, what was interesting in the Document is that it did *not* touch on religio-political doctrine. Careful as it is, Hezbollah named the document as *al-Wathiqah al-Siyasiyyah* (*Political* Document). 'What about your ideology?' asked one curious journalist. Unequivocally, Nasrallah replied: 'our [religio-political] doctrine is fixed'; it does not adjust to changing political circumstances (A. H. Fadlallah 2015).

Conclusion

Nasrallah's answer reflects the interpretation I advanced in this chapter. By 'fixed', I do not mean that the doctrine is frozen in time or closed to possible reinterpretation or development – indeed this chapter has shown that the theory of *Wilayat al-Faqih* has developed in ways that take into consideration contextual factors. The theory continues to be an area of contestations among Islamic, particularly Shi'a, scholars. Rather it is Hezbollah's *commitment* to its religio-political doctrine that is fixed. As I have argued in this chapter, religio-political doctrine is fundamental to Hezbollah's being and *raison d'être*. The doctrine combines the belief in Islam as a comprehensive value system, commitment to Shi'ism and acceptance of Khomeini's *Wilayat al-Faqih*. To demonstrate this, I first examined the Islamist movement's genesis: the religious, historical and political conditions that contributed to Hezbollah's emergence in the period 1978–85. I then moved on to show how these factors made Hezbollah an armed political movement.

Despite the many obituaries written for Hezbollah's Open Letter, this chapter shows that this document remains the main charter of Hezbollah's strategic goals. It is a product of both Hezbollah's religio-political identity and the political conditions the movement revolted against in the 1980s. These strategic goals – war-making against Israel, limiting Western influence in Lebanon and the region, aligning with the Islamic Republic and, ultimately, eliminating the Zionist occupation of Palestine – have motivated Hezbollah's socialisation in Lebanon and the region. Hezbollah, the chapter demonstrated, has connected these goals to religio-political elements, not least jihad, commitment to *Wilayat al-Faqih* and the preparation for the return of the awaited *Mahdi*.

These ideals and the struggle to realise them have shaped Hezbollah as an APM. The chapter shows that Hezbollah perceives itself as and is a member of a transnational movement tied organically to *Wilayat al-Faqih*. It is also an armed movement dedicated primarily, but not solely, to war-making with Israel. The chapter also highlighted Hezbollah as a political party that has used political avenues to realise its goals. Despite the analytical separation of these elements – armed, political, movement – in reality they are inseparable.

This chapter focused mostly on Hezbollah as an actor – its origins, identity, ideals. The following two chapters will explore how Hezbollah has attempted to realise its goals – purposeful socialisation – in domestic and international arenas, respectively. The last chapter examines some of the discontents this has generated.

Notes

1. I thank Moutaz Alkheder and Abla Mahmoud for offering their advice on the translation of this address. Any mistakes in the translations are mine and mine alone.

2. For the clip, see <https://www.youtube.com/watch?v=zWcRdOvH7ng> (last accessed 15 January 2017).
3. I will here use doctrine rather than ideology, given that Hezbollah's doctrine is based on both religious and political sets of beliefs that are not distilled or articulated into a clear-cut ideology. For an analysis of ideology as a modern concept and phenomena, see Baradat 1997.
4. For Saade (2016: 162) 'Hizbullah ideology, or what Hizbullah "is" in this sense, is the legacy of the resistance as a series of events, stories, people, and actions'.
5. Ali was among the first to convert to Islam and is celebrated by both Sunnis and Shi'as for his oratory, wisdom and religious commitment. For a collection of Imam Ali's major sayings including explanation by Muhammad Abdo, see his Ibn Abi Talib 2003.
6. According to the *Hadith* (a tradition based on a saying or deed of the Prophet), it is believed that the Prophet said: 'O people! Of whomsoever I am a master, Ali is his master. My Lord, befriend anyone who befriends Ali and make enmity towards anyone who makes enmity towards him' (Qassem 2010a, 48–9).
7. For a historical narrative, see Newman 2013, 18–21.
8. *Bala'* also means 'testing', in where God tests the believer's religious commitment in times of calamity. It is a notion that we will come back to when we examine Hezbollah's values and behaviour.
9. The sect is also called Shi'a Imamate or Ja'faris referring to Ja'far al-Sadiq, the sixth Imam who played a key role in establishing religio-legal codes.
10. There is also a religious interpretation for this *wilayah*. According to one *Hadith*, the Prophet told his followers that he is leaving behind him two 'momentous and trying things (*al-thiqlayn*)', which if followed believers would not go astray: the Holy Qur'an and his *Ahl al-Bayt*. For the actual *Hadith*s and sources, interpretation and dissemination by Hezbollah officials, see Qassem 2010a (45–9) and al-Sayyid 2008 (24–6).
11. Pro-Alid revolts under the Ummayad dynasty capitalised on Shi'a grievances and legitimacy and brought the Abbassid dynasty to power in 750 (Watt 1983: 22–4). In other instances, the Caliph capitalised on Shi'a sentiment – as in al-Ma'mun's case who announced the eighth Imam, al-Rida, as his heir – to legitimate his power.
12. Shi'as demarcate a Lesser Occultation and Greater Occultation. During the Lesser Occultation, *al-Mahdi* corresponded with his supporters through four *wakil*s, 'ambassadors' or 'agents': trusted men that carried messages and tithes back and forth between him and his followers. However, with the

death of the fourth ambassador in 940, *al-Mahdi* entered into the Greater Occultation.

13. These include guardianship over the Muslim community, administering and preserving its properties (mosques, schools, holy shrines, charitable endowments) and arbitrating communal disputes within and outside shariah courts. Notice, these functions of the *wilayah* dovetail with the description of the role of the religious scholar described above.
14. Shi'a *faqihs*, such as Sharif al-Murtaza (d.1044) and Ibn Hasan al-Tusi (d.1067), debated whether and to what extent Shi'as should serve under an 'illegitimate and oppressive' government (Rose 1983; Newman 2013); others, especially those associated with the Safavid period (1503–1722), such as Mohammad Baqer Majlesi (d.1699) and Sheikh al-Hurr al-Amili (d.1693), and ones that followed, such as Sheikh Morteza Ansari (d.1864) and Ayatollah Mohammad Naini (d.1936), advanced theories on the political role the *faqih* should take.
15. Khomeini was one amongst other scholars in Iran who sought to bring Islam back to politics. Others include Jalal Al-e-Ahmad (1923–69), Morteza Motahhari (1920–79) and Ali Shariati (d.1977) (Dabashi 2012: 268–75).
16. Khomeini's two-week lectures were a response to Ayatollah Abu al-Qasim al-Khoei, who did not believe that there was a religious basis for a political *wilayah* for the *faqih*.
17. Khomeini prescribed that 'Since the Islamic government is a government of law, those acquainted with the law, or more precisely, with religion – i.e. the fuqaha – must supervise its functioning. It is they who supervise all executive and administrative affairs of the country, together with all planning' (Khomeini n.d.: 46).
18. And for that matter other (Sunni) Islamist thinkers and activists of the twentieth century such as Imam Hassan al-Banna or Sayyid Qutb.
19. In an early sign of Shi'a discontent, Sayyid Sharafeddine sent a letter to President Bechara El Khoury complaining about the government's silence in the face of Israeli attacks against and the absence of socio-economic welfare in southern villages, which he described as the 'losing partner' in the nascent Lebanese republic (quoted in Kourani 2012: 141).
20. Such as the Lebanese Communist Party, Kamal (and later Walid) Jumblatt's Progressive Socialist Party, the Syrian Socialist National Party and even Palestinian political organisations which operated in Lebanon in the 1970s.
21. According to Chehabi (2006b: 210), Mohammad Montazeri, an Iranian

Islamist member of the opposition, who later established the Unit for Liberation Movements within the Islamic Revolutionary Guards in 1979, contributed to the strengthening of the Amal's Islamist faction as early as 1979.

22. Amal believes it is a 'national movement'. For its charter, see *Mithaq harakat Amal* [Amal movement charter] n.d.
23. The NSC included Bachir Gemayel, Walid Jumblatt, PM Shafik al-Wazzan and Nabih Berri, and was presided over by President Elias Sarkis.
24. Islamist figures who defected in various periods from Amal to later belong to Hezbollah, included: Hussein al-Musawi, Naim Qassem, Ibrahim Amin al-Sayyid, Hassan Khalil and Hassan Nasrallah.
25. The Dawa Party's public face was the Lebanese Student Federation. Dawa also tried to infiltrate Amal and to establish 'centres of power' in order to steer the movement in an Islamist direction (citing Nasrallah Mustafa 2003: 428).
26. Jaradi is head of Hezbollah's Ma'arif Institute for Religious and Philosophical Studies. The Ma'arif Institute produces a rich literature on religious and political issues that relate to Hezbollah's doctrine: <http://maarefhekmiya.org/author/shafik/> (last accessed 15 March 2017).
27. All quotes from the Open Letter are from H. Fadlallah 1994 (185–213) and are my own translation from Arabic.
28. These leaders include: General Secretary, Hassan Nasrallah, Deputy General Secretary, Sheikh Naim Qassem, Head of its Executive Council, Sayyid Hashem Saffiedine, member of its Shura Council, Sayyid Ibrahim Amin al-Sayyid, MP Hassan Fadlallah and others.
29. Article 5 of the constitution of the Islamic Republic of Iran recognises the *faqih* as the ulitimate authority in the age of occultation, echoing Khomeini's treatise: 'During the absence (ghaybah) of his holiness, the Lord of the Age, May God all mighty hasten his appearance, the sovereignty of the command [of God] and religious leadership of the community [of believers] in the Islamic Republic of Iran is the responsibility of the faqih who is just, pious, knowledgeable about his era, courageous and a capable and efficient administrator, as indicated in Article 107'. See the constitutions at <http://www.wipo.int/edocs/lexdocs/laws/en/ir/ir001en.pdf> (last accessed 16 May 2017) (Hamzeh 2004; Saad-Ghorayeb 2002; Jaber 1997).
30. *Shura* is an Islamic concept and it appears in the Holy Qur'an (42: 38), calling upon Muslims to seek consultation and discussion before taking decisions.
31. The councils are (1) *Vice-Secretary General*: takes-over the role of General

Secretary in his absence and supervises Hezbollah's work in parliament and government; (2) *Political Council*: incorporates members and units who are responsible for various political portfolios and relations with other political forces; (3) *Executive Council*: incorporates cultural, social, educational, professional and other units that execute Hezbollah's policies; (4) *Judiciary Council*: composed of Islamic judges and is one that adjudicates and resolves conflicts within the party; (5) *Jihadi Council*, which includes leading members of Hezbollah's armed unit (names of which are kept secret) and is presided over by Nasrallah; and (6) *Parliamentary Council*: composed of Hezbollah's parliamentary block. From available data we know that members are: Sayyid Hassan Nasrallah (Secretary General), Sheikh Naim Qassem (Vice-Secretary General), Sayyid Hashem Saffieddine (Executive Council), Sheikh Mohammad Yezbek (Judiciary Council), Sayyid Ibrahim Amin al-Sayyid (Political Council) and Muhammad Raad (Parliamentary Council). Nasrallah's political 'assistant' is Hassan Khalil.

32. I have chosen a random sample of thirty-three testaments of Hezbollah fighters from three different periods: 1980s, 1990s and since 2012. The sample is drawn from Al-Manar's programme *Ahya'a 'inda Rabihim* (Alive with God) and from YouTube. The programme episodes can be found via Al-Manar website < http://program.almanar.com.lb/program/1747>. The list of the examined testaments is found in the Appendix. I would like to thank Professor Talal Atrissi, of the Lebanese University, for suggesting that I should look at the testaments.
33. This extract is taken from the English translation of *Nahj al-balaghah*, found at <http://www.dawoodi-bohras.com/pdfs/Nahjul-Balagah-English.pdf> (last accessed 22 January 2017).
34. Available at <https://www.youtube.com/watch?v=vcW-kpEsmOA> (last accessed 12 June 2018).
35. This is different from *al-jihad al-ibtida'i* (or basic jihad), which is basically offensive jihad and involves Muslims confronting others and entering into their territories. The decision of this kind of jihad falls (according to Shi'a Islamists) with the Prophet or the infallible Imams, which does not apply in the age of Greater Occulatation (Qassem 2008a: 53).
36. For a long period, Fadlallah was inaccurately perceived as Hezbollah's 'spiritual father'. For a detailed study of Fadlallah's impact on and relationship to Hezbollah, see Saouli 2014a.
37. It is useful to note that the concept of Resistance Society started with Imam

Musa al-Sadr when he talked about *Mujtama'at al-Harb* (lit. a war society) (Mustafa 2003: 411). Later, in practice but also in theory, Hezbollah developed the concept to *al-Mujtama' al-Muqawamah* (Resistance Society), see Qassem 2008b.

3

Hezbollah Makes War, War Makes Hezbollah

> Each man, as it were, confronts himself. He 'conceals his passions', 'disavows his heart', 'acts against his feelings'. The pleasure or inclination of the moment is restrained in anticipation of the disagreeable consequences of its indulgence.
>
> Norbert Elias, *The Civilizing Process*

> After 2006 [war with Israel], each word, each letter, and each appearance was calculated. The positions [of rivals] were built on the speech; there were consequences. Speeches were placed under total scrutiny, and they were followed by friends and enemies and, thus, I have become critically more responsible. There was a higher level of expectations. This ceased to be about my personal mood, whether I like to give a speech or not. It was not personal anymore. I became conscious of the need to avoid committing mistakes . . .
>
> Hassan Nasrallah, *Al-Akhbar*, 15 August 2014

On 24 May 2000, reports of Israeli military withdrawal from occupied territories in south Lebanon began to flow to Hezbollah's leadership. Hezbollah was not surprised. Newly elected Israeli PM, Ehud Barak, promised to pull the troops out. But the withdrawal, which began in the middle of the night, was sudden and chaotic. Israel's proxy militia, the South Lebanese Army (SLA), collapsed. Thousands of its fighters fled to border crossings to seek refuge in Israel. The jailers of the Khiam prison, where Lebanese activists were detained and tortured, fled. Euphoric and in disbelief, many Lebanese flowed into the liberated villages. It was a historic day. But amidst the chaos and celebrations, Hezbollah had one major obsession: to prevent acts of retribution against Israeli collaborators and their families. It largely succeeded. A correspondent of *The Guardian* newspaper observed that after a twenty-two-year occupation, most liberated villages fell into Hezbollah's hands 'without a shot' (Goldenberg 2000). Hezbollah's behaviour refuted hitherto made predictions that Israeli withdrawal from Lebanon would generate bloodshed.

But why did Hezbollah not resort to executions of rivals as other triumphant movements (I am thinking of the French resistance after World War II or the Islamist revolutionaries in Iran) have previously done? Why did it prevent its own supporters from doing so? An answer to these questions takes us to the heart of this book's topic: Hezbollah's socialisation. This instance of restraint was neither an isolated nor a spontaneous act in Hezbollah's behaviour. It was, as I will demonstrate here and in later chapters, an integral element in Hezbollah's overall socialisation in Lebanon.

I suggested in Chapter 1 that Hezbollah's socialisation process (1985–2017) can be understood by situating the movement at the juncture of two interpenetrated 'anarchical orders': Lebanon and the Middle East region. War-making with Israel has determined the nature of Hezbollah's socialisation in both arenas. Hezbollah's socialisation reflects the Islamist movement's attempts to overcome constraints, both material and normative, and to appropriate opportunities as it aimed to realise its religio-political goals.

This chapter will explore Hezbollah's socialisation in the domestic arena. It divides chronologically into two phases that reflect Hezbollah's growth and development: 1985–90 and 1990–2005. Chapter 5 (*Tragic Ironies*) will resume the narrative and will look at the period 2005–17. Here I show that Hezbollah's socialisation in Lebanon is the continuation of war with Israel by other means. War-making has necessitated domestic security, socio-economic and political measures that have reinforced Hezbollah's external strategy. Hezbollah's socialisation in Lebanon, I demonstrate, has involved the use of violence, acts of self-restraint and varying presentations and re-presentations of its identity.[1]

Anarchy, Identity and Violence (1985–90)

I proposed above that socialisation is the purposeful participation of political actors in a society to preserve or alter political structures. Hezbollah's emergence in Lebanon in the early 1980s was one example of this attempt. To participate, Hezbollah needed the space to perform its identity, to mobilise support and to be able to act. The main goal was to weaken Western intervention in Lebanon and to establish armed resistance against the Israeli occupation. But in establishing this space and in attempting to realise its religio-political goals, Hezbollah threatened the power and goals of other groups in war-torn Lebanon.

It is well known that wars are the continuation of politics by other means. In many ways they manifest the failure of politics, pitting those who want to revise an existing political order against others who want to preserve it. In Lebanon, Muslims (and ambitious groups of leftist and secular forces) wanted to revise Lebanon's system to give them a more equitable share in the country's consociational democracy. Christians on the other hand, fearing that they may lose their political grip on Lebanon, fought against revising the system. The country's geopolitical location – a buffer zone and an area of contestation for Israel and Syria – in a highly polarised Middle East region, has moreover made it one of the most vulnerable and penetrated countries of the Middle East (Saouli 2006). The presence of a large community of Palestinian refugees and the dislocation of the PLO to Lebanon in the late 1960s and early 1970s, exacerbated Lebanon's domestic divide: many Muslim and leftist groups sided with the Palestinians; Christians resisted the Palestinian armed presence in Lebanon.

By 1982, Lebanon had become the arena for competing domestic, regional and international strategies. Syria perceived Lebanon as its underbelly (its Ba'athist regime did not formally recognise Lebanon's statehood until 2009). The Syrian strategy in Lebanon aimed to avert Western and Israeli influence and to prevent the emergence of a Lebanese hegemon. With Arab and US acquiescence, it militarily intervened in Lebanon in 1976 and prevented the victory of a coalition of Muslims/Palestinian/leftist forces against their Christian foes. Syrian intervention restored the Lebanese sectarian balance, bringing a short end to the so-called two-year war (1975–6). But Syria failed to lay the foundations for a political resolution.

The Israeli invasion in 1982 – coming after Egypt's signing of the Camp David Agreement and during the Iran–Iraq war (1980–8) – aimed to defeat the PLO, install a friendly regime in Beirut and curb Syrian influence. Put differently, the invasion wanted to relocate Lebanon into the Western-led camp of the US, France, Israel and their regional Arab allies, a prospect that would have alienated Assad's regime and paved the way for other Arabs (such as Lebanon, Jordan and the PLO) to sign peace treaties with Israel (Bregman 2016; Schiff and Ya'ari 1985).

Whilst some Lebanese Muslim leaders acquiesced with the Israeli invasion – speaking about the need to adapt to the forthcoming 'American epoch' in Lebanon – others refused to yield; the Israeli invasion, after all, was also a 'triumph' for their domestic Christian foes. The Israeli invasion also led to the defeat and expulsion of the PLO, which left a politico-military vacuum in Lebanon's Muslim areas. One outcome of the Israeli military advance was the signing of the 17 May agreement with the Lebanese government. Syria, Iran and the Islamists rejected the agreement. 'It was natural for the Islamists to reject the agreement', H. Fadlallah recalls, 'for any negotiations with Israel would entail a recognition of its existence, and thus its legitimacy' (H. Fadlallah 1994: 49). This placed Islamist groups (and, indeed, many secular movements), including the nascent Hezbollah, in confrontation with the Lebanese government.

By 1982 Lebanon was deeply divided among its Muslim and Christian parts (west and east Beirut, respectively). After a series of bloody battles, the Lebanese Forces managed to gain the upper hand in Christian areas, paving the way for its leader, Bachir Gemayel, to become president (Khalaf 2004: 241). The exit of the PLO, on the other hand, triggered a politico-military contest in Muslim areas. For Amal, who had become a formidable military power with strong roots in the Shi'a community, the withdrawal of the Palestinians presented an opportunity to gain control of Shi'a areas and to seek a political solution that would strengthen Shi'a representation in Lebanon's political system. For Syria, which was obsessively seeking to halt attempts to transform Lebanon into a threat to its security, Amal was a reliable ally that was able to contain potential rivals, including the PLO, and to form a bridge for Syria's return to Muslim areas.

By 1984, there were around 186 armed groups in Lebanon, each vying in endless bloody battles for its goals and interests and usually with the support of external patrons (Khalaf 2004: 240). This was the political world – Lebanon's Hobbesian anarchy – which the embryonic Hezbollah came to participate in. Conditioned by its religio-political identity and galvanised by the Islamic Revolution and the Israeli invasion, as we saw above, Hezbollah presented its own vision, or *al-Khiyar al-Akhar* (the alternative choice) for Lebanon (H. Fadlallah 1994). To realise its vision, it had to overcome major political and material constraints, ones that explain its first phase of socialisation in the 1982–90 period. In the 1980s, Hezbollah wanted to carve for itself a place in the divided country to achieve its aims: war-making with Israel, targeting Western influence in Lebanon and the re-location of Lebanon to the anti-Western camp.

If we were to venture and draw a line of causation of Hezbollah's socialisation in the complex and dizzying Lebanon war of the 1980s, we would find that Hezbollah attempted to realise its religio-political vision by the appropriation of political, social and territorial spaces that were necessary to realise its goals. It demarcated a separate socio-political identity, engaged in armed conflicts and supplemented these with the delivery of social services. This appropriation of socio-political space, however, challenged existing powers, especially Amal, leading to a bloody war between the two Shi'a movements in 1988–90.

In the first phase of its socialisation, Hezbollah aimed to demarcate a socio-political identity and doctrine in relation to others. This was not a mere political instrument; it was an expression and reflection of Hezbollah's religio-political identity and goals that set it *apart* from other political visions in Lebanon and the region. Hezbollah was carving the socio-political space as a *prerequisite* to act politically and militarily in Lebanon: namely, to recruit and indoctrinate fighters, mobilise the public and fight. Hezbollah presented itself as a victim of and a rebel against unjust political orders. Its young and very passionate founders (most of whom were in their twenties and thirties) believed they were not a 'typical' political party, a point that was highlighted in the Open Letter. Fighting Israel in Lebanon, they were keen to emphasise, was necessary to liberate Jerusalem from Zionist occupation. In the 1980s, some believed that Imam Khomeini was on his way to liberate Jerusalem and deliver the banner to the awaited *Mahdi* (A. Fadlallah 2015). These ideals set Hezbollah apart from Amal, Hezbollah's established rival within the Shi'a community. In an interview given to *Al-Ahed* in 1985, Hezbollah's mouthpiece and first Secretary General Subhi al-Tufayli emphasised the difference:

> Amal is a Lebanese movement; it seeks possible solutions for Lebanon within the existing balance of power in Lebanon. Hezbollah, on the other hand, perceives itself as an Islamic, not a Lebanese movement; the Lebanese problem concerns Hezbollah as much as it is a problem within the [broader] Islamic arena. (quoted in Abu Rida 2012: 372)

This is not surprising given what was presented in the previous chapter. But the timing of the interview and al-Tufayli's talk of '*tamayyuz*' (what separates or distinguishes) reveals Hezbollah's quest to set itself apart from its main rival. When Amal joined the government in 1984 amidst talks of negotiations between Lebanon and Israel under UN supervision, Hezbollah rebelled against the government. Abbas al-Musawi announced Hezbollah's revolutionary stance: 'We have no trust in this [political] system, and especially those who sat on the negotiations table' (quoted in H. Fadlallah 1994: 53). Hezbollah was now performing its identity or difference.

To demarcate its social space, Hezbollah disseminated its religio-political doctrine in society. In the 1980s, Lebanon – a country which found charm in all kinds of ideologies from China's Mao Zedong to America's Eisenhower – began through Hezbollah to be exposed to Khomeini's revolutionary Islamism. Revolutionary slogans, such as 'Death to America', or '*Nahnu Ummat Hizb Allah*' (We are the community of Hezbollah) or '*Ya Quds, innana qadimun*' (O Jerusalem, we are coming), began to appear in many Shi'a areas. To be fair, similar slogans were adopted previously by Arab nationalists and Islamists, but these political slogans now wore Hezbollah's own religio-political garb. In some areas the Lebanese flag was torn down (Abu Rida 2012: 372–3); instead, the flag of the Islamic Republic and the pictures of Khomeini symbolised the rise of Hezbollah. Slogans and songs demarcated Hezbollah's identity and goals:

> *Ya Aba 'Abd Allah, nahnu Ummat Hizb Allah* [O Hussein, We are Ummat Hezbollah]
> *Bi nahj al-Khomeini Namdi* [We pursue the path of Khomeini]
> *Fi sabil Allah* [For the sake or in the path of God]

This dissemination of these social norms was not alien to Shi'a-Islamist identity, but was nevertheless novel to Lebanese social traditions (Sharara

2007). The introduction of the *shador* (a black dress that covered women's body from top to the bottom) astonished many Shi'a and other Muslims – in denial about the religio-political commitment of these women, some alleged that they were paid money to wear the black garb. The religious veil (or headscarf) now had to comply with specific religious codes and standards. Hezbollah's men grew beards (which was not entirely astonishing given the leftist fascination with revolutionary beards) and introduced new dress codes: modest clothes with pale colours and tucked shirts that covered the waist. The concept of the 'committed' Muslim (or *multazim*) challenged traditional applications of Islam and reshaped social interactions. The committed believers now prayed in designated times, and no mundane obligation stood between them and God. Men and women stopped shaking hands or mixing in common places and events. Listening to music was frowned upon. Discussions about the religiously permissible (*halal*) or forbidden (*haram*) permeated social conversations. In many ways, the diffusion of Hezbollah's religio-political doctrine and norms re-defined socio-religious expectations and thus regulated standards of behaviour, particularly in Shi'a-dominated areas (Abu Rida 2012: 696–9).

The systematic diffusion of religio-political norms amounted to an 'Islamic Revolution', Hezbollah's slogan of the 1980s, if not in the political sense of the word, that is a revolution imposed from above, then certainly from below. After all, the Islamists, as Imam Khomeini (and others such as M. H. Fadlallah) had instructed them, wanted to bring Islam back to social life after it had been marginalised by modern secular movements and ideologies (such as Iranian or Arab nationalism and communism). In this regard, religious scholars and *hawzahs* (seminaries), which developed in the 1970s, played a key role in disseminating the doctrine. By 1993, there were sixteen *hawzahs* in Shi'a areas of Lebanon, four of which were directly controlled by Hezbollah.[2] By instilling Khomeinist doctrine in students, who would then become teachers, politicians and mosque leaders, Hezbollah reconstructed the politically neutral *hawzahs* of the past. By the late 1980s, religious men had re-established themselves as the vanguard of the Shi'a-Muslim society in Lebanon (Sharara 2007: 232–6; A. Amin 2013). M. H. Fadlallah, and Hezbollah's Sheikh Ragheb Harb (killed by Israel in 1984), Sheikh Subhi al-Tufayli, Abbas al-Musawi and the young Hassan Nasrallah, all played crucial roles in disseminating revolutionary Islamism. As Nasrallah recalls: 'In the 1980s I used to give a speech every night and move from Hay al-Saloum, to Ouzai, to [West] Beirut, to Chiah' (*Al-Akhbar* 2014). The focus was now on *harakiyyah* (activism) as opposed to the conformist Islam which Khomeini, Fadlallah and Baqir al-Sadr detested (Saouli 2014a). The commemoration of *Ashura*, once traditionally celebrated in small groups at homes or in a traditional performance in Nabatieh, became a major event for religio-political mobilisation – an institution in its own right, as I will elaborate below.

Religio-political doctrine, thus, formed an important bridge between Hezbollah and the mobilisation of Shi'a-Muslims. But the believer needed more than God's word and assurances about the afterlife. Like other communal political organisations in Lebanon (Cammett 2014), Hezbollah began as early as 1982 with the provision of social services. This was another means to mobilise and preserve a social base, particularly among poor Lebanese Shi'as. War-making with Israel had certainly been a key motivation in the provision of these services, but the collapse of the state and competition with Amal in the 1980s made the delivery of these welfare programmes a necessity. With direct Iranian help and in emulation of some of its agencies, Hezbollah founded the Imam Khomeini Imdad Committee, which had branches in Beirut, Tyre, Sidon and Baalbek, in 1982. Imdad (Assistance) offered thousands of scholarships, aid to the poor and interest-free loans. In 1984, Hezbollah founded the Islamic Health Unit to offer medical aid to the public, but especially Hezbollah's fighters and their families. By 2008, this unit was supervising a network of sixteen clinics and six hospitals in Beirut, Beqaa, and the south, including Imam Khomeini Hospital (established in 1982) and Rassoul al-Azam Hospital (established in 1988) in Dahieh (predominantly Shi'a southern suburb of Beirut) (Cammett 2014: 152–7). In the 1980s Hezbollah began to supply clean water and to collect garbage in Dahieh. Its education unit (*al-Hay'ah al-'Ilmiyyah*) supervises school networks, such as the al-Mahdi and al-Mustapha schools, also across several areas. Two units directly service Hezbollah's fighters and their families: Martyrs' Agency and the Agency of the Injured. These two units offer help for the families of Hezbollah's fighters who die in the battleground or, as in the latter, to those who are injured. In 1985 it established the *Jihad al-Bina'a* (Jihad for Construction) unit which has been tasked with the repairing of damage caused by wars and has been involved in major infrastructure planning in several areas of Lebanon (Harik 2005: 83–94; Qassem 2008a: 121; Cammett 2014: 152–7).

But was Hezbollah trying to establish *al-mujtama' al-naqid* ('antithesis society') or the Islamic state in this period as some have suggested (Sharara 2007; Hamzeh 2004)? To argue that Hezbollah was establishing an antithesis society, norms of which are all imported from Iran, would strip the movement of any agency and uproot it from its own Lebanese society. More accurately, Hezbollah 'activated' religio-political elements that were already latent in Shi'a-Muslim identity. Islam, the Imamate, *Ashura*, suffering, patience, restraint, revolution, dignity and freedom were not alien norms to Lebanese Shi'a-Muslims, as the previous chapter showed. Waiting for the return of the *Mahdi* is neither a Khomeini nor a Hezbollah invention: it is at the heart of Shi'a-Islamic doctrine (Newman 2013; Dabashi 2012; A. Fadlallah 2015). But what Hezbollah did was to give these norms a religio-political interpretation and meaning that was conditioned by the political goals the movement wanted to realise. Hezbollah, as Karl Marx once observed of revolutionary actors, attempts to 'anxiously conjure up the spirts of the past' (Marx 1963: 15) to the service of the present and future. Put differently, Hezbollah was reconstructing social reality to enable it to act within and through it. Hezbollah was laying the foundations to establish the Islamist and 'Resistance Society' (Qassem 2008b). As the previous chapter showed, this society forms an important springboard for the realisation of Hezbollah's goals.

Was Hezbollah trying to establish an Islamic state? Despite the recurrence of this proposition in the literature, there is no evidence to suggest that Hezbollah was willing, let alone able, to systematically attempt to institutionalise *Wilayat al-Faqih* in war-torn Lebanon. The previous chapter showed that in Hezbollah's mind there are impediments that prevent it from advancing such a project. Notwithstanding its growth and expansion in wartime Lebanon, Hezbollah did not have the power to realise such a monumental goal. The multiple visions and movements in Lebanon and international penetration therein prevented the emergence of a hegemon: no Lebanese or external force had the power to impose its will on others (that is the meaning of 'anarchy' in IR discourse). But where Hezbollah managed to lay control, some of its members or sympathisers attempted to impose their religio-political beliefs; they fanatically 'rejected everything/everyone that was different from their doctrine, ideas and behaviour' (Abu Rida 2012: 373). In some cases, shops selling alcohol were forcefully shut down or unveiled women were insulted. But in the 1980s, Hezbollah was still in formation; it still lacked the cohesion, discipline and restraint of the more mature organisation of the 1990s and thereafter. Moreover, these acts fell more within the expression of difference rather than attempts to impose an ideology. This was not different from other parties who imposed control – through taxation and the blackmailing and terrorising of rivals – in various areas of Lebanon. The erosion of social norms in wartime Lebanon and the fragmentation of its territorial space deepened the need for some form of social order. Sociologist Samir Khalaf observed that the Lebanon war 'did not only destroy common places. It also encouraged the formation of separate, exclusive, and self-sufficient spaces' (Khalaf 2004: 247). Hezbollah consciously or not was carving its own space.

The last, but certainly not least, factor that contributed to Hezbollah's growth, expansion and socialisation in Lebanon is war-making with Israel. The recruitment of fighters, the increasing number of operations against Israel and the rising number of Hezbollah martyrs all deepened Hezbollah's socio-political presence in Lebanon. Hezbollah's war-making with Israel challenged dominant political orientations in the Shi'a community. As Naim Qassem recalls: 'In general, the Lebanese were not convinced of the resistance against the Israeli occupation . . . some in our community opposed our vision and confronted us with a rejection' (quoted in Mustafa 2003: 457). The failure of the PLO's armed struggle against Israel from Lebanese territories, which among other things invited the Israeli invasion, and Shi'a disenchantment with Palestinian activities in their areas, militated against the use of violence against Israel. A telling insight of this feeling is the scene that showed some southerners welcoming Israeli soldiers when they entered Lebanon in 1982. To a large extent, Amal's political vision of the 1980s, and as we shall see shortly its collision with Hezbollah, was an expression of this general Shi'a feeling. By choosing to carry arms and fight, Hezbollah was running against a tide within its community. But that said, the nascent Hezbollah was not the only group to commit to armed resistance against Israel. Other secular movements, such as the SSNP or the Lebanese Communist Party, played a key role in the armed struggle against Israel for most of the 1980s (Mustafa 2003: 307–68).

Hezbollah's war-making involved armed resistance and constant preparation and mobilisation for war. Iranian backing was crucial. As early as 1982, the Iranian Revolutionary Guards (IRG) began to train Lebanese fighters, some of whom had already gained experience fighting with various Palestinian organisations and Lebanese secular movements (Norton 1987: 33–7).[3] The first group of fighters trained by the IRG comprised of around 180 men, including Abbas al-Musawi, Hezbollah's future Secretary General. It is believed, but cannot as yet be confirmed, that Hezbollah received about US$140 million annually in the 1980s and up to US$100 million in later years (DeVore and Stähli 2015). Financial backing from Tehran enabled Hezbollah to pay regular salaries to its fighters and the associated welfare units that supported them. In the 1980s war-making involved hit-and-run guerrilla warfare, martyrdom operations (or suicide bombings in common parlance) and hostage-taking. All these proved effective in driving Israeli troops and Western influence out of Beirut – we will explore in some detail how Iranian backing contributed to Hezbollah's strategy and successive wars with Israel in the following chapter. But it suffices here to say that war-making with Israel deepened and shaped Hezbollah's socialisation in Lebanon.

The period 1985–8 increased Hezbollah's influence in Muslim areas of Lebanon; however, the appropriation of socio-political space disrupted existing political configurations. Hezbollah's revolutionary fervour, its pan-Islamism, abhorrence of the Lebanese sectarian system, war-making with Israel, alliance with Iran and the perception of Amin Gemayel's regime as an enemy, all challenged Amal's and Syria's pragmatist approach to Lebanese and regional politics. In 1984, Berri became 'Minister of State for the South and Reconstruction' in the government and hoped to reach a political settlement to the Lebanese crisis. Amal also asserted Security Council resolution 425, which called for Israel's unconditional and full withdrawal from Lebanese territories. But these political approaches to the Lebanon war and the Israeli occupation challenged Hezbollah's militant strategy. By 1986, the ideological and political differences between Amal and Hezbollah (and their external patrons, Syria and Iran, respectively) would lead to a bloody conflict between the two actors: one that both parties, now in an indispensable strategic alliance, have invested dearly to overcome and one that they prefer to forget. Fighting over the political orientation Lebanese Shi'as should pursue, Amal and Hezbollah engaged in several cycles of violence in 1988–90. The war involved targeted assassinations of leaders, kidnappings, bombings, propaganda campaigns and the use of heavy weapons. Leading to the deaths and injuries of thousands, the war divided families, neighbourhoods and the Shi'a community at large.

The Israeli withdrawal to the 'Security Zone' by 1985 created a security and political vacuum in west Beirut, Mount Lebanon, Sidon, Nabatieh, Iqlim al-Tuffah and Tyre, which many forces sought to fill. Amal and Syria were particularly eager to fill the gap. But that also constituted an opportunity for Yasser Arafat and other Palestinian movements to re-establish a base in Lebanon after their 1982 defeat and expulsion from the country. These conflicting goals between a Lebanese force trying to gain control of its areas and Palestinian groups searching for space to exercise armed resistance against Israel led to bloody rounds of conflicts that would later be called the 'War of the Camps', in 1985–7. The presence of over 300,000 Palestinian refugees dispersed in various camps in Lebanon formed a social base for recruitment and political mobilisation, a condition Amal and Syria perceived as a threat. In 1984, Berri announced the 'Security Plan' for Beirut. With the help of the predominantly Shi'a 6th Infantry Brigade of the Lebanese army – which Berri had previously called upon to leave the Lebanese army during the 1984 uprising against the Gemayel rule – Amal placed several Palestinian refugee camps under siege. In aiming to control west Beirut, Amal clashed with the PSP, LCP and other pro-Palestinian groups such as the Arab nationalist Mourabitoun. The War of the Camps continued for over two years, with cycles of violence spreading to the Palestinian refugee camps in Sidon (Ain al-Hilweh camp) and Tyre (Rashidieh camp). In the first round (June 1985), for example, the war led to wide destruction of the camps located in west Beirut and to the deaths of 600 and injury of more than 2,000, before Syria stepped in to broker an agreement (Siklawi 2012: 18).[4]

The War of the Camps deepened the differences between Amal and the increasingly assertive Hezbollah. For Hezbollah, the War of the Camps was 'unjust'; from a religio-political perspective, Hezbollah stood with the Palestinians' right to fight Israel from Lebanon. The Islamist movement refused the killing among Muslim brothers, which, in the view of the armed movement, deflected from the focus on fighting the real enemy, Israel. As Hezbollah MP Ali Fayyad recalls:

> Hizballah stood strongly against this unjust war and played the role of mediator between the two sides. Even on some occasions Hizballah intervened militarily [to end the conflict between Amal and the Palestinians], as in the battle of Magdouche. (quoted in Siklawi 2012: 16)

But Hezbollah had considerations that transcended the role of mediation. Strategically, Hezbollah feared that if the Palestinians were disarmed, and if Amal and Syria reigned over the Muslim part of Lebanon, it might be next to be curbed and disarmed. Thus, both Hezbollah and Iran aimed to end the War of the Camps. In the battle for Maghdouche, which Fayyad refers to, Hezbollah had an interest in occupying this strategic area. According to Mamdouh Nofel (2006), of the Democratic Front for the Liberation of Palestine (DFLP), which fought with Fateh to occupy Maghdouche, Hezbollah secretly coordinated with the group to enter Maghdouche after the withdrawal of Palestinian armed groups. Hezbollah had to balance between its strategic goal of armed struggle against Israel and commitment to the Palestinian cause without alienating the Shi'a population that rejected the return of armed Palestinian organisations to their areas. It eventually controlled Maghdouche. The Amal–Palestinian war would finally end in April 1987, after 163 days of Amal siege of the camps. The Syrian deployment in west Beirut marked the end of Arafat's aim to return to Beirut and the 'Palestinian era' in Lebanon.

With Syria's and Amal's foes curbed, Amal now faced Hezbollah. The Amal–Hezbollah war, which continued for two years (1988–90), involved several rounds: April–May 1988; January 1989; and March–September 1990. In many ways, the war was a contestation over the soul of Lebanon's Shi'as: their national and religious identity; their political visions; and, ultimately, over the best political course to ensure their survival. But the war was also a manifestation of the varying visions of Iran and Syria in the war-torn country. By early 1987, Iran's interest in Lebanon had increased. As Goodarzi observes, after the Islamic Republic failed to capture Basra and to unseat Saddam Hussein's regime, it 'paid more attention to the Lebanese arena in 1987–8, channelled more resources there and showed sensitivity to other actors' attempts to undermine its influence' (Goodarzi 2009: 256). Syria, notwithstanding its alliance with Iran, was one of these actors. By 1987, it showed unease about Iran's ambitions in Iraq, which threatened the delicate balance Syria tried to establish between its alliance with the Islamic Republic, on the one hand, and the Arab nationalist identity of its regime, on the other. In Lebanon, Syria supported armed struggle against Israel for tactical reasons: to maintain pressure on Israel and to increase its diplomatic leverage with the West and Israel. This, however, contradicted with Iran and Hezbollah's strategic goal of liberating Lebanon and Palestine from Zionist occupation (Ehteshami and Hinnebusch 2002: 91). Capitalising on the violent confrontations between the vying militias in west Beirut, Syria, not without the request of some Lebanese factions, deployed there. In so doing, Syria hoped to increase its influence in Lebanon and thus to enhance its image as a stabilising actor in the volatile region. It exploited its ties to both Iran and Saudi Arabia, playing one actor off against the other to enhance its own autonomy and to make Damascus an inevitable channel for the resolution of regional conflicts – a role, which the US, to the chagrin of Iran, would acknowledge. Syria's goals, thus, challenged Iran's and Hezbollah's strategy in Lebanon.

An incident on 24 February 1987 reflected the rising tensions between the two actors. After a fifteen-month halt, in late 1986 and early 1987,[5] several Westerners were abducted in Lebanon. These abductions enraged Syria, which attributed them to Hezbollah. Two days after Syria's deployment in west Beirut, its troops reached Hezbollah's stronghold in the Bourj Abi Haidar district. After facing an initial resistance, Syrian troops attacked Hezbollah headquarters – Fathallah Barracks – and then rounded up twenty-two members, faced them to the wall and shot them. The Fathallah Massacre, as it came to be called, infuriated Hezbollah's growing constituency, which drew a crowd of 10,000 people to the funeral amidst shouts of 'death to Syria' and as its leaders began to call for restraint and prudence (Goodarzi 2009: 202). Fathallah had a disciplining effect on the revolutionary movement, making it conscious of the politico-military constraints it faced and the self-restraint it had to exercise to survive Lebanon's brutal war. On the other hand, the massacre also revealed the rising tensions among the anti-Western alliance (Iran, Syria, Amal and Hezbollah), but also the interdependence that locked them together. Iran, seeking to balance between its alliance with Syria and the protection of its Lebanese ally, increased its coordination with Syria and called upon Hezbollah to exercise restraint. One Iranian envoy, Ayatollah Jannati, vividly suggested to Hezbollah that: 'Revenge belongs to Allah. Your patience in this phase will merit Allah's best reward . . . victory is the ally of patience' (quoted in Goodarzi 2009: 205). Many years later, Nasrallah, still in alliance with the Syrian regime, would suggest that massacre was executed by 'certain members of the regime', dissociating Assad from the act.

But it would take much more blood before the contending allies resolved their politico-strategic differences. As signs of an increased US–Syrian coordination began to crystallise, in February 1988, Hezbollah abducted William Higgins, the American head of the UN Truce and Supervision Organisation, near the Amal-controlled southern city of Tyre. Hezbollah accused him of being a CIA operative and demanded the release of Lebanese and Palestinian prisoners in Israeli prisons in exchange for his release. Nabih Berri accused Iran of intervening in Lebanon and, capitalising on the act, Amal began to arrest Hezbollah officials in southern Lebanon, triggering the first and one of the bloodiest rounds of violence between the two movements. Amal managed to attack Hezbollah strongholds in Nabatieh, Jezzine and Siddiqin. The three-day fighting killed 50 and injured more than 120 before the violence spread to the Beqaa Valley and Beirut. After several clashes with the Syrian forces stationed in the Beqaa, on 2 May, Israel attacked Hezbollah's quarter in Maydoun (Beqaa) killing 40 of its fighters.

By May 1988, Hezbollah had lost its military presence in south Lebanon, its freedom of movement was curtailed in the Syrian-controlled Beqaa and was now besieged in Dahieh. Hezbollah must have sensed that both its allies and enemies wanted to at least disarm it and at worse eradicate it, an obsession that will continue with and define Hezbollah's socialisation in Lebanon and the region. The Islamic Republic, which had failed to impose a compromise on the two Shi'a movements, was walking a tightrope: 'Although it could not tolerate the elimination of Hezbollah, it was loath to jeopardize the partnership with Damascus' (Goodarzi 2009: 264). Iran moved in two directions, first it sought to prop up its Lebanese ally and second it aimed to reach a political settlement with Damascus. On May 6,

Hezbollah reacted. First it executed three Amal leaders, and with backing from the IRG, Hezbollah attacked Amal's strongholds in Dahieh. In a disciplined manner, which surprised Amal and the Syrians, by the end of May, Hezbollah managed to control the main districts of the southern suburb of Beirut: Bourj el-Barajneh, Hay Madi, Haret Hreik, Ghobeiry, Mouawad, Bir al-Abed and the coastal area of Ouzai – leaving Amal with control of Chiyah only. Hezbollah hoped to break its siege, increase its control of Dahieh and through that pave the way for its return to southern Lebanon. Amal also felt vulnerable having been in confrontation with the Palestinians and the PSP. The intense fighting killed and wounded more than 1,100 people causing immense destruction, and yet another round of civilian displacement in Lebanon's bloody war.[6] In a telling scene of the tragedy, a spontaneous demonstration by hundreds of women, mostly mothers of the fighting brothers, broke out in the end of the battle calling for 'Syrian forces to enter the southern suburbs'. Desperate, Amal made a similar plea. Nervous about the fall of its most loyal ally and keen on increasing its control of Muslim areas of Lebanon, Syria threatened to deploy its forces to Dahieh. But Hezbollah refused Syrian deployment and threatened to execute the Western hostages it held.

This first round of violence was a catalyst. It reaffirmed Hezbollah's politico-military presence in Lebanon, and also showed how far Iran was willing to go to preserve its main ally in Lebanon and thus its influence there. Notwithstanding their strategic alliance, from then on, all actors (Hezbollah, Amal, Syria and Iran) recognised the limits each rival was able to exercise on the other. Towards the end of May, Syria brokered a deal, one supervised directly by President Assad, who invited members of Hezbollah to Syria. Assad's invitation both reaffirmed Syria's influence in Lebanon and reflected Hezbollah's increasing political clout and relative independence. The deal, not without Iranian blessing, guaranteed Hezbollah's quest to pursue armed struggle from the south, Amal's freedom of movement in Dahieh and Syria's deployment of forces there (Goodarzi 2009: 275). On May 27, Syria deployed its forces in Dahieh. Several months later Hezbollah and Amal exchanged detainees.

Hezbollah and Amal, however, would clash again between May 1988 and September 1990, only to be curbed by Iranian–Syrian pressure. In January

1989, a new round of violence took place over the strategic, hilly area of Iqlim al-Tuffah, that tied Sidon to Nabatieh and Jezzine into Israel's occupied zone. This was followed by another, and last, round of violence that was triggered after protests in southern villages against the return of Hezbollah fighters – an illustration of the point mentioned above by Qassem about the hurdles Hezbollah's armed resistance faced. Regional and international factors, however, began to overshadow Lebanese domestic political dynamics, paving the way for the lasting (Second) Damascus Agreement that ended the Amal–Hezbollah war (Azani 2011: 80–2).

On 22 October 1989, under Saudi sponsorship, US backing and Syrian acquiescence, Lebanese MPs signed the National Reconciliation Accord, which is known as the 'Taif Accord'. The accord emphasised Lebanon's sovereignty as a 'final homeland' (dear to Lebanese Christians) and its Arab identity (which addressed one of the Muslims' grievances). It reduced the powers of the Maronite President, relocating the executive power to the government, led by a Sunni-Muslim, and divided the seats of parliament equally between Muslims and Christians (Saouli 2006). Iran aimed to mobilise Lebanon's Shi'a 'as part of a broad-based, pro-Syrian coalition . . . [that] coordinated its policies in Lebanon with Syria' (Goodarzi 2009: 288) and supported the Taif Accord. Syrian–Iranian coordination sealed the bloody war between the two movements and paved the way for a lasting and strategic alliance between the four actors. The strategic alliance preserved a role for Hezbollah's armed resistance against Israel. The Iraqi invasion of Kuwait in August 1990 contributed to end the Lebanon war. In search for an Arab coalition in its war against Saddam Hussein's invasion of Kuwait, the US exchanged Syrian support for its war for Assad's control of Lebanon. Among other things, this led to the termination of Michel Aoun's rebellion and the inauguration of Syrian control of Lebanon (Saouli 2006: 709–11; Goodarzi 2009: 287–8).

Interdependence, Social Re-presentation and Restraint (1990–2005)

After fifteen years of bloodshed, Lebanon's war came to an end in 1990. Syria emerged as the country's internationally recognised political master. With over 40,000 troops stationed in different parts of the country, an infiltrating intelligence network, and an adaptive political class, Syria managed to impose order on the divided country. Syria's – mainly – Muslim political allies reigned over the new order: Shi'a Nabih Berri, Sunni Rafic Hariri and Druze Walid Jumblatt. Christian mainstream political actors (Michel Aoun, Samir Geagea, Phalange) were either sent to exile or were excluded; Christian friends of Syria found a place in the new political pact (Leenders 2012: 122–32).

The post-war period ushered a new political phase in the country's history that necessitated political adaptation. For Hezbollah, which had endured the test of survival in the 1980s, the post-war political order presented new challenges, but also opportunities. Continued Israeli occupation, the Iranian–Syrian alliance and Assad's tactical goal of maintaining pressure on Israel enabled Hezbollah to continue its war-making against Israel. For many, the 1990s ushered the phase of Hezbollah's 'Lebanonisation'. Whilst this is partly accurate, it should not mean that Hezbollah abandoned its religio-political doctrine or war-making with Israel. As I will show, Hezbollah's socialisation in 1990s Lebanon served the strategic goal of war-making, but there was no 'transformation' in Hezbollah's religio-political doctrine. For Hezbollah members, the Islamist movement's integration in Lebanon was a 'tactical step' (Abu Rida 2012: 422), or part of Hezbollah's belief in the 'strategy of phases' (H. Fadlallah 1994: 90–6), in the realisation of strategic goals (set in the Open Letter). But we will see that Hezbollah's socialisation in Lebanon is itself *strategic*: establishing the basis of the 'Resistance Society', maintaining internal stability and acquiring legitimacy is a cornerstone in Hezbollah's broader strategy. Lebanon is both a sanctuary for Hezbollah and a springboard for its strategic, regional goals.

As such, in the 1990s Hezbollah rationalised its behaviour – remember, rationalisation, as discussed in the theoretical framework, is about the changes in the way people bond to each other. In post-war Lebanon, Hezbollah's ability to reconfigure the socio-political order was limited; thus, capitalising on available opportunities, it socialised in the new order. It is in this light that Hezbollah accepted the Taif Accord, with reservations about the re-arrangement of the sectarian system which it continued to reject. But the Syrian politico-military control of Lebanon – what Hezbollah depicts as the 'Syrian Management' – offered an important opportunity for Hezbollah: strategic backing and depth. Syria's control of Lebanon protected Hezbollah's war-making with Israel, giving it the opportunity to focus its energies on the armed struggle with Israel and not to be embroiled in Lebanon's divisive politics. You will see below that, when Syria left Lebanon fifteen years later, Hezbollah was obliged to fill the politico-security vacuum the Syrians left behind. That said, Hezbollah still had to *preserve* its social base and to *legitimise* its status as an Islamist and armed organisation in Lebanon. To do this, Hezbollah aimed to re-present its socio-political identity, deepen its social roots and to extend its political ties and alliances. All this served war-making: put differently, Hezbollah's socialisation in the 1990s was about the continuation of war through other, socio-political, means.

First, whilst in the 1980s Hezbollah was trying to demarcate itself as a different actor, in the 1990s Hezbollah wanted to be a part, not apart, from its society. The quest for legitimacy and social acceptance necessitated the performance of and emphasis on the Lebanese identity. In essence Hezbollah was now socialising in Lebanon's Lockean anarchy, as opposed to the Hobessian anarchy of the war (see Chapter 1 for the theoretical basis for this argument). Hezbollah was trying to *re-present* its image as an Islamist movement with local roots and interests that pertain to Lebanon. Hezbollah was also deconstructing labels ('Iranian proxy' or 'terrorist') others used to delegitimise it. As Hezbollah's MP Mohammad Raad recalls, among other goals, the Islamist movement's participation in the Lebanese political system aimed to 'correct the blurred image of Hezbollah' (*Ahzab Lubnan: Hizb Allah* [Parties of Lebanon: Hezbollah] 2003). But Hezbollah was involved in more than a correcting exercise; in virtue of its interdependence with other Lebanese forces, Hezbollah was seeking socio-political acceptance. In the early 1990s, Hezbollah changed its slogan from the 'Islamic Revolution in Lebanon' to the 'Islamic Resistance in Lebanon'. Its leaders ceased to publicly talk about the Islamic state as an ideal as they did in the 1980s, although this remained part of Hezbollah's religio-political doctrine as we shall see below. Hezbollah began to display the Lebanese flag along its own flag in official meetings and events. It was attempting to overcome political and normative constraints; and, in doing so, it was *internalising* Lebanese socio-political values and standards (Saouli 2003, 2011a).

After an internal debate, which was ultimately resolved by a religio-political *fatwa*, Hezbollah decided to participate in the Lebanese political system. Political participation served many goals: it paved an avenue for political openness to and dialogue with other political forces; contributed to the promotion and legitimising of Hezbollah's armed resistance; and helped to represent and voice the concerns of its constituency (Qassem 2008a: 280–3). In 1992, Hezbollah ran for parliamentary elections and won twelve seats (including eight of its members and four allies). It did this again in 1996, 2000 and 2004.

These electoral victories were enabled by an Amal–Hezbollah political alliance, one which will develop into a lasting strategic alliance. Whilst Amal appropriated Shi'a representation in state institutions and government, Hezbollah's participation in the political system was partial and cautious. Realising that the costs of participation in government outweighed the benefits, Hezbollah did not join any government until 2005 (Qassem 2008a: 292). Hezbollah's 'Loyalty to the Resistance' parliamentary block did not grant the governments of PM Rafic Hariri, who presided over most governments in post-war Lebanon, its vote of confidence. The Saudi-backed Hariri came to power in 1992 amidst increasing prospects for a resolution of the Arab–Israeli conflict after the Madrid talks and the Oslo Agreement of 1993. Focusing on economic reconstruction, Hariri must have believed that Hezbollah's role would be curtailed when Syria signed a peace treaty with Israel. His vision and close ties to Saudi Arabia and the US made him a rival of Hezbollah. When Yasser Arafat signed the Oslo Agreement on 13 September 1993, Hezbollah organised a rally to protest the agreement. Due to reasons that still have to be unlocked, the protesters clashed with the Lebanese army leading to the death of nine Hezbollah supporters. This deepened the division between Hariri and Hezbollah. In the funeral, Hezbollah's supporters called for the death of Hariri and his Defence Minister, Mohsen Dalloul (Saouli 2003: 74). But this incident also, like the Fathallah Massacre, showed Hezbollah's growing ability to exercise self-restraint, a trait that would only increase in post-war Lebanon. 'Despite the fall of martyrs', Qassem recalls, Hezbollah's Shura 'agreed to contain the *fitnah* [sedition] because some wanted us to enter into a confrontation with the Lebanese Army [and thus] to threaten the Resistance's activities' (quoted in *Ahzab Lubnan: Hizb Allah* [Parties of Lebanon: Hezbollah] 2003).

War-making with Israel also required domestic socio-political support. As most Lebanese political forces were enjoying the 'spoils of truce' (Leenders 2012), Hezbollah was carefully and strategically consolidating and expanding its social support base. In the 1990s, it deepened its ties with the Shi'a constituency by expanding it social provisions. The socio-economic – and one should say political – gap left by successive post-war Lebanese governments formed an opportunity for Hezbollah to fill, establishing a strong network of patronage. But unlike the traditional patron–client relations, Hezbollah's network in the 1990s was directly linked to war-making and the quest for legitimacy. Harik found that between 1988 and 1996, Hezbollah dug 57 artesian wells, fitted 15,000 metres of water pipes and installed 400 tanks of drinkable water in various districts of Dahieh (Harik 2005). The 'Martyrs Association for Social Welfare', which was established in 1982 with Khomeini's endorsement, provides 'comprehensive social welfare for the families of the martyrs'. These include: monthly salaries, accommodation (where needed), medical aid, free education (from school through to university) and social and psychological help to aggrieved families. When a fighter is killed, the Association pays a quick visit to the family, organises the funeral, documents the death and publicises the testaments of the martyr (several of which are sampled in this book). Additionally, the association has managed several major projects, including, Al-Rassoul Al-Azam Hospital, Beirut Heart Centre and Al-Rassoul Al-Azam College for Health Sciences.[7]

These provisions made a qualitative contribution to Shi'a socio-economic development in Lebanon and, specifically, to Hezbollah's own political base. Take the educational sector. To the shock, envy and fear of its opponents, in May 2009 Hezbollah held the 21st graduation ceremony of its university students. This round – named *al-Radwan* after Imad Mughnieh who was assassinated in Damascus a year earlier[8] – included a staggering 2,883 graduates. In the ceremony, Nasrallah emphasised the 'resistance's devotion to education', and confidently addressed the graduates telling them: 'you are today presenting a strong image and [sending a] clear message to those who doubt your ability to lead Lebanon in all fields and areas of specialisation'.[9] Educated members now play major roles in Hezbollah's numerous units. Some of these cadres went to play direct leading political roles in the party. For example, three of Hezbollah's MPs (Hassan Fadlallah, Nawaf al-Moussawi and Ali Fayyad) hold PhD degrees. Before becoming an MP, Fayyad presided over Hezbollah's 'Consultative Centre for Studies and Documentation', which was established in 1988. The centre, which many researchers utilise, plays an important role in making socio-economic and political recommendation to Hezbollah (A. H. Fadlallah 2015).

Key in the constructing of a socio-political base is Hezbollah's religio-political doctrine, which did not disappear as some have believed during the 1990s. The provision of social services and Hezbollah's war-making with Israel offered important channels to diffuse the doctrine within the Shi'a community. Throughout the year, Hezbollah celebrates many religio-political events and uses these occasions to increase its ties to its social base, to communicate its political message and to ingrain its religio-political doctrine. In addition to the celebration of the births of the Prophet and the Imams and the *Ghadir Day* (see previous chapter), Hezbollah organises several other events, including: Martyrs' Day, Martyred Leaders' Day, International Jerusalem Day, The Resistance and Liberation Day, July Victory Day and last, but not least, is the ten-day-long commemoration of *Ashura*.

These occasions usually feature Hezbollah's adored leader, Nasrallah (see book cover), who does not disguise his passion for giving speeches (*Al-Akhbar* 2014). The long speeches he delivers contribute to transmitting religio-political doctrine outside the confines of the organisation and thus reproduce the social base. In many of these speeches, Nasrallah lectures about *Taklif Shari'i*, the 'signs' of the return of the *Mahdi*, martyrdom, sacrifice, afterlife, war-making with Israel and other key topics, which we have explored in the previous chapter. These speeches serve several purposes. First, they socialise a broader audience into Hezbollah's religio-political doctrine. With time, this constituency begins to see the world through Hezbollah's religio-political lenses. As Qassem notes in his book *The Resistance Society*, the goal has been to establish a 'cohesive society' that can fight Israel – a strategy for the 'whole [society]', not just one part or party of it. Writing in 2008, he argued that the resistance has survived; now the 'question is: how can society integrate into the [project of] Resistance?' (Qassem 2008b: 3, 16). Second, and relatedly, speeches and the religio-political doctrine they imbue help to mobilise support for Hezbollah's war-making, justifying not only wars with Israel but also Hezbollah's interventions in Syria and other Arab countries. Lastly, speeches communicate political messages to Hezbollah's rivals and enemies that contribute to the deconstruction and the de-legitimisation of their narratives and actions.

These events and speeches have deepened Hezbollah's ties to its society, but one, *Ashura*, has had a particularly strong impact. Hezbollah leaders (such as Nasrallah, Qassem, Ibrahim Amin al-Sayyed or Mohammad Yezbek) give speeches to large congregations in different parts of Lebanon. The main congregation takes place in Dahieh in the purpose-built hall, Doyen of Martyrs, which accommodates thousands. The speeches are transmitted live by Al-Manar television station and Al-Nour radio, both Hezbollah's, to a Lebanese and international audience. In the speeches, Hezbollah leaders, like their Shi'a predecessors, revive the narrative of the Battle of Karbala and narrate the life and sayings of Imam Hussein. But unlike their predecessors, Hezbollah's *Ashura* commemoration serves immediate socio-political goals and needs of Hezbollah. Saffieddine notes that the commemoration of *Ashura* forms an 'important opportunity to enter into, analyse and understand [contemporary] political events in light of the Battle of Karbala' (Saffieddine 2007: 52). Talal Atrissi observes that since the Islamic Revolution, politics has overshadowed the commemoration of *Ashura*. The Israeli occupation in 1982 transformed *Ashura* into an occasion to wage 'jihad against Israel'. Although Musa al-Sadr invoked *Ashura* in his speeches to politically revive Lebanon's Shi'as and although Amal continues to commemorate it every year, it was Hezbollah that transformed Ashura into a full-fledged institution. Atrissi observes that:

> Hezbollah reproduced *Ashura* in a very distinguished way. [This] reached an extent that Hezbollah has established an institute to prepare narrators and to organise conferences that examine all facets of *Ashura*: the substance, its religious impact, the targeted audience; and the political, religious and social functions Ashura should serve. (Atrissi 2012: 344–7)

The institute in question, *Doyen of the Martyrs' Institute for the Husseini Forum*, was established after 2000. It publishes guidebooks for *Ashura* narrators, framing what can be said and how. 'Speeches in *Ashura*', one guidebook suggests 'should not be purposeless'. In 2003, the institute produced material on *Ashura* that targets specifically the youth. As Qassem notes:

> So the picture [Battle of Karbala] is not abstracted and is not left to history, it is important to connect the incidents of Karbala to a context that

> the child knows and understands . . . [For example] the experience of the Islamic Resistance in confronting the oppression of the occupation [which] recalls the story of Imam Hussein's companions who sacrificed and were martyred against Yazid and his oppressive aids. (quoted in Atrissi 2012: 356)

The commemoration of *Ashura* also performs Hezbollah's power. On the tenth day, Hezbollah organises huge processions in Beirut, Beqaa and the south. The biggest takes place in Dahieh, involving hundreds of thousands of people. The highly organised procession includes parades for youth, old men and women – emulating Imam Hussein's march to Karbala with his family. The picture of Hezbollah martyrs are displayed, connecting their struggle and martyrdom to Imam Hussein's battle at Karbala. Tens of teams are dressed in military fatigues of different colours and march like soldiers as they tour various districts of Dahieh. The stunning performance takes months to organise and attracts domestic and international attention. In the end of the procession Nasrallah delivers his political message, before reiterating the historical and traditional *Ashura* cry: *Hayhat min al-zillah*, Imam Hussein's slogan: 'we reject, or would never accept, humiliation' and other more immediate ones like 'Death to Israel' or 'Death to America'.

Hezbollah has also established institutes, such as the Centre for Islamic Studies or the Sapiential Knowledge Institute for Religious and Philosophical Studies. These centres focus on religio-political doctrine, hold conferences and publish manuscripts on various religious and political topics. The Institute publishes a monthly journal called *Baqiyat Allah*, that is devoted to religious studies and debates, usually featuring contributions of Hezbollah members and extracts from Imam Khamenei's writings and speeches on religious affairs.

But religio-political doctrine is disseminated via other avenues. Through its network of schools, institutes and other social welfare programmes, Hezbollah instils into its followers, particularly the youth, its religio-political doctrine. For example, the Martyrs' Association, discussed above, offers 'Cultural Welfare' programmes, which 'develop the spiritual connection' of the martyrs' children with religion. The programme encourages the memorisation of the Holy Qur'an; it promotes the 'culture of jihad, martyrdom and principles of good behaviour'; and organises religious trips to holy places in Saudi Arabia, Iran and Iraq and religious workshops.[10]

Through these provisions, Hezbollah has gradually been laying the foundations – Islamisation from below – of the Resistance Society in the Shi'a community. It has been mobilising the Shi'a community according to its religio-political visions, which, as argued in the previous chapter, is one of the strategic goals of Hezbollah.

Beyond the Shi'a community, Hezbollah has capitalised on post-war relative stability to increase its ties to different political groups in Lebanon. This formed the second strategic circle Hezbollah hoped to engage with, to ensure domestic legitimacy in Lebanon (the third circle is its international alliances, which we will explore in the next chapter). Hezbollah espoused the policy of 'dialogue' with and 'openness' to all groups 'except those who had or have relations with Israel' (H. Fadlallah 1994: 95). Hezbollah hoped to expose these parties to its political mission and to widen its 'social safety net', as a domestic bulwark in its war-making with Israel. In a demonstration of Hezbollah's political pragmatism in this period it aimed to neutralise ideological and/or religious difference 'to mobilise energies to combat the [Israeli] occupation'. In 1997, it convened seventeen Lebanese political parties 'to revive party politics in Lebanon and to support the resistance in the south' (Qassem 2008a: 115–16). It then announced the birth of the 'Lebanese Brigades for the Resistance of the Occupation'. This organisation formed a military umbrella for individuals who shared the goal of resisting Israel, but differed ideologically with Hezbollah. Hezbollah trained and funded this organisation; its members also benefitted from Hezbollah's social provisions (Mustafa 2003: 531). This offered Hezbollah the opportunity to ingrain the culture of resistance in Lebanon and 'to constrain [the] non-objective rejections of the resistance' (Qassem quoted in Mustafa 2003: 536).[11] But on a different level, this was another way for Hezbollah to normalise its status as an armed movement in a pluralist society. The policy of establishing parallel armed groups is one that Hezbollah and Iran will extend to other countries in the region, as we shall see in Chapter 5.

All of the policies that Hezbollah pursued internally, in the Shi'a community or Lebanon at large, served the purpose of war-making with Israel, the strategic motivation of Hezbollah's socialisation process. Nasrallah cannot be clearer:

> The main aim of the social, educational, political, media, cultural, organisational and service-related aspects which Hezbollah undertakes in all the regions and with all the political forces, is to support and reinforce the resistance and preserve its continuity. (quoted in *Ahzab Lubnan: Hizb Allah* [Parties of Lebanon: Hezbollah] 2003)

And the resistance it was. In the 1990s, Hezbollah sustained an armed resistance against Israel, which also involved two wars in 1993 and 1996 and the Israeli withdrawal in 2000 – details of which we will examine in the following chapter. Military operations against Israel, Hezbollah's changing political image, the armed movement's refrain from direct involvement in Lebanon's corrupt politics and Israel's withdrawal from Lebanon have all contributed to increase Hezbollah's legitimacy, particularly among the country's Muslim community. When Israel withdrew from Lebanon, Hezbollah distributed billboards throughout the country celebrating its loss of '1,281 martyrs' in the war with Israel (and probably other battles in the domestic arena). Legitimacy, Hezbollah wanted to bring to the mind of compatriots, is not granted; it is extracted. By 2000, Hezbollah had secured a strong position amongst Lebanon's political parties and a unique place in the heart of the Shi'a community.

In this regard, it is important to underline that the Shi'a community was not a mere passive vassal for Hezbollah's indoctrination and mobilisation. On the contrary, Hezbollah's emergence, growth and socialisation in the 1980s and 1990s was conditioned by the socio-political expectations of the Shi'a community. Hezbollah's growth spoke to at least three areas of Shi'a religio-political identity. First, as should be clear by now, Hezbollah activated salient elements in Shi'a religious identity, presenting one amongst other interpretations of what it means to be a Shi'a. In this way, Hezbollah contributed to the reproduction of Shi'a communal identity. Second, at a political level, Hezbollah consolidated and reinforced Shi'a political revival in Lebanon, which was triggered in the 1950s. By 2000, the Shi'as had two strong political movements, which in their various ways and means – Amal through its appropriation of state positions and Hezbollah through its armed resistance against Israel – have transformed Lebanon's Shi'as from a victim to a victor. In Lebanese parlance and perceptions, the Shi'as ceased to be *Ta'ifat al-Mahrumin* (the community of the deprived) and became *al-Ta'ifah al-Sa'idah* (the rising community). (Though the culture of '*mahrumin*' still lingers in the minds of many, sometimes serving as a justification for the absence of economic development in Shi'a areas, political negligence or corruption of Shi'a leaders.) Thirdly, Hezbollah's armed resistance and the Israeli withdrawal in 2000 spoke to Shi'a's pride and confidence. In the eyes of many Shi'as, this was not only a unique event in the rather depressing Arab–Israeli conflict which saw many Arab defeats and few moments of pride, but it was also a genuine struggle for Lebanese independence. Amin Mustafa (2003: 517), who studied various forms of resistance in Lebanon from 1948 to 2000, described the feelings of many Shi'as in the wake of the Israeli withdrawal from Lebanon:

> It felt like we were watching a movie that was produced to surprise all people, whether in Lebanon, the Arab world or the world at large. No one could have imagined that the largest military machine in the Middle East, the most well-equipped regular army in the region, well-provided by air and naval coverage, fully-protected by advanced technology and satellites, and boasting wide-patronage of the superpowers, would fall before a fraction of *mujahidin* who gave up their worldly life in exchange for the eternal afterlife. The scenes kept moving before our eyes like a dream. The pattern of the defeat of the Israeli army and the escape of the collaborators in the district of Jezzine under the cover of darkness to the farthest end of the occupied territory was repeated before our eyes.

But there are other contributing factors to Hezbollah's political consolidation in post-war Lebanon. One is the Nasrallah factor. 'Sayyid Hassan', as many refer to him in Lebanon, has a strong charisma. His leadership of Hezbollah played a crucial role in the legitimisation of the movement. His numerous appearances have made him the unquestionable public face of Hezbollah: one that encapsulates Hezbollah's religio-political doctrine, political pragmatism, restraint, rage, modesty, pride and anxieties. We could have studied Hezbollah's long-term socialisation through this man alone. He was born in 1960 to a poor Shi'a family in the district of Karantina, where many Shi'a migrants from southern Lebanon resided. Inspired by Imam Musa al-Sadr, he joined Amal in 1975. Nasrallah recalls how he always glanced at the picture of al-Sadr which was posted in his father's shop. In 1977, following the paths of students of religious studies, Nasrallah left for Najaf to obtain his studies, but the Ba'athist political pressure on the Iraqi *hawzahs* obliged him to return home. In Lebanon, Nasrallah continued his studies under the supervision of Sayyid Abbas al-Musawi in Beqaa, before graduating as a religious scholar. He was Amal's representative in the Beqaa before he defected to what would become Hezbollah. In Hezbollah, he made his way gradually to the top. Initially he was a member of the armed resistance and then became Hezbollah's representative in Beqaa. He later headed Hezbollah's influential Executive Council and, thus, became a member of the Shura Council (Abu Rida 2012: 504–10). After Israel assassinated Musawi in 1992, Hezbollah's Shura Council unanimously elected the 32-year-old Hassan Nasrallah as its General Secretary.

Despite his young age, Nasrallah left a strong impact on his party and social base. Qassem notes that Nasrallah was even a candidate for the Secretary General position when Musawi was elected. With Musawi's death, Nasrallah incontestably emerged as the strongest candidate. His comrades (Ibrahim Amin al-Sayyid, Naim Qassem, Hashem Saffieddine, Hassan Khalil) describe him as someone 'with a high level of [religious] belief, honesty, wisdom, courage; and one that possesses a collective mind'. His transparency and honesty with the people and the trust he has gained from other political parties in Lebanon played a crucial role in Hezbollah's quest for acceptance. Nasrallah's social status as a turbaned religious man, a '*Sayyid*', who is believed to be a descendent of the Prophet, has also reinforced his leadership and charisma, especially in the Shi'a community.

Nasrallah's leadership of Hezbollah in war and peace earned him the label of '*Sayyid al-Muqawama*' (Leader or Crown of the Resistance). But there was one event that transformed him from a Shi'a leader to a highly respected Lebanese, Arab and Islamist figurehead: the death of his son on the battleground in 1997. Hadi Nasrallah was 18 years old when news broke out that he was killed in Iqlim al-Tuffah during a confrontation with the Israelis. Hadi's death exposed Hezbollah in a new light. Here was a son of a leader who was not sent to London or Paris (or Tehran for that matter) for an elite education; who was not enjoying any political privileges; who was not groomed to inherit the leadership of his father, as is common with other political parties (or regimes in the Arab world). Rather, Hadi, like other Hezbollah fighters, was ready to sacrifice his life on the battleground. The teenager's testament reflects his beliefs in Hezbollah's mission:

> I am, God willing, one of the *mujahidin* of the Islamic Resistance. I have joined the resistance for liberation and to defend the Almighty God's religion . . . I ask God to grant me martyrdom . . . Our path is difficult; I ask you [his brothers in Hezbollah] to persevere: fight and do not fear their mighty weapons, for you possess the power of *Allahu Akbar* (God is Great!) . . . I ask you to read about *Ashura* and [recite] the verses of the Qur'an every day. I [also] ask for your forgiveness.

Hadi's martyrdom reinforced Nasrallah's credibility as a leader and strengthened the political effect of his vision and speech. Nasrallah has a strong capacity for self-control, a penetrating knowledge of the political moment in which he is delivering his message and a perceptive understanding of his targeted audience. A journalist with close ties to Hezbollah observed that Nasrallah has undergone a major development since becoming General Secretary particularly on

> how he absorbs [political] developments, how he calmly responds to these developments, how he assures everyone around him that things are under control, how the mind controls the nervous system; the heart is not paralysed, nor is his [Nasrallah's] deep belief in God's will, but these are balanced with the mind that takes control of the situation . . . before a decision is made. And, above all, how he is prepared to carry the responsibility [for the decisions he makes]. (I. Amin 2014)

His speeches have with time developed into a political event in their own right. However, notwithstanding these personal traits, Nasrallah's development cannot be stripped out of its context. His imposing performances – his chosen rhetoric, body gestures or volume of the voice – reveal and mirror Hezbollah's goals and interests in particular periods, its religio-political identity and its overarching socialisation process. The volume of the voice during speeches, he discloses, is 'of course intentional and depends on the nature of the event and audience'. Mostly, Nasrallah's appearances reflect Hezbollah's political consciousness: the armed movement's anxieties in its war-making with Israel and its political vigilance as it seeks political acceptance, recognition and legitimacy in Lebanon and the Arab world. 'I do not just go out and say whatever I want', he reminds, 'without any restrictions or discussions with my brothers [members of the Shura Council], especially in sensitive speeches that deliver political decisions' (*Al-Akhbar* 2014).

Whilst Nasrallah's appearances have played a key role in communicating Hezbollah's political message and in the mobilisation of the base, as we have explored so far, they have also contributed to *regulating* the emotions and actions of his supporters. This regulation has contributed to restraining the passions and potential use of violence by his followers, to diffusing tensions, and to boosting confidence when the movement faces challenges. In the 'Liberation Speech', which Nasrallah delivered after the withdrawal of Israel from Lebanon in 2000, he assured collaborators and their families that Hezbollah will not engage in acts of retribution: 'there should be no fear, neither by Christians nor by Muslims . . . We in Hezbollah are not a substitute for the state, nor are we a security authority' (quoted in Saouli 2003: 75).

But Nasrallah's message was, again, a reflection of Hezbollah's strategy in post-war Lebanon. Hezbollah in all its party organs prepared well for the Israeli withdrawal. It established checkpoints in several areas to 'control the situation'. Fear of retributions against collaborators, Hezbollah feared, might steer attention away from the major achievement of the resistance and create *fitnah* (sedition), which Israel would benefit from, in Lebanon. Hezbollah's 'major achievement', according to Saffieddine, was to convince the 'supporters of the resistance and the families of martyrs and detainees' that the 'preservation of this victory requires additional sacrifice and patience' (quoted in *Ahzab Lubnan: Hizb Allah* [Parties of Lebanon: Hezbollah] 2003).

Conclusion

Going through Hezbollah's socialisation process in Lebanon – its birth, growth and development – you will agree that the Islamist movement has overcome major obstacles and appropriated useful opportunities before it established a foothold in the divided society. Hezbollah, this chapter has found, first carved for itself a place within its Shi'a (and broadly Muslim) community in war-torn Lebanon of the 1980s. The process required a demarcating of different religio-political identity and the fighting of bloody wars against internal and external opponents.

Hezbollah's survival in the 1980s then paved the way for its political integration in post-war Lebanon. In the 1990s, Hezbollah benefitted from Syrian security and political backing to focus its energies on fighting Israel, contributing to Israel's withdrawal in 2000. But Hezbollah also benefitted from the relatively stable political order to deepen its roots in society: it disseminated its religio-political doctrine; built social institutions to buttress the Resistance Society; and by re-presenting its religio-political identity, it widened its political alliances. By 2005, Hezbollah had deepened its socio-political ties to Lebanon, establishing what I termed as interdependence, in Chapter 1, with this arena, one which will have a lasting impact on Hezbollah's decision in later stages.

Hezbollah's socialisation in Lebanon served the armed movement's endless 'quest for survival' (Saouli 2003) and the preservation of the resistance, thus realising one of its religio-political main goals: war-making with Israel. War-making with Israel has shaped how Hezbollah socialises in Lebanon. Socialisation in Lebanon has shaped Hezbollah: rationalising its actions, restraining its behaviour and reformulating its image. To get a wider and deeper picture of Hezbollah's domestic socialisation, we will now flip the analytical coin to its other side and examine Hezbollah's international socialisation.

Notes

1. The title of this chapter is, of course, inspired by Charles Tilly's famous dictum 'War made the state and the State made war' (Tilly 1985). This is, however, a treatment of an armed political movement, Hezbollah. The chapter shows how war-making with Israel has directly shaped Hezbollah's socialisation in Lebanon and, thus, remade the movement.
2. For a well-researched study on the influential role of *hawzah*s and Shi'a clerics, see Abisaab 2006.
3. One example was Imad Mughnieh, who was a member of its Fateh elite corps, Force 17, and who would later become Hezbollah's highest-ranking soldier. Mughnieh was assassinated in Damascus in 2008. Hezbollah accused Israel of

the killing and celebrated him as the leader of Hezbollah's military successes in 2000 and 2006.

4. For a detailed analysis of the PLO policy in Lebanon and of War of Camps, see Brynen 1990; Siklawi 2012.
5. Three Americans were kidnapped in the period 9 September and 21 October 1986; in early 1987, eight more: four Americans, two Germans, one Frenchman and Terry Waite (envoy of the Archbishop of Canterbury).
6. For a detailed analysis of this round of the Amal–Hezbollah war, see Goodarzi 2009 (263–77).
7. For more details of the work and activities of the Martyrs' Association, see <https://www.youtube.com/watch?v=NGTq73fu7d8> (last accessed 14 April 2017). See also the official website of the Association: <http://www.shaheed.com.lb/> (last accessed 14 April 2017).
8. 'Hajj Radwan' was Mughnieh's partisan name. He was killed in Damascus in 2008. Hezbollah accused Israel and the CIA of the assassination.
9. For the ceremony and speech, see <http://www.moqawama.org/essaydetails.php?eid=14799&cid=210> (last accessed 13 April 2016).
10. For more details on this programme, see the Association's promotion via <https://www.youtube.com/watch?v=NGTq73fu7d8> (last accessed 14 April 2017).
11. For an elaborate analysis of the Brigades, their origins, make-up and military operations, see Mustafa 2003 (527–58).

4

War-making as International Socialisation

> In the culture of the Resistance, if you continue to believe in what you do, in the sacredness of what you do, in the greatness of what you sacrifice for; if you do what you do from the position of consciousness and will, then you will be unconcerned about what they say about you in the Security Council, in the US or the world media – terrorist, mad, primitive.
>
> Sayyid Hassan Nasrallah

> Sadly, we live in a world where the law of the jungle applies – that is the stronger will always try to dominate the weaker. We see ourselves as a people whose rights have been taken away and so we need to have a force to help us. Jihad is a fundamental basis for us. We do not use it as a means of imposing our views on others, but consider ourselves in a position of jihad to defend our rights.
>
> Sheikh Naim Qassem

> The defence of the West Bank starts in West Beirut.
>
> Yitzhak Shamir, Former Foreign Minister of Israel

On 10 June 2000, almost two weeks after the Israeli withdrawal from Lebanon, President Hafez Assad of Syria died. Nervous about the political uncertainly Assad's death would incite, his Lebanese allies hurried to Syria to deliver their condolences. But this was more than a social occasion to pay respect to Syria's strongman and Lebanon's actual political master. Funerals of dictators are passages of a known past to an uncharted future. Assad's funeral was such a passage. It offered Assad's Lebanese allies the opportunity to pledge allegiance to his soon-to-be president son, Bashar Assad. Tucked in fancy suits and armed with poetic words, Lebanese politicians, one after the other, condoled and greeted Bashar Assad. But suddenly, one group broke the monotony of the scene and words. Here was Nasrallah, a relatively short man in his cloak and black turban commanding a large Hezbollah delegation and distinguished with a group of disciplined fighters all dressed in black military fatigue. After offering his condolences, and with a guarding eye over his fighters, Nasrallah stood between the 34-year-old Bashar Assad and Syria's aging Minister of Defence, Mustafa Tlass. Then each fighter passed by and offered his military salute to Bashar Assad.[1]

Like other Hezbollah performances this was immersed with political symbolism. It spoke to the past and to the future, to friends and to enemies. Hezbollah's alliance with Syria, the armed movement emphasised, was strategic: born out of war not political opportunism. The presence of Hezbollah's fighters at the funeral signalled the primacy of war-making. The military salute was not a pledge of loyalty to the Assad regime that intervened in the most minor, day-to-day affairs of Lebanon's politics; nor to the regime that turned a blind eye to or engaged with Lebanon's corrupt political class. Rather, it was a pledge of allegiance to Assad's Syria that formed the vital geopolitical link to the Islamic Republic of Iran and to the only Arab regime to back Hezbollah's armed resistance politically and militarily. Hezbollah hoped for an orderly transition to power in Syria, one that maintained Syria as a member of the self-proclaimed 'Resistance Alliance' – the regional camp that tied together Iran, Syria, Hezbollah, Hamas and Islamic Jihad – and one that has constrained the US-led attempts to control the region.

Hezbollah's performance in H. Assad's funeral was also symbolic of its overall international socialisation. In many ways, Hezbollah's international socialisation is similar to its domestic socialisation. Here, too, Hezbollah tried to establish and maintain political alliances, overcome and reconstruct normative structures, and engage in violence – war – to realise its goals. But whilst the domestic system – Lebanon – was regulated by the Syrian hegemony (until 2005) and a set of normative and institutional structures (a system we depicted as a 'Lockean Order' in Chapter 1), the international system is the realm of war and survival (a 'Hobbesian Order'). To examine Hezbollah's international socialisation, in this chapter we first look at how Hezbollah perceives this international system and, second, how Hezbollah has engaged in the system through war-making and alliance formation.

Once again, we are here separating Hezbollah's socialisation in the international sphere only for analytical purposes. This will give us the opportunity to understand Hezbollah's behaviour at an international level, especially at the Middle East regional level until 2005. It will also pave the way to explain in the next, and last, chapter (*Tragic Ironies*) some of the unintended consequences of Hezbollah's socialisation in the two orders in the period 2005–17.

Seeing like Hezbollah

Hezbollah's international socialisation, like the domestic process, has spurred diverse or even opposing interpretations. Some depicted the Islamist movement as the 'Global Footprint' of terrorist and criminal activities (Levitt 2013). Others have shown that during Hezbollah's international socialisation, international norms – statehood, nationalism, sovereignty – have become 'progressively constitutive of Hezbollah's action'. The Islamist party has undergone a 'transition' from a pan-Islamist ideal of the *Ummah* to one centring on the 'Lebanese nation' (Dionigi 2014: 7, 169). But my point of departure here is, rather, to examine Hezbollah as a revolutionary, non-conformist armed political movement that is fighting a perceived unjust international order and to trace the ideational and material origins of this non-conformism (Saad-Ghorayeb 2002: 88–168; Jaber 1997: 7–97). This is what we started exploring in Chapter 2 (*Being Hezbollah*) and what we will elaborate on here, but with more focus on Hezbollah's perceptions and war-making and alliance formation. Such an examination will help us understand how a revolutionary actor, which perceives itself as a victim of an oppressive system, begins with time to conform to existing practices as it socialises in the anarchic international system.

Hezbollah's perception of and behaviour in the international sphere are conditioned by two factors: one falls in the realm of ideas and ideals, that is Hezbollah's religio-political doctrine; the second in the realm of practice, namely socialisation: accumulated experience in war-making and political alliances. Hezbollah's identity and world vision have informed its behaviour, as we have seen so far, but the Islamist movement's interaction with the political world has also *reinforced* certain elements of its *own* world vision. (The philosophically and theoretically curious will want a more elaborate statement on the relation between ideas, ideals and practice, but the purpose and scope of the book curb further elucidation.)

Let us start with its religio-political identity. First, as we have seen in Chapter 2, Hezbollah subscribes to Islam as a 'comprehensive' and universal system of values and rules that offers answers to the cultural, social, educational, psychological, economic and political needs of humanity. Islam is God's gift to the world that enables human beings to overcome their fears, egos, pride and greed in this world and ensures they are saved in the afterlife. Like other universal value systems, Islam highlights the dichotomy between good and evil; Islam is naturally on the side of good and is always in a struggle to rid the world of evil. As God's ultimate message to the world, Islam is juxtaposed in relation to other universal religions. Good Muslims, whether through a social organisation or day-to-day individual deeds, should promote (through *da'wah*, religious propagation, or jihad if the right conditions are present) Islam and protect it against corruption from within or infiltration from without. The interests of Islam and the *Ummah* of Muslims should form the principal goals of all Muslims.

But in itself, Hezbollah's Islamist belonging does not determine whether its relationship with the 'other' is one of enmity or consent. It takes the consideration of other contextual factors – economic, political, cultural – to determine the nature of the relationship between Hezbollah and others. But this belonging locates Hezbollah as a member of the broader Muslim community (Jaradi 2014: 56–8), as we saw above. It is also where Hezbollah converges with other Islamist resurgent movements in the twentieth century and one that forms the basis for Hezbollah's perception of the international system.

But beyond this general level, Hezbollah's perceptions are also shaped by its own, specific Shi'a religio-political doctrine. The martyrdom of Hussein, 'a major historical trauma', forms an important critical juncture not only in the making of the Shi'a as an identity group within Islam, but also in shaping their world vision (Dabashi 2012: 23). The brutal murder of Imam Hussein has first presented the world in Shi'a consciousness as unjust and oppressive and the Shi'as as victims; but, second, the Battle of Karbala also cultivated a feeling of revolution ('a perpetual defiance' (Dabashi 2012: 81)): a struggle to overcome the oppression and to realise God's 'true' mission. These two drives form important ingredients in Hezbollah's worldview. In Hezbollah's view, life is a struggle between good and evil, between *Ahl al-Iman* (believers) and *Ahl al-Kufr* (infidels). 'There is no choice for human beings except through two directions', maintains Qassem:

> Either the path of God or the devil; either life in its shallowness or the afterlife in its eternal truth. There is no room to fuse the two or to lose sight of the direction by trying to combine them; fighting and confronting evil is a necessary step to bring forth good. (Qassem 2010a: 118)

Given these restricted choices, life becomes a temporary sphere of *bala'*: as you will remember from Chapter 2, this is God's way to test the believers' faith, perseverance and preparedness to sacrifice oneself and one's family in the realisation of God's will. The Holy Qur'an, *Hadith*s and, once again, the epic of Imam Hussein's martyrdom serve to reinforce this worldview (Qassem 2010b, 2010a; al-Sayyid 2008). For Hezbollah, Imam Hussein's martyrdom was one, among other, critical turning points when Islam's 'authentic' spirit was lost to the forces of corruption, oppression and violence – namely, the Ummayads. What was lost is the 'authentic Muhammadi Islam' (*al-Islam al-Muhammadi al-Asil*), the Islam of *Ahl al-Bayt*. For many centuries, as we saw in Chapter 2, Shi'as – as supporters of Imam Hussein, as the 'proof' to his victimhood, and as vulnerable minorities – perceived the dominant political orders as illegitimate, unjust and oppressive. But with Imam Khomeini's intellectual and political revolutions, this feeling of victimhood transforms into a mission against oppression and a struggle for good against the 'evil': an attempt to restore 'authentic Islam' and to prepare the ground for the return of *al-Mahdi*. This religious mission, for Ibrahim Amin al-Sayyid, is the 'beginning of hope in the path towards the return of the saviour [*al-Mahdi*]; it is 'God's plan for the world' (al-Sayyid 2008: 74–7). In Hezbollah's mind, there is a teleological, 'continuous line' in history:

> The mission starts with the Prophet, then . . . Ali, and then *al-Mahdi* brings the mission to its conclusion. Theirs is Islam's mission, the mission of *Hizb Allah* [the party of God]; their enemies are the *Hizb al-Shaytan* [the party of the devil]. They represent the path of light, their enemies the path of darkness. (Qassem 2010a: 123)

The *Hizb Allah* that Qassem refers to is mentioned in the Qur'an and *Hadiths* of the Prophet and his imams. Two verses in the Qur'an (5: 55, 56) subscribe *Hizb Allah* to: 'whoever is an ally of Allah and His Messenger and those who have believed - indeed, the party of Allah - they will be the predominant'.[2]

The emergence of *al-Mahdi* will be preceded by 'signs' or 'indications'. One is the appearance of a group of genuine believers, *al-thullah al-mu'minah*: 'these are the *Mumahhidun* [those who pave the way] – with them the conditions of the Greater Occultation will be completed' (Qassem 2010a: 200). They will emerge in *Bilad al-Sham* (Greater Syria) and uphold jihad and persevere in the face of harsh difficulties. And another group (Ta'ifah), carrying black banners, the belief goes, will emerge in Khorasan (contemporary Iran) and will fight enemies to revive Islam and promote its virtues. This group will persevere 'until it is joined by the Imam [al-Mahdi], who will carry the banner and lead the struggle' (Qassem 2010a: 202).

Drawing on various *Hadiths*,[3] in Hezbollah's belief, the emergence of the Messiah will be accompanied by drastic changes towards the 'end of times': the diffusion of oppression and corruption; a major struggle between those who promote virtue and others who promote vice; the rise of a group that will steer Islam away from its true path; a major *fitnah* in Bilad al-Sham; and the presence of *al-thullah al-mu'minah* (Qassem 2010a: 159–208).[4] Hezbollah leaders, including Nasrallah,[5] occasionally discuss the 'indications' of the end of time. But they go a little bit further. They sanguinely but cautiously suggest that we might be living in the age preceding the emergence.[6] They can never be certain, they acknowledge, for this is God's will. After all, it this uncertainty surrounding the emergence of *al-Mahdi* that has kept the belief in his return alive and the whole Shi'a religio-political doctrine intact. Shi'ism prospers on this hope.

But Hezbollah make daring suggestions on this level, ones that give an interesting insight on how they see the world now. Speaking during *Ashura* in 2006, on the anniversary of the Islamic Revolution, Ibrahim Amin al-Sayyid asked: what does the victory of the Islamic Revolution actually mean?

> We have no doubt that what we witnessed was a great event [Islamic Revolution], which resembled an earthquake; but the importance of this

> event – its honour, sacredness, greatness – is that this revolution is one step in the path of the divinely and just plan [that culminates] with *al-Mahdi*. (al-Sayyid 2008: 86)

So was the Islamic Revolution the Khorasan that *Hadith*s had for long predicted? 'God knows', Qassem cautions. But his reserved stance is followed by a more reassuring belief: the Islamic Revolution, which upholds Islam and virtue, 'is certainly a step in the way to the [*Mahdi*'s] emergence' (Qassem 2010a: 203). The world, he contends, has now reached unprecedented levels of corruption and oppression. The materialistic culture – 'a deepening lust for the body, erosion of boundaries, elimination of prohibitions and the collapse of virtue into vice and vice into virtue' – may be the signs of the end of times (Qassem 2010a: 199).

Is Hezbollah *al-thullah al-mu'minah* in the 'sea of disbelief' (Qassem 2010a: 138) that the *Hadith*s claim will emerge in Bilad al-Sham and will precede the emergence of the *Mahdi*? Again, although Hezbollah cannot strongly claim to be the 'Hizb Allah' the religious texts refer to, it certainly aspires to be that group (Qassem 2010a: 149; A. H. Fadlallah 2015). In Hezbollah's eyes, the emergence of the movement, its struggle against Israel, oppressive regimes and the unjust international order are, like the Islamic Revolution, yet other signs of and progress in the road to the return of the *Mahdi* (al-Sayyid 2008; Qassem 2008b, 2010a).

But here the lines between religious prophecy – God's predetermined plan for the world – and Hezbollah's own efforts to realise it begin to be blurred. Belief in the prophecies of the return of the *Mahdi* begin to take the form of prescription for a plan of *action*. This return, Hezbollah leaders remind their supporters and potential recruits, cannot be materialised by prayer and wishes alone: it requires actual religious, cultural and political preparation – *tamhid*, of which jihad is the most important element – as our discussion highlighted in Chapter 2. Hezbollah uses its own experience, particularly war-making with Israel, to reinforce these beliefs. Hezbollah's success in forcing Israel out of Lebanon in 2000 and its survival in the 2006 war (depicted as a 'Divine Victory') are examples of how *Rijal Allah* (or God's soldiers) confronted the 'invading Zionists': 'for if it was not their belief in God, the Prophet's approach, *Ahl al-Bayt* and their awaiting for the emergence of the *Mahdi*, they would have not accepted this *bala'* or presented these sacrifices' (Qassem 2010a: 149).

But you might ask, how do these beliefs and perceptions translate into actual behaviour? How do they shape Hezbollah's international socialisation? The cynical might argue that these are just ideas that Hezbollah carries, instruments to realise its political interests and ones that have no bearing on reality. When I asked one political observer in Lebanon (I keep their name anonymous) about Hezbollah's belief in the *Mahdi*, the brief answer, which axed the discussion on this theme, was: *sallim 'ala al-Mahdi* ('send my regards to the Mahdi!'). Nevertheless, Hezbollah is not, nor the student of Hezbollah should be, naïve about the direct translation of these beliefs into concrete policies. In other words, whilst Hezbollah believes it is preparing the ground for the awaited *Mahdi*, and does that at an organisational level as we saw in Chapter 2, it does not construct its political strategy on these beliefs. This is for two reasons. First, at a doctrinal level, whilst Hezbollah believes in preparing for the *Mahdi*'s return, it cannot be sure about the actual timing. Jaradi cautions that: 'if you stick to the past, you will freeze; but if you focus on the future, you will become utopian' (Jaradi 2015). Thus, these beliefs cannot be seen through the narrow lens of strategic or political planning and calculation (Qassir 2015). But there is a second reason why there are limits to a potential utopia: war-making. Hezbollah was born, as we have seen so far, from the midst of war, which socialised it in concrete geopolitical and military realities. This socialisation cannot afford any speculation – religious or otherwise.

So, how exactly do these beliefs shape Hezbollah's behaviour and perception? Based on what has been presented so far, one can deduce that these beliefs bestow religious meaning and significance on Hezbollah's actions and identity. War-making with Israel thus becomes not only a national liberation struggle, but as Qassem believes a 'part of the practical and realistic operation of *tamhid*' (Qassem 2010a: 102). Hezbollah's perceived successes on the battleground are interpreted as 'Divine Victories' and God's 'promise' to his believers, 'al-Mahdi's soldiers' (Jaradi 2014: 74–9; Qassem 2008b; al-Sayyid 2008: 81). These beliefs are reflected in the fighters' testaments. In one, a fighter (Qassem Ezzealdine) urges his brothers to transform the love for Hussein into practice, for 'the path of Hussein is continuous, for every day is *Ashura* and every land is Karbala'. Another (Asa'ad Atat) urges his brothers to 'pursue the path of the Islamic Resistance and to be the *Mumahhidun* for *al-Mahdi*'.

This religio-political doctrine, thus, offers Hezbollah with one lens to see the world. The ingrained universal beliefs bestow meaning on Hezbollah's actions and identity and imbue the Islamist movement with a sense of righteousness. In 2017, Muhammad Ibn Salman, the young Saudi deputy crown prince, contended that Iran believes 'the Imam Mahdi will come and they must prepare the fertile environment for (his) arrival . . . and they must control the Muslim world' (Aboudi and Fahmy 2017). Nasrallah retaliated a few days later, suggesting that the prince should seek religious education. The return of *al-Mahdi*, he noted, is not an exclusive Shi'a belief, it is an Islamic one.[7] (Indeed, the self-proclaimed Islamic State has also anticipated the return of *al-Mahdi*.) But Nasrallah did not mince his words on who the Messiah will side with: 'When the *al-Mahdi* emerges in Mecca, there will not remain any unjust king or a despotic prince . . . this day is coming: neither you, your forefathers or grandsons will be able to change anything in this divinely will' (Nasrallah 2017).

But there is a second lens that Hezbollah sees and interprets the world through, specifically the international political order.[8] Here, Hezbollah appears more as a product of Islamic revivalism of the twentieth century, which aimed to bring Islam back into political life and to combat Western domination (Abu-Rabi 1995). This is the layer that many students of Hezbollah have focused on to explain the Islamist movement's motivations and goals (Hamzeh 2004; Saad-Ghorayeb 2002; Jaber 1997). It is also one that sheds more light on the politics and strategy of Hezbollah's international socialisation.

To use the terminology of Social Movements Theory, this worldview involves both diagnostic and prescriptive elements. As mentioned previously, Hezbollah's worldview is shaped by revolutionary Islamist thinkers and activists, such as Imam Khomeini or Ayatollah Fadlallah. Hezbollah has adopted many of the diagnostic and prescriptive principles of these thinkers. It perceives Arab-Muslim weakness and subservience as a result of two interrelated factors: Western hegemony and the retreat of Islam. The latter enables the former. To counter Western hegemony, Islam needs to be activated in all social spheres.

Hezbollah perceives itself both as a victim of and a revolutionary force against Western hegemony. For Hezbollah, Western hegemony pervades all spheres – cultural, economic, military and political – of the life of Muslims. It strips these societies from their authentic identity: Islam. At a cultural level, Hezbollah associates the West, particularly the US, with the corruption of human values and dignity. Capitalism, with the forces of marketisation, individualism, materialism and objectification of human beings (especially of women) that it spurs, constitutes the antithesis of Hezbollah's religious and cultural identity. This socio-economic system, Hezbollah believes, is the cause of wars, poverty, hunger, oppression and corruption in the world. There is, thus, a 'cultural conflict' with the West (Saad-Ghorayeb 2002: 102–6).

There is also a Western 'cultural invasion' (al-Sayyid 2008: 58). This point draws us closer to the crux of the issue: perceived Western political hegemony. By sending diplomatic missions, establishing schools, cultural centres, media offices and economic units, the West's main intention is to 'impose its own ideologies in our region', claims Qassem. Hence, 'it is our job to invalidate their concepts, to prove their evil and to spread our vision instead' (quoted in Jaber 1997: 56–7). For Saffieddine, the West is engaged in a 'soft war' against Iran and Hezbollah.[9] This strategy serves to weaken Hezbollah's religio-cultural foundations, which is key in Hezbollah's 'defensive' struggle with the West.[10] In the Islamic Government treatise, Khomeini had warned against 'orientalists serving as propaganda agents for the imperialist institutions' (Khomeini n.d.: 79). These orientalists, adds Ayatollah M. H. Fadlallah, produced studies and reports that aimed to weaken the Islamist identity and authenticity, thus aborting the potential for Islam's revival (M. H. Fadlallah 2003: 80–2).

What Hezbollah and other Islamists particularly abhor, however, is how the colonial powers divided the Arab region into weak polities in the post-Ottoman period, treating them 'as political and economic dependencies'. The West, Qassem warns, 'utilises slogans such as modernity, democracy, human rights to dilute Islam's potential for leadership and to keep it away from the social sphere' (Qassem 2008a: 364). American foreign policy, he observes, is enacted 'with no consideration to any ethical, religious, humane or political considerations – even if this were to cost the lives of a thousand or hundred thousand innocent people, as the attacks on Nagasaki and Hiroshima attest'.

What about Western values (democracy, human rights, freedom), do they constitute an appropriate basis for the US-led international order? Qassem believes these values are for US domestic use only; internationally, they are 'used to blackmail [enemy] states, organisations or individuals . . . and are a means to realise other goals such as the control of human, political and natural resources' (Qassem 2008a: 365). Hezbollah accuses the West of double standards. The US fights Iraq or Iran, Hezbollah observes, for possessing or building capacity for weapons of mass destruction, but Israel is protected despite its possession of nuclear weapons (Saad-Ghorayeb 2002: 93). The US labels Hezbollah as a 'terrorist' organisation, but does not recognise the violence Israel inflicts on the Palestinians and Lebanese as terrorism, Saffieddine complains. The US backs Arab dictators if they are allies, but imposes sanctions on regimes that challenge it.[11]

However, if there is one area where the confrontation between Hezbollah and the US is the most intense, then it is in relation to the Arab–Israeli conflict. In Hezbollah's view, it is even wrong to talk about the 'Arab–Israeli conflict', for the establishment of the Israeli state, and the support this state garnered from world powers (the Soviet Union, US, Britain and France), amounts to a 'major crime against humanity':

> The establishment of the Zionist entity in Palestine is a clear aggression against the innocent Palestinian people. It exchanged one people for another: it transformed the real owners [the Palestinians] of the land into refugees dispersed around the world and in return congregated invaders [Jews] from around the world [in Palestine]. This is not a struggle over borders between two neighbouring countries: it is the uprooting of a state and a people and the establishment of another in its place. (Qassem 2008a: 240)

The Zionist goal, Qassem believes, is to control the land between the 'two rivers: Euphrates and the Nile', which has a religious basis in the Torah. Zionist success is due to unfettered Western, particularly American, military, economic and political backing. From the Balfour Declaration (1916), which promised the Jews a home in Palestine, to the recognition of Israel after its founding (1948), through the series of wars it fought with the Arabs (1948, 1956, 1967, 1973, 1982), the West has contributed directly to Israel's expansion in Palestine and to the suffering of the Palestinians. Thanks to the 'Zionist lobby' in the US, America has made Israel a main pillar in its Middle East strategy, which divided Arab ranks. The West, including the UN, revolts Qassem, have been totally silent about Israel's 'aggressive policies against the Palestinians and Lebanese'. UN security council resolutions (such as 194, 242 or 425) have all failed to liberate the occupied territories, return the refugees or deter Israel from further expansion (Qassem 2008a: 223–42). All this leads Qassem to deduce that without armed resistance: 'we will see our existence eroding . . . and this would be a humiliating life that has no meaning' (Qassem 2008a: 252).

These perceptions and war-making, as we shall see below, reveal a Hobbesian, realist construction of the world order. As Nasrallah notes:

> We live in a world of wolves: there is no international law; there is the law of the jungle; the strong preys on the weak. If we are weak, we will fall prey to the strong. If we are strong, the world will respect us, [especially] when we influence the balance of power and interests. This world searches for [and is driven by] interests, not by values. Thus, our power, interests, destiny and future stand on our capabilities, our unity, our peoples' determination, their consciousness.[12]

But the intellectual (and you could say more sober) ground for this realist view was laid before the emergence of Hezbollah. It is one that aimed to offer prescriptions to overcome Islamic decline, weakness and victimhood. Islamist thinkers called for a religio-political awakening. One, Ayatollah M. H. Fadlallah, called for Islamic liberation. In his *Islam and the Logic of Power*, published in 1973, Fadlallah called for the 'empowering' of Islamist movements. Islamists, he recommended, should hold a clear vision. The vision should not be reactive. This he believed was important for the 'authenticity' of the Islamists' identity and message. An understanding of power should be 'connected to the Muslims' fateful social, political and military causes' (M. H. Fadlallah 2003: 12–13; see also Saouli 2014a: 5–7). Islamists should 'rebel against oppression and injustice and work to change it' (M. H. Fadlallah 2003: 61). The starting point is to gradually accumulate power by investing in cultural and socio-economic spheres and to create the space for the rise of Islamist power. The aim is to defeat feelings of weakness. But Fadlallah cautioned against unrestrained enthusiasm. Islamists should be cognisant of the socio-political constraints it faces and build its strategies accordingly. Accumulating power serves two interests: self-reliance and determination, namely to control the *Ummah*'s resources and to determine its political choices; and, second, to deter enemies from attacking it. (M. H. Fadlallah 2003: 332–7).

Islamic liberation, M. H. Fadlallah and Khomeini believed, involves freedom from (Arab/Islamic) oppressive regimes and colonialism. It is the Muslims' religious duty to struggle for freedom, to 'promote virtue and prohibit vice'. Fadlallah called for 'Islamic unity' to fight colonialism and enforce the *Ummah*'s liberation (M. H. Fadlallah 2004: 183–98; Khomeini n.d.: 71–2). Echoing these perceptions, Saffieddine argues that Hezbollah perceives 'Western culture' with suspicion and doubt. 'Our main duty is to bring confidence and belonging back.' Cultural revival here is crucial for the 'confrontation with the arrogant and Zionist plans in our region' (Saffieddine 2007: 57).

Fadlallah, who mobilised many of Hezbollah's cadres, believed that the Israeli occupation of Arab territories can and should be liberated by armed resistance. Liberation of Jerusalem, he reminded fellow Muslims, is a religious duty (M. H. Fadlallah 2004: 91). Like Fadlallah, Imam Khomeini treated the liberation of Jerusalem as a religio-political duty calling upon all 'Muslims to eradicate this concentration of corruption [Israel] and to assist the *mujahidin* [fighters] in doing so' (quoted in Qassem 2008a: 250–1). The testimonies of Hezbollah fighters also attest to these beliefs. One (Muhammad Srour's) calls to 'join the ranks of the Islamic Resistance . . . to destroy the Great Satan, the US, to uproot the Zionist cancer from this earth'.

Webs of Interdependence: War-making and Political Alliances

Hezbollah's worldview, its religio-political doctrine and understanding of current world affairs have, thus, placed the Islamist movement in confrontation with the dominant forces in the international order and their allies in the region. This is key to understand Hezbollah's war-making and political alliances at an international level. The Open Letter offered clear indicators of Hezbollah's politico-strategic goals (see Chapter 2): 'We declare that our ambition is to make Lebanon an invisible part of the geopolitical landscape that is ruled by Islam and its just leadership [Khomeini] and that is in opposition to the US, the arrogant world and world Zionism'. Hezbollah's socialisation has since been committed to the realisation of these goals. A demonstration of its war-making and alliance formation will reveal this commitment.

War-making

One can think of war-making as a process that involves constant preparation for and occasional engagement in armed conflict with an enemy with the purpose of realising a political goal. Hezbollah's war-making with Israel aimed to drive Israel out of Lebanon as a stepping stone to liberate Palestine. This strategy had its social, religious and political dimensions, many of which we have already examined in previous chapters. But the military dimension is the building-block of this strategy. Strategy is the 'link between military means and political ends' (Betts 2000: 5). In its war-making with Israel, Hezbollah has attempted to utilise available military means to achieve short- and long-term political goals. The choice of means is borne from Hezbollah's context: an armed guerrilla group fighting a strong standing army within a specific topography; the availability of and access to weapons; and the accumulation of knowledge through improvisation and innovation on the way. As in the political battlefield, Hezbollah's military strategy has aimed to overcome military constraints and to appropriate opportunities in the struggle against Israel.

One way to understand Hezbollah's war-making is to first identify Israel's politico-military goals in Lebanon, especially in the wake of the 1982 invasion. Israel wanted to protect its northern border by neutralising any threats coming from Lebanon and to maintain its deterrence reputation. The invasion aimed to defeat the PLO and its allies, install a friendly regime, establish economic ties and, ultimately, sign a political agreement with Lebanon. Such a goal served Israel's broader Middle East strategy, which aimed to divide the opposing Arab camp by signing individual treaties with Lebanon and Jordan and, thus, deepening Syria's isolation in the region (Schiff and Ya'ari 1985; Lieberman 2012: 178–80; Bregman 2016: 152–87).

Now turn to Hezbollah, and it is not difficult to realise that the Islamist movement hoped to hamper these Israeli goals. Hezbollah's asymmetrical struggle with Israel involved a sustained and protracted war of attrition. The aim was to make Israel's occupation of Lebanon as costly as possible and to oblige the enemy to reconsider its strategy and options. Through religio-political mobilisation, Hezbollah also wanted to thwart any social, economic or political naturalisation of the Zionist state. This strategy aimed to keep Lebanon out of the Western and Israeli camp in the region. To realise these goals, Hezbollah initially utilised several military means: martyrdom operations, military ambushes, roadside bombs and anti-tank and anti-armour capability.

Martyrdom operations, as Hezbollah calls them (commonly known as suicide bombings), offered the Islamic Resistance with a military advantage over Israel. This military tactic combined two elements. The first involved the car bomb, which was regularly used during the Lebanon war by various actors to assassinate and terrorise foes. The first to use this military tactic in Lebanon was Israel when it assassinated a Palestinian official in 1972. But the second element involved Hezbollah's development of this tactic by adding a driver to the car who was willing to sacrifice his life to become a martyr. 'With drivers', observes DeVore and Stähli, 'car bombs became vectors that could deliver heavy explosives against both secure and mobile targets' (DeVore and Stähli 2015: 346–7). The 'main pillar' of these military operations is the 'human factor', for it requires someone who is willing to sacrifice his life to realise it.[13] The religio-political culture of martyrdom, which we have explored above, enables this military tactic. According to H. Fadlallah, these operations are usually undertaken by 'elite members of the resistance who possess high spiritual, cultural and religious commitment'. One aim of this means was to 'inflict heavy losses [on the enemy] in addition to the psychological and moral impact [this causes]'. Another was to boost people's morale and prevent them from engaging with the enemy (H. Fadlallah 2009: 129; Mustafa 2003: 459).

Hezbollah carried out 12 suicide bombings in the period from 1982 to 1999.[14] These attacks targeted Israeli military headquarters, posts and motorcades in various parts of southern Lebanon. On 11 November 1982, a car bomb targeted the Israeli military headquarters in Tyre, demolishing the eight-storey building and killing 75 Israelis and 15 Palestinian and Lebanese detainees (DeVore and Stähli 2015: 347).[15] The driver was the 17-year-old Ahmad Kassir, from the village of Deir Qanoun En Nahr. Kassir was working in Saudi Arabia before he decided to go back home in the wake of the Israeli invasion of Lebanon and enrol in the resistance cells in his village. Known to his comrades and family as modest, religiously committed and spiritually and psychologically pure, Kassir expressed an interest in 'pursuing the path of martyrdom'. After undergoing several 'tests' – including attempts by his comrades to dissuade him from undertaking the operation – he was chosen to undertake the operation (H. Fadlallah 2009: 130–2). With a *fatwa* in hand, information about the Israeli headquarters gathered by a surveillance team and a car loaded with explosives, Kassir inaugurated a series of car bomb attacks against Israeli and Western targets in Lebanon.

Kassir is celebrated by both Amal and Hezbollah as 'their' martyr, though it was more likely that he belonged to cells connected to what would become Hezbollah (Mustafa 2003: 459–60). Al-Manar recently disclosed information revealing that Imad Mughnieh masterminded the attack.[16] The new information resonates with Hala Jaber's narrative on other similar attacks against Western targets in Lebanon. On 18 April 1983, a jihadi attacked the American embassy at a time when the CIA Beirut bureau was holding a meeting. The attack killed 63 people, including 17 Americans. Six months later, on 23 October 1983, two simultaneous but separate attacks targeted the US marine barracks and French troops, killing 241 US personnel (including 220 marines) and 58 French paratroopers (Jaber 1997: 76–82). Jaber reports that Imad Mughnieh and Mustafa Badreddine, who would both become military chiefs in Hezbollah, planned the 'Syrian-Iranian-backed operation' (Jaber 1997: 82–3). However, unlike the Tyre attack, Hezbollah never claimed responsibility for these operations. Another group, the Islamic Jihad, claimed responsibility. Was Imad Mughnieh a member of Hezbollah in the 1980s? It is very likely that Mughnieh belonged to the cells that worked directly with the Iranian IRG, which aimed to realise specific politico-military goals in Lebanon, including hostage-taking (Norton 2014: 71).

Although these cells shared similar religio-political goals, the extent to which they connected to Hezbollah remains unclear. Many years later, Nasrallah revealed the Mughnieh was not a member of Hezbollah in the 1980s and that he belonged to another organisation, 'regardless of whether this organisation still exists today'. Hezbollah remains very cautious in revealing information on these attacks of the 1980s. The way, for example, Al-Manar's documentary recounts Kassir's story reveals some inconsistencies.

On the one hand, the organisers, including Kassir, are portrayed as enthusiasts who collected money (which one claims they borrowed) to buy the dynamite for the explosives. On the other hand, the story reveals Mughnieh as a key player in supervising and coordinating the logistics of the operation, which echoes H. Fadlallah's narrative of the presence of organised cells who carefully considered various means and targets. When Kassir was ready to conduct the operation, he and his group realised that they required a religious mandate (or *fatwa*) first, especially since the Azmi building included Lebanese and Palestinian detainees on the top floor who could be killed in the attack. The group, the story goes, sought this *fatwa* from 'brothers in Iran'. If this is accurate, then the group certainly was part of an organisation, even if loose at this stage, that was in a close coordination with the IRG.

These questions aside, these attacks served the goal of Hezbollah (and Iran and Syria). What is also clear is that Hezbollah was the one to innovate and pass on to other movements the military means of suicide bombing.[17] Many years later, as we shall see in the following chapter, Hezbollah would itself fall victim to suicide bombings. But in its war-making with Israel, the effectiveness of this military tactic began to erode as Israel started to take strict precautions to protect its soldiers, not least in its phased withdrawal to its 'security zone' in 1985 and its backing of the SLA as a buffer between itself and the enemy. For example, whilst the first attacks in 1982 and 1983 generated 75 and 29 Israeli losses, respectively, the last two attacks in 1996 and 1999 led to the killing of two and seven Israelis, respectively.

Other military means that Hezbollah utilised involved guerrilla and irregular tactics, such as military ambushes and roadside bombs. Military ambushes targeted Israeli military motorcades by using light-to-medium weaponry, such as automatic rifles, grenades or road bombs. After careful surveillance of Israeli movements and manoeuvres, a team of Hezbollah's special forces would prepare the ambush and execute the operation (Mustafa 2003: 470; H. Fadlallah 2009: 127–8). These 'small units proved that they could strike quickly at targets of opportunity and then, just as suddenly, disappear into Lebanon's population' (DeVore and Stähli 2015: 345). With time, these kinds of attacks became more complex with the initiation of the 'dual ambush': first, one group attacks a convoy and as an Israeli support unit joins it, it in turn comes under attack by another Hezbollah unit

(H. Fadlallah 2009: 128). Ambushes formed the majority of the attacks against Israel, with around 545 in the period 1982–2000. The biggest of these attacks was the 'Ansariya Ambush'. On 5 September 1997, Hezbollah prepared an ambush in the coastal village of Ansariya in the expectation that the Israeli commandoes were planning to attack the village to detain or assassinate one of Hezbollah's military leaders. When the Israeli soldiers arrived these road bombs were detonated all at once before the two parties clashed for many hours leading to heavy Israeli losses (Mustafa 2003: 471–4). Many years later, in 2009, for purely domestic reasons, which we will look at in the following chapter, Nasrallah would disclose that Hezbollah had in fact intercepted communications of Israeli reconnaissance planes to learn about the planned Israeli attack (Saouli 2011: 939). The number of military ambushes averaged around 23 in the period 1982–92, bearing in mind Hezbollah's embroilment in the war with Amal in 1988–90 (see Chapter 3). The number would increase to 129 in 1993–4 then gradually decrease to 47 (1996), 68 (199–8) and 24 (1999–2000) the year of the Israeli withdrawal (Mustafa 2003: 470–1).

But as Hezbollah was developing various means to cope with the Israeli military challenge, Israel in turn was adapting to the challenges posed by the armed resistance in Lebanon. After intense internal debates about its embroilment in Lebanon, the Israeli government decided in favour of a phased withdrawal. The goal was to ensure that the PLO or other threatening parties did not establish a base in southern Lebanon and to preserve Israel's deterrence reputation. Israel withdrew to a 'Security Zone' in 1985 and supported the SLA as a buffer zone between it and its enemies. On the other hand, 'Israel tried to deter further attacks [from Hezbollah and others] on its forces . . . by punishing the civilian population' and using 'arrests and targeted killing' (Lieberman 2012: 178–9). Through these policies Israel aimed to create a wedge between armed groups and their local social base.

As we saw in the previous chapter, Lebanese southerners were reluctant to accommodate armed struggle against Israel having grown disenchanted by the previous Palestinian experience. But, paradoxically, these Israeli measures reinforced Hezbollah's narrative and religio-political mobilisation efforts in the 1980s that called for resistance as the most viable politico-military strategy. For example, on 16 October 1983, the Israeli army clashed with

Shi'a mourners during the commemoration of *Ashura* in Nabatieh leading to the death of two people and the injury of fifteen. This incident, in addition to Israel's separation of south Lebanon from the rest of the country by installing checkpoints, generated a defiant reaction and led even moderate Shi'a scholars, like M. M. Shammesdine, to call for 'civil resistance' (Jaber 1997: 18–19).

The Israeli retreat to the Security Zone after 1985 offered Hezbollah opportunities to occupy strategic areas and posts. Hezbollah's new strategy involved the protection of these posts, to prevent the IDF from getting in, and also using them as springboards to attack the enemy in the occupied zone (Gabrielsen 2014: 263). Hezbollah established four major positions that covered the area extending from the coast near Tyre to western Beqaa. (In Chapter 3 we saw that Hezbollah's domestic strategy aimed to consolidate these areas, which generated violent confrontations with Amal.) One main bunker was in the strategic Mleeta Mountain, which acts as a natural barrier to invasions. After 2006, Hezbollah transformed the bunker into a military museum – the Mleeta Resistance Tourist Landmark. The museum exhibits some of Hezbollah's weapons, military equipment taken from the Israeli army and the bunker where Hezbollah fighters, including their leader, Sayyid Abbas al-Mussawi, prayed, ate and prepared for military operations. With this transformation, observes H. Fadlallah, the Islamic Resistance began to merge conventional warfare with guerrilla tactics: sometimes it would conduct military operations in the classical style – using intensive shelling before the arrival of infantry – and at other times it reverted to ambushes and roadside bombs. This obliged the Israelis and the SLA to remain continuously on alert and within their own fortresses (H. Fadlallah 2009: 162–3; Gabrielsen 2014: 263–4).

Another military tactic involved the so-called 'secret' or 'security war'. This involved the infiltration of the SLA, the recruitment of some its members and the assassination of others. The aim was to break the shield – the SLA – Israel imposed and to expose the Israeli army (H. Fadlallah 2009: 141; Lieberman 2012: 179; Gabrielsen 2014: 258; Mustafa 2003: 494–8). Through assassinations, Hezbollah hoped to instil fear in SLA members and their families, to encourage defections and ultimately to delegitimise the group as collaborators. For example, between 1982–92, Hezbollah killed 368 members of the SLA (Mustafa 2003: 498), including high-ranking officials.

Between 1993 and 2000, SLA lost on average 57 soldiers per year (Mustafa 2003: 498).

But many of these operations required thorough surveillance. Hezbollah's development of its intelligence services was yet another indispensable outcome of its war-making with Israel. The need for such a capacity initially emerged when Hezbollah gathered information before it performed military ambushes or suicide attacks. This did not require sophisticated information gathering and analysis (H. Fadlallah 2009: 147). However, with the growth of Hezbollah, with the organisation becoming a public one in 1985, the war with Amal and the assassination of Mussawi in 1992, the need for more institutionalised intelligence service units became one of strategic relevance. The goal was to debilitate Israel's intelligence network in Lebanon and, thus, to prevent it from realising its politico-military goals there (H. Fadlallah 2009: 145–51). Israel – not unlike other actors involved in Lebanon's convoluted wars – had a strong spy network in Lebanon. Its war with Palestinian organisations required intelligence infrastructure which enabled it to realise its goals. One such operation – conducted by Israeli commandoes including the future PM of Israel Ehud Barak – was the assassination of three Palestinian leaders in the Verdun area of Beirut in 1973 (Bregman 2016: 154).[18] Hezbollah, which initially was not under the Israeli radar, learned from the successes and flaws of Palestinian military activities in Lebanon. By the mid-1990s, Hezbollah's intelligence network grew to cover key areas in Beirut and Lebanon as a whole. Special focus has been on Dahieh, where Hezbollah leaders are based in its self-proclaimed 'Security Zone' (or *al-Muraba'a al-Amni*). There, Hezbollah regularly dispatches surveillance teams that gather information on residents, their ages, occupations, and so forth. According to Fadlallah, this has prevented many Israeli infiltrations, including an assassination attempt against Nasrallah (H. Fadlallah 2009: 148–9). By 2010, Hezbollah could claim that it had the 'strongest counter-intelligence agency' in Lebanon. This celebratory announcement came after several Israeli spy networks were uncovered in Lebanon in the period 2008–10 (Saouli 2011: 939).

Another way to combat Israeli and Western intelligence activities in Lebanon was the tactic of hostage-taking, which was used in the 1980s. As we saw in Chapter 3, this was one of the factors that contributed to Hezbollah's wars with Amal and Syria. More than 87 Europeans and Americans were taken as hostages during the 1980s. Although Hezbollah never claimed responsibility for this tactic, as we saw above, many believed that it or groups associated with the IRG played a key role in these activities. The tactic contributed to weakening Western influence in the war-torn country and 'sparked an exodus of Europeans and Americans from Lebanon'. Hostage-taking also involved exchanging hostages for prisoners in Kuwaiti, Israeli or French jails; obliging the US or France to expel Iranian dissidents; and the generation of ransoms (DeVore and Stähli 2015: 348–50).

But Hezbollah does claim responsibility for abducting Israeli soldiers. These operations, highlights H. Fadlallah, served two principal goals: one, psychological, to inflict fear in the ranks of Israeli soldiers, to expose their weakness and to interrogate them; and, second, to exchange them with Lebanese and Palestinian detainees in Israeli prisons (H. Fadlallah 2009: 142). Between 1982 and 2000, Hezbollah abducted 12 Israeli soldiers. Through these abductions, Hezbollah managed to bring back all, or most, Lebanese detainees in Israeli prisons.

Hezbollah has also relied on another key area of war-making: psychological warfare. In 1986, it began to film its military operations against Israeli and SLA fighters. The filming of operations served Hezbollah's campaign to mobilise and recruit the public against the Israeli occupation (H. Fadlallah 2009: 151). To the pride and increasing confidence of Hezbollah's supporters, some films showed how Hezbollah fighters attacked and occupied an Israeli or SLA outpost and implanted the Hezbollah flag. Hezbollah distributed these films to various media outlets and displayed them on Al-Manar. The films are then reproduced in promotional video clips to ingrain the 'culture of resistance' and to deconstruct Lebanese and Arab perceptions of Israel as the 'army that cannot be defeated'. The message was clear: 'Yes we can!' The aim, as one Hezbollah member puts it, is to preserve the memory of these operations and to 'emphasise the need to establish the resistance society' (Mustafa 2003: 487). The footage challenged and in some cases discredited Israel's narrative and information on its own losses on the battleground. As Gabrielsen explains:

> Hezbollah carried out an attack and claimed that its fighters had penetrated an IDF position, but initially only provided limited footage of the assault.

> Then, when the IDF subsequently denied that Hezbollah had managed to breach the position, Hezbollah released more footage clearly showing that its fighters indeed had entered the IDF outpost. (Gabrielsen 2014: 259–60)

The psychological impact of this footage might be more forceful than the actual military operations (Gabrielsen 2014: 259). The factor that enables this form of psychological warfare is Israel's democracy and its polarised politics, especially in the 1980s and 1990s. Hezbollah's psychological warfare, whether in the form of footage of military operations or in the speeches of Nasrallah, has with time become a factor in Israeli political dynamics – call it the 'Hezbollah factor'. In many ways, Hezbollah has established a balance of (psychological) power with Israel. The latter has historically used a combination of means to shape the domestic politics and orientations of its enemies: war and violence in their various forms, divide-and-rule tactics and propaganda campaigns. The aim was to maintain military superiority and a reputation for deterrence (Aran 2012; Schulze 2008; Lieberman 2012). But Hezbollah's military challenge and its psychological warfare against Israel have in turn transformed it into a factor that shapes Israeli politics. Various wars – 1993, 1996, 2006 – demonstrate this change, as we shall see.

Finally, is Hezbollah's rocket warfare. The development of this military means is, yet again, borne out of the battle. In wars, competitors want to find ways to at least constrain the movements of their enemies or, better, to paralyse their military capacity. They want to deter the enemy, and in doing so want to defend themselves. Hezbollah's war-making with Israel, at least in its short-to-medium term, can be condensed to simply that. Ironically, it is Israel's quest to maintain military superiority over its enemies and its occupation of Lebanon that has triggered Hezbollah's own quest for deterrence. H. Fadlallah explains the rationale for the development of rocket warfare, namely the Katyusha. After having developed irregular and conventional means to fight Israel, he notes that:

> the remaining challenge for the resistance was Israel's targeting of civilians, which it [Hezbollah] began to search for ways to terminate. It found that it had to treat the Israelis in the same manner: to disrupt the stability/security of Israeli settlers in the north [of Israel]. The [only] available weapon in this context is the Katyusha rocket. (H. Fadlallah 2009: 164)

The Katyusha was used in World War II. It is 288 centimetres, has a reach of 20 kilometres, and a speed of 690 metres per second. Triggered from mobile launchers that are hard to locate, Hezbollah first used the Katyusha in 1992 to avenge the killing of its leader. However, with time, Hezbollah began to use the Katyusha to target military outposts in the occupied zone to 'paralyse the capacity and free movement' of these positions. But, as Nasrallah explains, the use of the Katyusha required a political decision, usually made by the Shura Council: 'To maintain its deterrent quality, we did not always use it' (*Ahzab Lubnan: Hizb Allah* [Parties of Lebanon: Hezbollah] 2003).

It was during high-intensity conflicts that this and other military tactics were combined to challenge Israel's military superiority. Between 1982 and 2005, two such wars, 1993 and 1996 (and the 2006 war, as we shall see in the following chapter), demonstrated the increasing challenge Israel was facing in Lebanon and the constraints it faced in trying to consolidate its deterrence policy. There are striking similarities in these wars. In 1993, Israel hoped to get rid of Hezbollah or at least to paralyse its military capacity. This came after a salient increase in the number of Hezbollah attacks on Israel and increasing support of Hezbollah in Lebanon. As we saw above, the period 1990–3 brought political stability to Lebanon, enabling Hezbollah to focus on war-making efforts. This led Israel to launch what it called Operation Accountability on 25 July 1993. The military campaign involved intensive attacks from land, air and sea against Hezbollah and civilian targets. The seven-day war had a devastating impact on Lebanon's southern villages and led to the deaths of 130 civilians (Jaber 1997: 172). Israel's policy in Lebanon, which would endure in the following two decades, aimed at the 'exacerbation of the opponent's internal contradictions' (Aran 2012: 841). Through Operation Accountability, Israel wanted to displace many southerners, and in doing so increase the pressure on the Lebanese government to halt or disarm Hezbollah (Ynetnews n.d.; H. Fadlallah 2009: 167). Such pressure, Israel calculated, would also foment divisions between Hezbollah and its Shi'a supporters (Bregman 2016: 271; Jaber 1997: 172).

The 1993 war had its regional and international dimensions and implications. The US, its regional allies and Israel had an interest in promoting the peace process between the Arabs and Israel (the secret Oslo negotiations between the PLO and Israel were close to completion). The strategic goal of detaching Lebanon from Syria or, at least, weakening Syria's bargaining power by defeating Hezbollah – as one of Syria's 'negotiating cards' – played a key role in the intensifying of the conflict in July 1993.

But Hezbollah hoped to thwart the Israeli war aims. As Fadlallah recalls, the armed movement prepared for the 'worst scenario': ground invasion. But this did not materialise. Israel instead relied on long-range fire from aircraft, tanks, artillery, missile boats, targets which were beyond the reach of Hezbollah. To counter Israel's campaign, Hezbollah leaders decided to attack Israeli and SLA military outposts, use rocket fire against Israeli positions and northern settlements and to offer help for civilians to 'keep them in their villages'. On the first day of the war, Hezbollah fired around 50 rockets on northern Israel (H. Fadlallah 2009: 166–70). But as the war developed, it became clear that Israel was unable to either defeat Hezbollah or deter it from targeting its citizens in the north. The military stalemate then gave way to a political resolution. Under US and Syrian auspices, Israel agreed that it would halt its military campaign against Lebanese civilians in return for Hezbollah stopping its use of Katyusha against Israeli civilians. The 1993 war displaced around 200,000 people, demolished thousands of homes, killed 140 and wounded 500 (Bregman 2016: 271).

Three years later, in April 1996, Hezbollah and Israel entered into a new war. Once again, this came after an increase in Hezbollah attacks on Israeli and SLA fighters in the occupied zone (and a wave of Palestinian suicide bombers inside Israel). In March 1996, Hezbollah's attacks, including one suicide bombing, killed five Israeli soldiers and injured others. On 30 March, IDF missiles killed two Lebanese civilians in the village of Yater, outside the occupied zone. Hezbollah quickly, and to pre-empt any 'political intervention that would constrain its decision' (H. Fadlallah 2009: 185), called upon Israeli civilians to seek refuge and started to fire Katyusha rockets on northern Israel. Prime Minister Shimon Perez – who was attempting to consolidate his power in Israel after the assassination of Yitzhak Rabin by an Israeli extremist – launched 'Operation Grapes of Wrath'. Indeed, it was.

To start with, Israel targeted Hezbollah's political command (Shura) offices in Dahieh. But Hezbollah leaders had vacated most of their offices and resorted to secret locations (H. Fadlallah 2009: 184–6). Israel's bombardment of Dahieh, however, preluded a more comprehensive and devastating military campaign in Beirut, Beqaa and the south that lasted for sixteen days. To put pressure on the Lebanese government and people, Israel bombarded the newly constructed power station, put Lebanese ports (including Beirut, Sidon and Tyre) under siege and blocked the Beirut–Tyre coastal highway. In the south and Beqaa, Israel gave ultimatums to civilians to leaves their homes. But, yet again, Israel's military campaign failed to stop Hezbollah's attacks on its troops in Lebanon or citizens in northern Israel. In the war, thirteen Hezbollah fighters were killed; but most of the damage fell on Lebanese civilians. Israeli missiles and bombs targeted civilian cars, ambulances and buildings, killing more than 165; over 200,000 people fled their homes. One attack was horrendous. At around 2 p.m., on 18 April, Israel attacked a UN base in the village of Qana (Jaber 1997: 173–95), which hosted the UN peacekeeping Fijian contingent. When the war started, more than 850 civilians sought refuge in the UN compound, assuming it would be safe from the Israeli onslaught. It was not. In a span of seventeen minutes, Israel shelled the base killing 109 civilians and injured 150 others (including four Fijian soldiers) (Jaber 1997: 171; Bregman 2016: 272). Among the dead were many children and in some cases whole families. One was the Balhas family, which lost 28 members. The youngest, Mussa Balhas, was two years old and the oldest, Muhammad Balhas, sixty.[19] Israel first denied committing the crime, but then acknowledged it was a mistake (Jaber 1997: 171).

During the war, Hezbollah continued its attacks on Israeli and SLA positions and the shelling of Katyusha, which now acquired an improved precision, on northern Israel. This, Fadlallah perceived, 'contributed to instilling fear in the northern settlements and, thus, imposed a relative balance [of power]' (H. Fadlallah 2009: 190). Whilst in 1993 Hezbollah launched 151 rockets (21.6 on average per day), in 1996 it launched 639 increasing the daily average to 39.9 (Gabrielsen 2014: 266). Indeed, the rockets had a psychological impact. During the war, many Israeli civilians either resorted to underground shelters or fled southward. After the war, 'the Israeli government had to offer large economic incentives' to keep its own citizens in their northern towns (Gabrielsen 2014: 261). During the war, Nasrallah promised to avenge the killing of Lebanese civilians and Israel's bombardment of Dahieh. As part of Hezbollah's psychological warfare, Al-Manar distributed a clip showing more than seventy men in military fatigue taking the vows before Nasrallah and displaying their readiness to commit suicide attacks (Jaber 1997: 187; *Ahzab Lubnan: Hizb Allah* [Parties of Lebanon: Hezbollah] 2003).

The US did not immediately seek a diplomatic resolution to the war, which reflected its regional strategy. In March 1996, the US, Egypt, Jordan, the PLO and leaders of twenty-nine world countries met in the Egyptian resort of Sharm El Sheikh to revive the peace process. One goal of the conference was to isolate Syria (and Iran), which was not invited to the conference, and to oblige it to give up its support for Hezbollah, Hamas and Islamic Jihad (Jaber 1997: 176). Israel's military campaign attempted, once again, to destroy Hezbollah and gradually dissociate Lebanon from Syria. However, Hezbollah's survival in the war and Israel's failure to stop it from launching its rockets on northern Israel led to a military stalemate. The Qana Massacre, however, formed the turning point: 'it was an attack of such magnitude that it prompted President Clinton to call for an immediate cease-fire' (Jaber 1997: 193).

Hezbollah's survival, Israel's failure to realise its military goals and the US quest for an immediate ceasefire steered regional and international actors back to Damascus. Assad's politico-military influence in Lebanon, his strategic relations with Iran, cordial relations with Arab states and the leverage he possessed over armed movements in Lebanon and Palestine, all made him a key actor to negotiate an end of the war. After more than a week of negotiations, the parties (including the US, Israel, France, Russia, Iran, Hezbollah, Lebanon and Syria) reached a deal that came to be known as the 'April Understanding'. It was a developed and written version of the 1993 agreement and one that reflected Hezbollah's growing military effectiveness. It called upon both actors to ensure 'that under no circumstances will civilians be the target of attack'. Crucially, it emphasised that 'nothing shall preclude any party from exercising the right of self-defence' ('Text of Israel-Lebanon Cease-Fire Understanding' n.d.). Hezbollah considered this to be a moral and military victory: its military survival and use of Katyusha rockets, the Islamist resistance believed, had now guaranteed that Israel would not target Lebanese civilians. Crucially the world now 'acknowledged its right to perform military operation against the occupation' (H. Fadlallah 2009: 200).

The 1996 war had an unintended effect on Israel. The devastating damage to Lebanon's infrastructure and the targeting of civilians increased Hezbollah's popularity in Lebanon and the Arab world; it reinforced Hezbollah's domestic strategy – see previous chapter – to establish the 'Resistance Society' and to increase its ties to other Lebanese religious and political forces (Gabrielsen 2014: 261). In the funeral of the innocent lives lost in the Qana Massacre, many people showed defiance. Placards read: 'The massacre of Qana is a real witness of Israeli terrorism'; people screamed 'Resistance, Resistance, all of us are Resistance! Our children are Resistance!' (Jaber 1997: 170, 190–9). On many of the demolished buildings, Hezbollah posted placards that read: 'Made in the USA'.

Moreover, Hezbollah's survival in the 1993 and 1996 wars, ones which the movement and its supporters have celebrated as victories in their long-term struggle with the Zionist state, reinforced Hezbollah's religio-political doctrine, political choice (armed struggle against Israel) and worldview. In Hezbollah's eyes, Israel has exposed its weaknesses and failure to deter its enemies. After 1996, Hezbollah and its pundits spoke of a 'balance of fear' between Hezbollah and Israel. In the 1996 war, H. Fadlallah observes, Israel lost its ability to 'surprise' its enemies or to conduct 'swift' wars to realise its political goals. Unlike the 1967 war when in a matter of six days Israel managed to occupy the Sinai Peninsula, Golan Heights, the West Bank and Gaza Strip, when many Israelis believed that a 'divine intervention' had come their way, the 1996 war took sixteen days and Israel did not manage to realise its goals. For several Israeli military scholars, these occasions became 'reputation-eroding events': 'Once Israel was unable to achieve a military victory, deterrence eroded' (Lieberman 2012: 175).

After the end of the 1996 war, Hezbollah resumed its attacks against Israel and the SLA in the occupied zone. By 2000, the year Israel withdrew from Lebanon, Hezbollah had executed 6,786 military operations against Israel and the SLA, with around 5,282 between 1994 and 2000.[20] In May 2000, Hezbollah executed 323 attacks against the IDF and SLA (Gabrielsen 2014: 262); the goal was to hasten Israel's withdrawal and to prevent the SLA from filling the void Israel was going to leave. Between 1982 and 1992 the SLA lost 368 fighters and in 1992–2000 around 456 (Mustafa 2003: 498). In January 2000, Hezbollah assassinated Aql Hashem, a high-ranking SLA officer, by a roadside bomb close to his home. This operation left a major psychological and military impact on the SLA (*Ahzab Lubnan: Hizb Allah* [Parties of Lebanon: Hezbollah] 2003), whose members began to defect in greater numbers, until the organisation's total collapse in May 2000 (Bregman 2016: 274–80).

The increase in Hezbollah's military operations began to reshape Israel's domestic politics, leading to the withdrawal. Here it is worth noting that the Israeli military was divided about the efficacy of its presence in Lebanon. If the available information on the dilemmas the Israeli leadership faced is accurate, then this paints a different picture from the one Hezbollah has harboured on Israeli intentions in Lebanon. In 1985, the IDF General Staff debated whether to withdraw from Lebanon or maintain a presence there. Moshe Levi (Chief of Staff) wanted to establish a 'security zone' as a buffer between Israel and Lebanon and to deploy Israeli troops and the SLA to guard it. The aim was to prevent the enemy from attacking Israel. The other proposal came from Ehud Barak (then Director of Military Intelligence) who called for a total withdrawal from Lebanon to the international border, whilst maintaining the readiness to intervene in Lebanon if the need arises.[21] Levi's proposal won.

However, Hezbollah would argue that the Israeli debate was because of the resistance Israel faced in Lebanon. Indeed, the Israeli invasion of 1982 led to 'more than 700 deaths' (Bregman 2016: 184). Between 1985 and 2000, Israel lost 265 soldiers in Lebanon, averaging 17–18 per year (Bregman 2016: 273).[22] Israeli public opinion began to shift, generating a majority of 55 per cent who supported withdrawal from Lebanon in 1999; in 2000, the percentage increased to 62 (Gabrielsen 2014: 262). Barak believed that an Israeli withdrawal from Lebanon would strip Hezbollah of any justifications to target Israel, creating, as he would explain later, an 'invisible barrier between the IDF and Hezbollah forces' (quoted in Aran 2012: 840). Having failed to defeat Hezbollah, Israel now opted to contain the armed political movement. It withdrew its forces on 25 May 2000 (Bregman 2016: 288; Aran 2012).

Hezbollah and its many supporters in Lebanon and the Arab world considered Israel's withdrawal from Lebanon as a historic moment of strategic relevance: for the first time in the Arab–Israeli conflict, Israel withdrew from an Arab-occupied territory, not through negotiations, but under fire. This corroborated and legitimated Hezbollah's religio-political choice. In his 'Liberation Speech', delivered in the city of Bint Jbeil in southern Lebanon,

Nasrallah reflected on the origins of this 'historic and great day'. The 'victory', Nasrallah emphasised, was realised through jihad, *Shahadah*, and deep belief in God;[23] not by the implementation of UN resolutions (425), the adjudication of a biased actor (US) or by negotiations. 'The times when we were terrorised by Israeli threats is over', he asserted. 'Any attack on Lebanon will not be faced by a complaint to the UN Security Council. It will only be confronted by [military] resistance.' Towards the end of his speech, Nasrallah urged the Palestinians to pursue the path of armed struggle, adding that Israel 'which possesses nuclear weapons' is 'by God I swear weaker than a spider-web'.[24]

Nasrallah's description of Israel as a spider-web – one, as we shall see in the following chapter, that Israel tried to militarily debunk in the 2006 war – temporarily sealed a phase of the Hezbollah–Israel rivalry. In this last phase, Hezbollah emerged as a confident armed political movement. For Israel, the rivalry with Hezbollah questioned the Zionist state's military capacity: 'The general image of the invincible Israeli soldier', observes Elli Lieberman, 'began to erode during the daily struggle between Israel and the civilian population'. As the Israeli military and society were exposing 'high sensitivity to casualties', Hezbollah's 'religious beliefs conditioned their soldiers to sacrifice their lives for the attainment of their goals' (Lieberman 2012: 187–8).[25]

Hezbollah's war-making with Israel is a form of (international) socialisation that has conditioned the behaviour of both Hezbollah and Israel. In the period leading to 2000, Lieberman demonstrates how the two actors have shaped one another:

> Interestingly, Hezbollah adopted a strategy that was very similar to the Israeli strategy. Israel's national security doctrine argued that Israel's reputation for toughness would be created and demonstrated over a long period of time in which victory after victory would eventually convince the Arabs to abandon the military option to solve the conflict. Hezbollah argued that over a long period of time and through a long series of minor defeats, it would be able to weaken Israel's resolve. (Lieberman 2012: 187)

Political alliances: the Resistance and Refusal Axis

But Hezbollah's war-making with Israel required more than military preparedness and resolve. It required a conducive geopolitical environment: geographic depth, secure lines of communication, military support and political and diplomatic backing. Hezbollah has secured all of this through its alliance with Iran and neighbouring Syria. After recalling the sacrifices of Hezbollah's leaders and its martyrs in his 'Liberation Speech' (2000), Nasrallah singled out two actors: Imam Khomeini's Islamic Republic and 'Assad's Syria'. Khomeini 'supported, backed and prayed for the *mujahidin'*. Iran, Nasrallah reiterated, 'did not abandon Lebanon, Syria and the Palestinian people'. As for Damascus, it 'protected, embraced and guarded the resistance': 'who could forget President Assad's firm' stand in the 1996 war, asked Nasrallah, when the world met in Sharm El Sheikh to condemn the resistance movements and to praise Israel.[26] When Nasrallah led a delegation to H. Assad's funeral, he was delivering the same message in Syria.

Nasrallah did not utter any exaggerations, neither in the speech nor during his visit to H. Assad's funeral. Hezbollah's war-making with Israel could not have been possible without Iran's material and religio-political patronage and Syria's political and military backing. As we saw in Chapter 2, a combination of factors made possible the rise of the armed political movement: commitment to armed struggle by a domestic group; patronage from the Islamic Republic; a collapsed Lebanese state; and a Syrian–Iranian alliance, despite some of the strategic differences between the two actors. Both domestic and external factors were important in the making and survival of Hezbollah. In Chapter 3, we saw how war-making shaped Hezbollah's domestic socialisation. We identified two 'circles' of strategic importance for the movement: the Shi'a constituency and Lebanon as a whole. These formed the first and second protective layers for Hezbollah's war-making with Israel. To understand Hezbollah's international political alliances and socialisation, we need to focus now on the third protective layer, namely the Middle East region.

International alliances offer armed political movements, such as Hezbollah or Hamas, the opportunity to amalgamate resources and capabilities in order to counterbalance and deter mutual threats. Alliances emerge when at least two actors develop common perceptions of political threats, opportunities and interests and then transform these perceptions into political and military strategies (Darwich 2016; Booth and Wheeler 2007; Barnett and Levy 1991). Whilst a common ideology or identity can contribute to the making of alliances, this is usually not sufficient.

What came to be known as the Resistance Axis, also known as the 'Resistance and Refusal Axis', originated in 1979. The two main pillars of the alliances were Iran and Syria. With time, Hezbollah, Islamic Jihad, and Hamas would join the axis (Hamas would tactically move away after 2012). The alliance has four main origins. First, the Islamic Revolution, which shifted Iran's foreign orientations to become a staunch rebel against Western influence in the region. Second, Syria's isolation in 1978, which gradually intensified since its fall-out with President Sadat's Egypt (who opted for a political settlement of the Arab–Israeli conflict) and with its Ba'athist counterpart in Iraq. Islamic Iran offered Syria a strong regional ally first to replace Egypt, which by 1979 had withdrawn from the Arab–Israeli conflict, and as a counterbalance to Saddam Hussein's Iraq, which was seeking a dominant role in the Arab world. Under Hafez Assad, Syria pursued a realist-pragmatist foreign policy that aimed to diversify its foreign allies (Soviet Union, Arab Gulf states, Libya, etc.) to boost external aid, prevent Syria's regional isolation, and to maintain regional influence (Ehteshami and Hinnebusch 2014). Assad's alliance with Iran, thus, aimed to increase Syria's political leverage at a regional level. Syria was the first Arab country to recognise the Islamic Republic (Goodarzi 2009: 18).

For Iran, Syria formed a major ally in the Arab region and, thus, strategic depth in the Levant. This contributed to thwarting US and its regional allies' attempts to isolate it or topple its revolutionary regime. The alliance with Syria became especially crucial after the Iraqi invasion of Iran in 1980, which triggered the Iran–Iraq war (1980–8). Syria, thus, formed a critical avenue tying Iran and Lebanon, which formed a fertile ground for Iran to disseminate its revolutionary Islamism (Goodarzi 2009: 12–23; Ehteshami and Hinnebusch 2014). The alliance is thus based on 'convergence of vital strategic interests', with the most important being opposition to Israeli and Western penetration of the region (Ehteshami and Hinnebusch 2002: 88).

Thirdly, the Israeli invasion of Lebanon in 1982 did not only reinforce the emerging alliance between the two actors, it also enabled the birth of Hezbollah, the third main pillar in the alliance (see Chapter 2). The Israeli invasion and threat of shifting Lebanon to the Western camp increased Syria's vulnerability and deepened its need for Iran. Iran, which by 1982 had turned the tide to its advantage in the Iran–Iraq war, was ready to come to

Syria's assistance. The Syrian–Iranian alliance shared the goal of weakening and even defeating the Western presence in Lebanon. The attacks against Western targets in Lebanon satisfied these interests in the period 1982–4 (Jaber 1997: 82–3) and 'precipitated the MNF's [Multinational Force] withdrawal from Lebanon; paving the way for Syria's eventual return to Beirut' (DeVore 2012: 97).

But Syria was also nervous about the rise of a strong Islamist movement in its Lebanese backyard, especially in the Beqaa region, or initially in Zabadani in Syria (Chehabi 2006a: 214–16; H. Fadlallah 2009: 60–1). (During this period, Assad was repressing an Islamist rebellion in Syria (Van Dam 2011: 105–17).) As we saw in Chapter 3, Hezbollah's growth in Lebanon disrupted Syria's and its allies' attempts to establish order in the war-torn country, leading to bloody clashes between the two actors. Despite their common strategic vision, Iran and Syria differed in their approaches to Israel: as Ehteshami and Hinnebusch (2002: 91) observe: 'Syria's interest in carefully pressuring Israel in southern Lebanon only partially coincided with Khomeini's desire to make Lebanon a base for an anti-Zionist crusade'. Hezbollah and Amal's ideological and turf wars were a reflection of these differences. But these differences also offered opportunities for deeper coordination between Iran and Syria (Goodarzi 2009).

Fourthly, the failure of the state-to-state wars and the PLO to liberate Palestine gave rise to Palestinian Islamist movements, namely Islamic Jihad and Hamas, who challenged the PLO, rejected the Oslo Agreement and preferred armed struggle against Israel. Among other things, this offered Iran and Syria the political avenues to shape the behaviour of these movements and, thus, to maintain an influence in the Palestinian–Israeli conflict. The Islamic Jihad movement and, until 2012, Hamas were based in Damascus (Saouli 2013).

Thus, by the late 1980s the main pillars of the Resistance Axis were constructed. Despite the varying ideological backgrounds of the members – Shi'a-Islamism (Iran and Hezbollah), Arab nationalism (Ba'athist Syria), and Muslim Brotherhood (Hamas and Islamic Jihad) – they all, to varying degrees, shared common perceptions of the Middle East regional order and goals, including the weakening of Western influence and liberating Israeli occupied territories (Saouli 2013; Ehteshami and Hinnebusch 2002: 88–91).

The relationship between Iran and Hezbollah, however, warrants some further elaboration, for this *partly* challenges our common understandings of alliances. We have already seen in Chapter 2 that there is a strong, organic religio-political connection between Hezbollah and the *Wilayat al-Faqih* in the Islamic Republic. We have seen that the *faqih* defines the broad religio-political strategy, which Hezbollah abides to. But we also saw that the *faqih* confers a wide margin of freedom to Hezbollah. In that sense, the *faqih* is both a religio-political patron of and an ally to Hezbollah. Of the five actors that make the Resistance Alliance, Hezbollah and Iran have the strongest ties. The doctrinal ties notwithstanding, the relationship between Iran and Hezbollah should not demolish our understanding of alliances. As with other state sponsorships of armed groups, Iran's patronage has been vital for Hezbollah's war-making and, indeed, survival. Financial and military assistance, sanctuary and political backing have enabled Hezbollah to 'pursue long-range strategic planning' (DeVore 2012: 87–8), which is necessary for war-making as we saw previously. To debunk and deny US allegations about Hezbollah's money laundering and drug smuggling activities (Levitt 2013), in 2016 Nasrallah formally admitted that Hezbollah's entire budget and the rockets and weapons it possesses 'come from the Islamic Republic' (Rafizadeh 2016).

On the other hand, Hezbollah offers Iran a strategic presence in the Levant. Hezbollah's growth, development and major role in driving Western and Israeli presence in Lebanon did not only realise Hezbollah's goals, but also were integral to Iran's strategy in the region. Hezbollah, thus, reflects Iran's military and political reach in the Levant, one that is not only located on the Lebanese–Israeli border, but is, as we shall see, crucial for the survival of the Syrian regime. Therefore, the relationship between Iran and Hezbollah has with time developed into one of *interdependence*.

Geopolitics matters. Hezbollah's long-term strategic ties with Iran were made possible by Syria's geopolitical location. Syria is both a conduit for the transfer of weapons from Iran and source of arms. Syria is pivotal, as Qassem stresses; Lebanon has limited options: 'either Israel or Syria' (Qassem 2008a: 360). 'Consolidating' Hezbollah's relationship with Syria 'amidst the changing international conditions', argues Hezbollah's Sheikh Hassan Ezzeddine, is 'a major goal' for the movement (quoted in Mustafa 2003: 509). Hezbollah served more than one purpose for Assad's Syria. Frist, its war-making kept the pressure on Israel and its Western supporters, offering Assad political and diplomatic leverage, a 'net profit' for Syria, as Salman notes (Salman 2015; see also Leenders 2012: 154–6). As we saw above, Hezbollah's interests within Lebanon, such as weakening of Western influence and the constraining of strategies to establish peace with Israel, are to varying degrees congruent with Syria's. Second, Hezbollah's strategy contributed to Syria's aims to avert strategies of encirclement by its regional adversaries. Hezbollah served to break this encirclement (see below). Finally, at a domestic level and within Arab political dynamics and discourse, Syria's support for Hezbollah and other resistance movements boosted the legitimacy of Assad's regime, presenting it as the 'bulwark of steadfastness'.

On the other hand, Hezbollah's alliance with Palestinian movements offers it strategic depth in Israel and the occupied territories. For Hezbollah, the attacks Hamas and Islamic Jihad inflicted on Israel increased the pressure on the Zionist enemy and kept the 'culture of resistance' alive against the 'culture of submission' of the Palestinian Authority. As such, Hezbollah backed Palestinian movements with both words and deeds. In his liberation speech, Nasrallah dedicated the 'triumph . . . to the deprived people in occupied Palestine'. He urged the Palestinians to pursue armed resistance: 'Your fate is in your own hands', he prompted: 'The road to Palestine, O people of Palestine, the road to freedom, is the road of resistance and *intifadah* [popular uprising]' (see also Qassem 2008a: 259–63).[27] Shortly after the Israeli withdrawal from Lebanon, Al-Manar began to broadcast to the rest of the Arab world, with special emphasis on the occupied territories. Al-Manar offered strong coverage of the second Palestinian intifada and was a forum for anti-Oslo Agreement Palestinian activists and leaders (Saouli 2003: 76). Al-Manar produces several programmes, such as *al-Mash'had al-Falastini* (The Palestinian Scene) or *al-Zakirah Miftah al-'Awdah* (Memory: the Key for Return), that particularly focus on the Palestinian cause.

But solidarity with the Palestinians goes beyond rhetoric. Whilst Israel has tried to divide Arab ranks, Hezbollah has aimed to connect its struggle to that of the Palestinians. For example, on 7 October 2000 Hezbollah captured three Israeli soldiers in a military operation it executed in the disputed area of Shebaa Farms. Hezbollah hoped to exchange the three soldiers with Lebanese and Arab detainees in Israeli prisons. In the conference that Nasrallah held after the capture, he said that any future prisoners' swap would have to include Palestinian detainees in Israeli jails. Hezbollah was exposing the leadership of the late Yasser Arafat as weak, incapable of freeing Palestinian detainees. Once again, Hezbollah was juxtaposing the approach of resistance against the political track, which Arafat pursued and which many pro-Western Arab regimes encouraged.

Militarily, Hezbollah has played a key role in the 'transfer' of knowledge, experience and weapons to Palestinians (Qassem 2008a: 336). Whilst Damascus formed the centre for these exchanges, Hezbollah has attempted to transfer weapons, including 'Kornet missiles to Gaza' as Nasrallah disclosed (Khoury and Reuters 2017). In 2009, the Egyptian authorities arrested Sami Shihab who was accused of smuggling weapons into Gaza, which, in the war of words with the former President Hosni Mubarak's regime, Nasrallah would later acknowledge (Slackman 2009).

Beyond the Resistance Axis, Hezbollah has aimed to increase its ties with various political movements in the Arab world, especially groups that share its vision in the Arab–Israeli conflict. But unlike the domestic setting, where, as we saw in the previous chapter, Hezbollah re-presented its identity and internalised Lebanese values and discourse, in the regional order Hezbollah has rebelled against the dominant discourse represented by Arab allies of the West who subscribed to the political solution with Israel. Egypt's defeat against Israel in 1967, and its failure to consolidate its initial advances in the 1973 war due to US support of Israel, led it and many others in the Arab world to conclude that a political settlement with Israel was the only route to restoring the occupied territories. President Sadat of Egypt, who argued that '99 per cent of the cards are in America's hands' and who promoted the 'Egypt First' policy, contributed to gradually shifting Arab discourse to the language of settlement. By the time Sadat visited Israel in 1980 and signed a peace treaty with his former enemy, the Arab world was giving way to a new division, which continues to shape Arab discourse and dynamics until this moment. Arab allies of the US (namely, Egypt, Saudi Arabia, other Gulf states, Jordan, Morocco and the Palestinian Authority) have expressed readiness to recognise and normalise relations with Israel in exchange for Israel's withdrawal from occupied territories. Recognised by the US as the 'moderates', these states have encouraged negotiations with Israel as the only 'possible' option. Syria (and to varying degrees Algeria, Libya (under Muammar Gaddafi), Iraq (under Saddam Hussein) and Yemen), on the other hand, have stood against normalisation of relations until land is restored. Whilst Syria accepted peace talks with Israel in the 1990s on the principle of 'Land for Peace', Iran, Hezbollah, Hamas and Islamic Jihad refused the political process.

Hezbollah believes that the Oslo Agreement, even if it was going to be fully implemented, will create a Palestinian state that is devoid of real sovereignty. Through Al-Manar, the self-designated 'Channel of Arabs and Muslims', and the discourse of its leaders, Hezbollah has aimed to deconstruct the moderates' approach and policy. It, thus, joined traditional discursive battles surrounding the question of who represents the 'genuine' Arab voice and interest (Valbjørn and Bank 2012; Barnett 1998). Hezbollah has been challenging and reformulating the dominant discourse through a set of concepts, such as 'resistance', 'liberation', 'dignity' and Arab and Islamic 'unity'. As we have seen, these conceptual elements are integral to the Islamist movement's own discourse and identity (Qassem 2008a: 333–7). The aim was to overcome sectarian, national and ethnic divisions within the Arab and Muslim worlds and to demarcate friends/allies (such as Iran) from the rivals/enemies (such as Israel and the US). War-making with Israel and Hezbollah's discourse, which resonated with Arab popular views, contributed to increasing its support and legitimacy in the Arab world (for figures see the Introduction).

Conclusion

This chapter focused on Hezbollah's international socialisation: how Hezbollah perceives the international system; how religio-political doctrine gives its actions meaning in that system; its war-making with Israel; and on the armed political movement's international alliances. This chapter complements the previous one and takes us to the final chapter of this book.

But before we turn the page, I want to pause for a theoretical interval, which relates to the central argument of the book. Hezbollah's purposeful socialisation – the attempt to be part, preserve or alter social reality – as we have seen so far, has conditioned the behaviour and identity of the Islamist movement. This conditioning offers important insights. You notice that as the oppressed, or weaker actor (Hezbollah), revolts against a perceived oppressor, they activate and demarcate their agency – identity, history, ideals, motivations – against an 'other'. Liberation from oppression requires self-reliance, which necessitates the amassing of (ideological, social, military) power. Amassing power requires the recruiting and indoctrinating of members – the establishing of an organisation – and the mobilisation of a political support base. Combatting the oppressor, whether for defensive or offensive reasons, requires the building of military capacity. Delegitimising the oppressor, which is necessary for justifying actions towards it, strips the enemy of its own agency and of any values it may carry. In the process, in this war for survival, the weaker party begins to learn from its enemies and to internalise the rules of military, ideological and political combat. Gradually, the non-conformist actor begins to conform to the rules of the game set by the 'self-help' international anarchic order (see Chapter 1 for definitions). Socialisation in this system – whether it is by Mao's China, Thatcherite Britain or Lebanon's Hezbollah – invites conformism. The deeper the actors' socialisation in the system, the more conformist they will become (Waltz 1979: 128). The deeper the socialisation, the more actors become locked in 'webs of interdependence' limiting and shaping the scope of their actions and discourse (Elias 2000: 14–15). Hezbollah's socialisation process reveals a similar trajectory. The instruments of power it develops, the actions it has to take and the discourse it uses, begins to resemble those of its enemies. This forms what I call in this book socialisation and its tragic ironies, which we will now explore.

Notes

1. I first came across this scene on Lebanese television during the funeral of Assad in 2000. For a glimpse, see Al-Mayadeen's *Khiyar al-Darurah* (The Necessary Decision) documentary available via YouTube at <https://www.youtube.com/watch?v=p4zVpsfdUc8> (last accessed 16 September 2017).
2. These verses are taken from the English translation of the Qur'an, available at <https://quran.com/5> (last accessed 6 May 2017). According to a *Hadith*, the Prophet is believed to have said: 'O Ali, your Shi'as [supporters] are the victorious in the Day of Judgment, so who humiliates them, humiliates me. Who humiliates you, humiliated me . . . tell your Shi'as, O Ali, they are the Shi'as of

God, your *Ansar* [supporters] are the *Ansar Allah* . . . your allies are the allies of God, your party is the party of God' (Qassem 2010a: 121–2).

3. According to one *Hadith*: 'The time will only come when the world is dominated by oppression and aggression, then there will emerge a man from my family (*Ahl al-Bayt*), to fill it with justice, after it was filled with oppression and aggression' (quoted in Qassem 2010a: 127–8).
4. For a longer discussion, including the Qur'anic verses and *Hadiths* about these 'indicators', see Qassem 2010a (112–16).
5. See, for example, Nasrallah's speech on 5 June 2015, shown on Al-Manar, in which he reiterates narratives about the 'signs' related to the emergence of the *Mahdi*.
6. Hezbollah, it is worth noting, is not alone in making such interpretations. The diffusion of these beliefs and ideas have led many to make predictions about the 'signs' of the time or to predict the date of the emergence. One was worryingly specific: the *Mahdi*, he claimed in 2004, will appear on Saturday, 19 January 2008 (Hassan 2006: 175).
7. Both Sunnis and Shi'as believe in the emergence of the *Mahdi*; both agree that the *Mahdi* will come from the Prophet's family. But between them and among the Sunnis, there is a disagreement on who the *Mahdi* is; for the Shi'a, the *Mahdi* is the Twelfth Imam who went into occultation. Both Sunnis and Shi'as draw from similar *Hadiths* to construct their interpretations, one of which was made by the so-called 'Islamic State', which, like Hezbollah, also bestows religious meaning and significance in its battles, especially in Syria, to highlight the end of times. The group has also anticipated the return of the *Mahdi*; see Wood 2015.
8. As Qassem Qassir, a journalist and researcher of Islamist movements including Hezbollah, observes there is a 'common area between the main idea [layer one in my framework] and the political practice of Hezbollah, which is real work: the building of the just state, developed society and the establishment of justice are all goals that of the Imam al-Mahdi, which Hezbollah aims to realise' (Qassir 2015).
9. The concept of soft war was promoted by Ayatollah Khamenei (it should be differentiated from Joseph Nye's 'soft power'). Soft power aims to increase awareness of the 'instruments' (media; UN Security Council; cultural, academic and think tank centres; economic pressures) the US uses to delegitimise the Islamic Republic and movements such as Hezbollah.
10. See the interview with Saffieddine via Al-Manar, available at <http://program-

sarchive.almanar.com.lb/pdetails.php?pid=3549&eid=157584&wid=4332> (last accessed 15 June 2018).

11. See ibid.
12. See Nasrallah's speech, available at <https://www.mediarelations-lb.org/article.php?id=14605&cid=94#.WQrpeFPyuV4> (last accessed 4 May 2017).
13. The first to use such a combined tactic was the Iraqi Da'wah when one of its members attacked the Iraqi embassy in Beirut in December 1981 in protest against Iraq's invasion of Iran in 1980 (Norton 2014: 71–2).
14. For a detailed list of these and military operations, see Mustafa 2003 (458–90).
15. Some sources put the figure to 141 deaths among the Israelis (Mustafa 2003: 460).
16. Mughnieh personally surveyed Azmi building, the base of the Israeli headquarters, and held meetings with Kassir in Kfar Ruman and Tar Diba in preparation for the attack; see the documentary – 'The Martyr Ahmad Kassir' – available at <http://programsarchive.almanar.com.lb/pdetails.php?f=1&pid=4231> (last accessed 15 June 2018).
17. On 16 June 1984, Amal's Bilal Fahs conducted a martyrdom operation against an Israeli patrol. Sana'a Mehaidli of the secular SSNP also conducted such an operation against an Israeli target. After that Palestinian Islamic Jihad, Hamas, Al-Qaeda, Al-Nusra and ISIS, among others, would use this military means against both military and civilian targets.
18. The three Palestinian leaders were Kamal Nasser, Kamal Udwan and Abu Youssef Al-Najjar.
19. For the list of those killed in the Qana Massacre, see Mustafa 2003 (581–5).
20. The number of operations was constantly increasing in this period. For example, in 1994 Hezbollah counted 378 attacks, whilst in 1999 the number increased to 1,528. For a detailed description of these see Mustafa 2003 (494–7).
21. For a more elaborate discussion of these debates, see Bregman 2016 (266–8).
22. Citing the IDF information branch, Mustafa (2003: 587) notes that the number of Israeli deaths between 1982 and 1998 was 886, with the largest number (655) in the period 1982–5.
23. He added that it was 'God who showed us the path of resistance; God filled our hearts with security and . . . instilled fear in the hearts of our enemy; He is the one who shot, He is the one who demolished [military] positions'. Nasrallah went on to recall the sacrifices of all the martyrs and Imam Khomeini who 'prepared, nurtured and established in this jihadi path in Lebanon'.

24. Nasrallah's speech is available at <https://www.mediarelations-lb.org/article.php?id=1564&cid=144#.WTqiaxPyuu5> (last accessed 11 June 2017).
25. Ahron Bregman (2016: 272) adds that opposition in Israel to continued presence of troops in Lebanon grew in 1997 and 'seemed to symbolize a shift in thinking and was a constant reminder to the Israelis of the grim reality in southern Lebanon'.
26. Available at <https://www.mediarelations-lb.org/article.php?id=1564&cid=144#.WTqiaxPyuu5> (last accessed 11 June 2017).
27. Ibid.

5

Tragic Ironies

> Structures limit and mould agents and agencies and point them in ways that tend toward a common quality of outcomes even though the efforts and aims of agents and agencies vary.
>
> Kenneth Waltz, *Theory of International Politics*

> A revolutionary power believes it has a mission to transform international society by conversion or coercion, and cannot admit that its neighbours have the same right to continued existence which it assumed for itself.
>
> Martin Wight

> The road to Jerusalem goes through Qalamoun, Zabadani, Homs, Aleppo, Sweida and Hasaka.
>
> Hassan Nasrallah

On 15 October 2000, Hassan Nasrallah gave a talk to the Arab Nationalist and Islamist Conference. Never short of surprises, he announced to a delighted audience that 'the Islamic Resistance succeeded in abducting an Israeli soldier in the rank of colonel' in what he described as 'a very complex security operation'. The audience was stunned; one week earlier Hezbollah had abducted three Israeli soldiers in a military operation in the Israeli-controlled Shebaa Farms. Sensing that the audience wanted to applaud, Nasrallah granted the permission. They did. Traditionally, Hezbollah preferred to loudly recite 'O God, send blessing upon Muhammad and the family of Muhammad' instead of clapping hands. But times had changed. This came after eight years of Hezbollah's peaceful socialisation in Lebanon and five months after Israel's withdrawal from Lebanon. Nasrallah now possessed the means to exchange the Israeli soldiers for Lebanese and

Arabs in Israeli jails. This was Hezbollah's latest performance of power and confidence.[1] The 40-year-old General Secretary had become one of the most respected leaders in Lebanon and the Arab world: a national liberation hero who stood above the rotten daily politics and sectarianism of Lebanon and the Arab world; one who revived old, buried dreams of independence and dignity; and one whose movement had managed to reconcile an Islamist ideology with the complex politics of the modern world – not least, Lebanon's consociational democracy.

Now fast-forward fifteen years. It is 18 October 2015. Here is the same, but somewhat older, Nasrallah speaking from behind a screen (since the 2006 war, discussed below, Nasrallah's public appearances became scarce). Nasrallah was commemorating the death of one of Hezbollah's fighters in Syria. To his right stood an elegantly designed banner that read: 'We will be where it is necessary to be'. Defiant, confident or maybe anxious, Hezbollah was now announcing to the world and to its many critics that it was ready to intervene in any country of the region to defend its interests, to back its allies and to deter its enemies. The time to be contained in Lebanon had lapsed. Security threats have no political boundaries, the movement dared to announce intellectually and politically (H. Fadlallah 2015: 218–20). By 2015, Hezbollah had completed its third decade of socialisation in Lebanon, but arguably its most difficult. In 2015, Lebanon was everything but a totally collapsed state. The country was divided politically and on sectarian bases. Its institutions were paralysed. As ever, and true to its schizophrenic behaviour in the Middle East, Lebanon split in relation to regional upheavals taking place in the Arab world since 2011 – which one ventured to call the 'Arab Spring'. By 2015, Hezbollah became Lebanon's most controversial political party. Former supporters of Nasrallah dropped and tore his pictures in many, especially in non-Shi'a, areas of Lebanon and the Arab world.

This was certainly not the result Hezbollah had hoped for. But it is one, as this chapter will show, that Hezbollah was drawn into as the armed political movement was seeking survival in the two anarchical orders of Lebanon and the Middle East. The period we will examine in this chapter is roughly from 2005 to 2017. This phase exposes some of the unintended consequences Hezbollah faced as it tried to survive and realise its goals. They reveal the limits actors have over the political world they want to conquer and the inconsistencies – or 'fortuitous incongruities', as Niebuhr calls them – that they have to stand defending. They ultimately show how revolutionary and ideological actors, moulded by the orders they seek to socialise in, begin to conform to traits held by the once powerful enemies they struggled against.

I argue that the deeper Hezbollah's socialisation process became, the more it got locked into domestic and international webs of interdependence in Lebanon and the region. I demonstrate that Hezbollah's quest to deter threats and attempts to appropriate opportunities in Lebanon and the region have generated security paradoxes and ethical quandaries for the Islamist movement. Despite that, the chapter also shows that Hezbollah has painfully managed to overcome many of the threats it faced.

This chapter brings the story of Hezbollah's socialisation process to its end. My intention here is to overcome the analytical separation of the domestic and international arenas that I adopted in the previous two chapters. Rather, I show how *interaction* among the two orders has presented challenges for Hezbollah and how the armed political movement has, successfully or otherwise, tried to reconcile and overcome pressures emanating from each order.

Security Paradoxes

Towards the end of his book on Hezbollah, published in 2002, Naim Qassem identified two sources that may strategically threaten Hezbollah: a domestic conflict with the Lebanese army or other forces; or, international pressure on Syria to abandon Hezbollah and the Resistance Axis (Qassem 2008a: 388–9). We saw in the previous chapters that Hezbollah followed separate, but cohesive, strategies in Lebanon and the region to thwart threats and realise its goals. But by 2005, the potential for the materialisation of Qassem's concerns was real.

The American and Israeli strategic goal to break up the Iran-led alliance, which Qassem feared, did not subside. However, from 2001, developments in the Middle East and internationally provided new opportunities for this goal to be achieved. The 11 September 2001 terrorist attacks on American soil offered the Republican administration, which was influenced by Neo-Conservative figures, the opportunity to wage an international 'war on terrorism'. The Middle East was a major theatre for neo-conservative adventures, paving the way for the US invasion of Iraq in April 2003. The US hoped that its occupation of Iraq would give it unprecedented influence in the oil-rich region, one that could diminish its dependence on allies, particularly oil-rich Gulf states, and discipline rivals, namely Syria and Iran (Fawn and Hinnebusch 2006).

As ever in regional politics, the US strategy invited accommodation from allies and resistance from rivals. Syria and Hezbollah rejected the US-led invasion of Iraq, fearing that this would shift the regional power balance in favour of the US (Engel 2003). Though it was reluctant to see US troops stationed in neighbouring Iraq (and Afghanistan since 2001), the Islamic Republic saw an opportunity to remove an old foe from Baghdad (and an enemy, the Taliban, from Afghanistan) and to pave the way for the Shi'a majority to come to power in Iraq; the US would achieve what Iran hoped but failed to realise in its war with Saddam Hussein's Iraq. Iran and the US secretly coordinated their differences in the build-up to the invasion of Iraq (and Afghanistan) (Filkins 2013).

Capitalising on its military presence in Iraq, the US began to put pressure on Syria and its Lebanese allies. Colin Powell, US State Secretary, who visited Damascus and Beirut in May 2003, urged Bashar Assad to close the offices of Palestinian movements in Syria, recognise the Palestinian Authority, stop all forms of political and military backing for Hezbollah and redeploy or withdraw troops from Lebanon. Syria, which feared that the US was intent on curtailing its regional influence, rejected Powell's requests (Pakradouni 2009: 284–6). In November 2003, the US Senate passed the 'Syria Accountability and Lebanese Sovereignty Restoration Act', which transformed Powell's political demands into law. Among other elements, the law continued to identify Syria as a 'state sponsor of terrorism until it ends support for terrorism, including its support of Hizballah' (Engel 2003). In June 2004, Presidents George W. Bush and Jacques Chirac called for Lebanese 'independence' and for Syrian withdrawal from Lebanon. Finally, in September 2004, the UN Security Council passed resolution 1559 that called for 'free and fair' presidential elections, disarmament of 'militias' and the withdrawal of all foreign troops. The resolution clearly targeted President Lahoud, Assad's strong ally, Hezbollah and Syria's presence in Lebanon (Saouli 2006: 712–13).

The US Middle East strategy divided Lebanon. The country's vulnerability to external influence has with time made its political elites masters in the art of political adaptation. For Christian movements (such as the LF, FMP and the Phalange), who were politically excluded from the post-war political accord, the US strategy – expelling Syria from Lebanon and curbing Hezbollah – served their interests. On the other extreme, for Hezbollah the US strategy aimed to achieve the constant goal of isolating Iran, weakening Syria and disarming the resistance – all to the benefit of Israel (H. Fadlallah 2015: 140–50). These polarising responses exposed Prime Minister Rafic Hariri's position in Lebanon. By 2004, despite Damascus's attempts to check his power, Hariri had dominated over Lebanon's Sunnis, who traditionally stood with Syria. His relations with Syria deteriorated after the coming of Bashar Assad to power in 2000, but especially after Assad exercised pressure to extend his rival Emile Lahoud's presidential tenure for three years (until 2007). Aware of the changing regional dynamics, Hariri wanted to see Syrian troops withdraw from Lebanon. However, it is also very likely that he wanted an orderly transformation: one that would neither humiliate or radicalise the Syrian regime, nor affect Lebanon's own stability. Hariri, thus, attempted to maintain his political ties to Syria's allies; before his assassination he held several meetings with Nasrallah to discuss post-Syrian Lebanon. But Hariri was also engaging with the anti-Syrian opposition in Lebanon. In 2004, he delegated one of his Christian MPs to participate in the meetings of the opposition. His Druze ally, Walid Jumblatt, who was one of the major beneficiaries of the Syrian control of Lebanon, spearheaded the opposition to Syria. A master in the art of political adaptation, Jumblatt aimed to reposition himself in the new Middle East. He called for Syria's withdrawal from Lebanon and for Lahoud's resignation. Unlike Hariri, Jumblatt rebelled against Syria's dictates and voted against the extension of Lahoud's tenure. Whether it was political prudence or mere political opportunism that motivated Hariri, his actions exposed him to various interpretations and to the political abuse of his adversaries.[2] Syria's allies in Lebanon accused the Saudi-backed billionaire of turning against Assad and of engineering resolution 1559 (Pakradouni 2009: 311; Saouli 2006: 712–13).

On 14 February 2005, Hariri was assassinated, with another 21 people including his bodyguards, a former minister and bystanders, when 1,000 kg of explosives detonated as his motorcade passed by the St George Hotel in central Beirut. Hariri's shocking and brutal murder put paid to Lebanon's relative stability since 1990 and inaugurated a new chapter in the country's turbulent history. Regardless of the perpetrator, the assassination was strategic and served more than one party. First, it aimed to split the ruling Muslim majority in Lebanon, moving beyond the Christian–Muslim schism, which characterised Lebanon's politics since 1920. By dividing the majority, the assassination kept Lebanon exposed to external penetration. Second, the assassination turned Lebanon's Sunnis against Syria and its firm ally, Hezbollah. According to one poll of the time, 88 per cent of Lebanon's Sunnis and Druze stood against disarming Hezbollah in 2004, but only 55 per cent of Sunnis and 26 per cent of Druze shared this sentiment after the assassination of Hariri (Saouli 2006: 713). For the US and Israel, the assassination exposed Hezbollah and enabled its potential isolation in Lebanon, which would also weaken Syria and Iran. Third, for Syria, despite its loss of direct influence on Lebanon, the assassination left Lebanon divided and incapable of potentially turning against its eastern neighbour for regime change, as Assad feared. The assassination increased Hezbollah's vulnerability and, consequently, its dependence on Syria. With Syrian withdrawal from Lebanon, Hezbollah would check attempts to turn Lebanon against Syria's Assad or in support of the Western camp.

However, whatever the motivations, Hariri's assassination sharpened the divide between the pro-Syria and anti-Syria camps (Saouli 2014c). Hariri's political camp called for Syria's withdrawal from Lebanon and for Hezbollah to disarm. They hoped to weaken and incorporate Hezbollah into a political regime of their own design. They accused Hezbollah of wanting to draw Lebanon into the Syrian–Iranian alliance, whilst their rivals accused them of working to implement the US strategy in the region (*As-Safir* 2006a). This political polarisation was also giving way to sectarian mobilisation, both inevitable and politically indispensable in the religiously divided country.

On 26 April 2005 Syrian troops left Lebanon. For the opposition this was the dawn of a new independence. But for Hezbollah it was a testing political juncture in its endless quest for survival. The politico-military backing Syria had offered Hezbollah in Lebanon since 1990 was by 2005 threateningly lost. Syria's withdrawal created a vacuum, which the Saudi-

and Western-backed Sunni–Christian coalition was racing to appropriate. Hezbollah reacted in two ways. First, to prevent Lebanon from slipping into the US camp, it joined the government in 2005. This presented a qualitative change in Hezbollah's socialisation, bringing the Islamist movement to the heart of political decision-making in Beirut. Second, Hezbollah continued the strategy it had pursued since 1990, which, as we saw in Chapter 3, aimed to increase its domestic legitimacy. To thwart Israeli and US attempts to 'exacerbate' its domestic tensions, Hezbollah's Lebanese strategy focused on the exercise of restraint (especially in the use of violence), and the resort to political, civil and discursive means to realise its goals (Saouli 2011: 934–6). But, despite Hezbollah's best intentions, as we shall see, this period revealed the limits Hezbollah possessed over its and Lebanon's political fate.

After enduring three weeks of political rage by Hariri's supporters against Syria, which was accused of the Sunni leader's assassination, Hezbollah responded. Again, not without a telling and strategic symbolism, on 8 March 2005, Hezbollah called for a mass demonstration. The Islamist movement did not organise the demonstration in Dahieh, the south or Beqaa, where it usually held events, but in the heart of Beirut. This, Hezbollah was hoping to show, was not a traditional Shi'a peripheral outburst against an authority. It was, rather, a national performance that signalled Hezbollah's growing political clout in Lebanon and its ability to shape the country's political orientation. Hezbollah asked the demonstrators to carry Lebanese flags only.[3] 'Today', Nasrallah informed the large crowd, 'you are deciding the fate of your country.' To the US and France, who advanced UN resolution 1559, Nasrallah said 'the people are telling you we want to maintain our historical relations with Syria, we support the Resistance and reject 1559.' To the many Syrians who witnessed the forced and humiliating withdrawal of their troops from Lebanon, the March 8 demonstration said: 'Thank you Syria.'

Hitherto one of the largest political rallies, the March 8 demonstration was a performance of power: a reminder of and a pointer to Hezbollah's actual influence in Lebanon. 'Lebanon is not Ukraine' (many believed that the 'Colour Revolutions' in Eastern Europe were orchestrated by the US), Nasrallah reminded his critics; a few protests (by the opposition), he threatened, will not alter the strategic choices of Lebanon – that is, the choices that Hezbollah and its allies embrace. The US 'lost in Lebanon' in the 1980s and will not control Lebanon again. Lebanon will remain loyal to Syria, he concluded.[4]

The March 8 demonstration, one observer recalls, 'encapsulated Hezbollah's influence over half of the Lebanese [political] formula' (Pakradouni 2009). Whilst many believed that the Syrian withdrawal would curb Hezbollah's influence in Lebanon, it actually had the reverse effect. Syria's retreat liberated Hezbollah and Amal from the dictates set by the Syrian presence in Lebanon, and increased Shi'a influence in the divided society. A decade later, Hezbollah would confess that in some respects Syria's influence in Lebanon had constrained the Islamist movement (H. Fadlallah 2015: 118–21).

But there was another 'half' of the Lebanese political equation. As Nasrallah was reassuring his allies and power base, he was also, unintentionally, inciting his rivals. The huge March 8 demonstration provoked another, probably larger, demonstration on 14 March 2005 (the debate over the size of each demonstration continued unabated for a while in Lebanon). Lebanese from different sectarian groups and areas crawled in the hundreds of thousands to Martyrs' Square in Beirut. The rally amounted to a quasi-national uprising, which Syria's opponents unduly depicted as the Cedar Revolution. The March 14 uprising exposed accumulated grievances against Syria's excessive political control of Lebanon *and* fears of Hezbollah's political awakening. Some treated the March 14 demonstration as opportunity to, finally, transform Lebanon into a sovereign nation; others saw it as an occasion to adapt Lebanon to regional changes and to score political gains against opponents in Lebanon. In politico-sectarian terms, the rally represented a broad coalition of forces: the majority of Sunnis, represented by the FM; the majority of Druze in support of Jumblatt; the vast majority of Christians supporting the resurgent Christian parties (such as, FMP, LF, Phalange); and a tiny minority of Shi'a figures. Lebanon's Shi'as, including Hezbollah, emerged isolated and on the defensive.

Angry with the assassination of Hariri, galvanised by the international and Arab support for their movement and hopeful that Syrian troops were on their way out, March 14, as Syria's opponents came to be known, advanced new political claims. They called for Syria's withdrawal, for Hezbollah's disarmament and/or its incorporation in the state, for the prosecution of heads of security agencies (all allies of Syria), for the deployment of the Lebanese army into the south and for an international investigation in the Hariri assassination. Like March 8, March 14 also represented itself as a genuine national movement: 'You are the genuine representatives of the national line', noted Ahmad Fatfat of the Future Movement.[5] Akram Chehayeb, a member of Jumblatt's PSP, told the crowd that you are now 'establishing the building blocks for the future of Lebanon: the free, independent and sovereign Lebanon'.[6]

Rhetoric aside, the two demonstrations exposed the contours of a deeply divided country that was facing stark strategic choices. For a whole decade (2005–15), Lebanon would be divided between the March 14 and March 8 camps. Each camp had its own national security culture: visions on Lebanon's regional role; a discursive toolbox to legitimise its actions and to demonise the actions of its rival; and, as ever, external allies and sponsors. Of the two, Hezbollah had the weapons, a source of strength and a cause of contention with its compatriots.

Reflecting the traditional Christian vision for Lebanon (Saouli 2014c), March 14 wanted to dissociate Lebanon from the Arab–Israeli conflict and to align it with 'moderate' Arab allies of the West (Saudi Arabia, Jordan, Egypt). March 14 preferred the diplomatic and political approach to dealing with the Israeli threat, especially since Israel had withdrawn from Lebanon. If Arab states signed a peace treaty with Israel, Lebanon would be the last Arab country to do so. The assassination of Hariri led many Sunnis to adopt this vision. The FM espoused the 'Lebanon First' slogan, bringing them closer to Christian political parties. (Some FM officials, such as MP Ahmad Fatfat (2015), called for total 'neutrality' in the Arab–Israeli conflict.) The US strategy in the region, on the other hand, offered a perceived opportunity to free Lebanon from external intervention and to build a state that, above all, monopolises the use of coercion: namely, to disarm Hezbollah or to incorporate its 'armed wing' in the state (Costanian 2015; Qatisha 2015; al-Sayed 2013).

March 8, and Hezbollah as its strongest force, embraced a different national security culture. As we have seen in the previous chapter, war-making with Israel, membership in the Resistance Axis and religio-political doctrine place Hezbollah at the opposing end of March 14. Syria's withdrawal from Lebanon offered an opportunity for, and even pushed, Hezbollah to attempt to *nationalise* and promote its own strategic vision. Lebanon's strength,

Hezbollah envisioned, was by preserving the armed resistance, by ingraining the culture of resistance in the national consciousness and by maintaining strong ties with Syria and Iran. In a 'weak state', which in Hezbollah's view had failed to defend Lebanon against the Israeli onslaughts, an armed resistance was the best form of (asymmetrical) force to defend Lebanon's independence (A. H. Fadlallah 2015; H. Fadlallah 2015). Hezbollah tried to reconcile its own religio-political goals with the politics of the divided state of Lebanon. It called for a 'strong and effective state', one that would 'guard' the resistance (A. H. Fadlallah 2015). It promoted the slogan and concept of: 'People, Army and Resistance'.

These two opposing visions, political opportunism on each side, and heightened regional rivalry over Lebanon, generated security paradoxes: as each camp attempted to guarantee its own security and to advance its own political standing, it increased the fear in the other and created a situation of overall instability, short of war (see Chapter 1 for the theoretical basis of this argument). As with Hezbollah's war-making with Israel, its relations to its Lebanese rivals has with time become one of interdependence. In this relationship, each group had a function for the other and using that function, each group tried to withhold power from the other. Hezbollah had two main powers: weapons and a strong influence in the Shi'a community, a main constituent of Lebanon's multiconfessional society. Through these, Hezbollah could check March 14's quest for political hegemony. March 14, on the other hand, had the power to mobilise their politico-sectarian groups against Hezbollah and, thus, to question or withhold the legality and legitimacy of Hezbollah's resistance. Each camp mobilised its power to the best of its abilities.

Until the July 2006 war, March 14 was on the offensive. Exploiting the political tide triggered by Hariri's assassination, it aimed to deconstruct the political and security regime Syria installed in Lebanon. It first succeeded in toppling the pro-March 8 government of PM Omar Karami and brought to power Hariri's ally, PM Najib Mikati. After the Syrian withdrawal, four heads of security agencies,[7] who had come under a relentless onslaught by March 14, and the General Prosecutor resigned. March 14 then appointed allies in various key security positions. On 7 April 2005, the Security Council adopted resolution 1595. In agreement with the Lebanese government, the resolution called for an 'international independent' commission to investigate Hariri's assassination, which in effect internationalised Hariri's murder and paved the way to establish the Special Tribunal for Lebanon, the first of its kind. In June 2005, the commission indicated that the former four security heads may have had a role in Hariri's murder and were arrested for investigation.

On 7 May 2005, Michel Aoun returned to Lebanon and emerged as the uncontested Christian leader when he won most Christian seats in the June 2005 elections. The results of the elections gave March 14 a parliamentary majority.[8] Following the elections, Prime Minister Fouad Siniora, of the Future Movement and Rafic Hariri's close friend and ally, formed the government. Despite the results, Amal and Hezbollah, given Lebanon's consociational democracy, were represented in government.

These developments placed Hezbollah (and Syria's allies) under a political siege. This was the first internal strategic challenge the armed political movement faced since its war with Amal in 1988–90. But for March 14's Cedar Revolution to materialise, they had to overcome two other impediments: the toppling of Lahoud and the political subduing of Hezbollah. Hezbollah's responses to these challenges explain the Islamist movement's deeper socialisation in Lebanon in this period. Hezbollah walked a tightrope: on the one hand, it wanted to abort the March 14 goals; but on the other hand, it strove to avoid a political and military conflict with its adversaries that would exacerbate its vulnerability to external forces (primarily Israel, but also the US and its Arab allies). Hezbollah's behaviour in the period 2005–15 can be encapsulated by its attempts to reconcile these two goals.

To realise its goals, Hezbollah utilised all non-violent weapons it possessed: political mobilisation and protest, institutional means and discourse. These political tactics contributed to a deeper internalisation of Lebanese political values and symbols, but they also offered a possibility to *contest* the meaning of these norms. Initially, Hezbollah aimed to break its political isolation. To defuse the increasing politico-sectarian tension and divides, it called for a dialogue as the best means to resolve issues of major disagreement, such as Lahoud's presidency, Hezbollah's weapons and the international tribunal for Hariri's assassination. It attempted to reassure its rivals that its weapons would not be employed for political gain in Lebanon. In the parliamentary election of June 2005, it ran on the same platforms with March 14 candidates, including former enemies, the Lebanese Forces. In July 2005, Hezbollah joined Siniora's government.

However, Hezbollah's ability to contain the political strategy of March 14 or to control political developments was limited. In June 2005, Samir Kassir, a journalist, was killed. This inaugurated a series of more than a dozen political assassinations. In July, an assassination attempt targeted the Minister of Defence, Elias Murr, which was followed by another assassination attempt on May Chidiac, a journalist. Gebran Tueni, a journalist and arch rival of Damascus, was assassinated in December. Unlike Hariri's assassination, however, most of these crimes targeted anti-Syrian figures who did not have strong influence on the political balance in Lebanon. But they had the capacity to fuel emotions and to deepen the political divide in the country. These tragic incidents offered numerous opportunities for political exploitation. Each camp accused its external enemies of perpetrating the murders. March 14 accused Syria of the assassinations; Syria, they believed, had an interest in terrorising March 14 for daring to stand against it. These allegations served to increase international pressure on the Syrian regime and to extract political concessions from its domestic allies, namely Hezbollah. March 8, on the other hand, accused Israel, who, they believed, had an interest in dividing Lebanon and creating a wedge between it and Syria.

Political trust among the two camps began to erode as each was accusing the other of 'treason', which also paralysed the capacity of state institutions to regulate conflict in the country. In December 2005, Amal and Hezbollah suspended their participation in the government in protest against March 14's attempt to legalise the Special Tribunal for Lebanon (STL). They also requested that the government consider Hezbollah as a 'resistance movement' not a militia, thus annulling resolution 1559, as a condition to return to the government. But Siniora rejected the request (Pakradouni 2009: 413). Resolution 1559 offered March 14 international backing and contributed to the isolation of Bashar Assad and Emile Lahoud. On the other hand, March 14 wanted to retain the label of 'militia' as a weapon to politically discipline and to potentially delegitimise Hezbollah, effectively rolling-back Hezbollah's political investment to legitimise itself since the early 1990s (as we saw in Chapter 3). By questioning Hezbollah's armed status, March 14 constrained the armed movement's ability to use its weapons internally, for using them would give credit to March 14's arguments. Fear of conflict, particularly a Sunni–Shi'a one, restrained Hezbollah. Despite this, Hezbollah could not offer any concessions regarding its 'sacred' possession of weapons. The words of Nasrallah in March 2006 reflected the security fears of the armed political movement: 'I, the resistance, have a gun directed at my head, the Israeli is directing a gun, and the American is directing a gun, and others. I, the resistance, cannot expose my destiny to the unknown' (*As-Safir* 2006b).

But Hezbollah continued to employ political means to contain March 14 and to break its isolation. Exploiting a political crack in the March 14 Alliance, in February 2006, Hezbollah struck a 'Memorandum of Understanding' with Michel Aoun's predominantly Christian FPM. Symbolically signed by Nasrallah and Aoun in a church located on the fault-line (Ain al-Rumani) that once divided Beirut's Muslim West from the Christian East, the memorandum called for upholding 'Lebanon's consociational democracy' and for integrating Hezbollah's armed wing in a 'national defence strategy' (Raful 2015). The memorandum, which with time developed into a strategic alliance between the two movements, helped to break the political isolation of both actors. Aoun shared the political principles of March 14; indeed, his political exile in 1990–2005 is a testimony to this orientation. Aoun's strong Christian following and aspirations to become president had alarmed his Christian March 14 allies. Muslim leaders (namely Hariri, Siniora and Jumblatt), who in the post-Taif Lebanon enjoyed uncontested power, were reluctant to elect an influential Christian president, not least one like Aoun who called for political reform and accountability for governments in post-1990 Lebanon. Aoun was excluded from Siniora's government.

But Aoun differed in other important ways that were particularly relevant to Hezbollah and its allies. He believed that the issue of Hezbollah's weapons should be resolved by dialogue and not by force or division. After having played a key role in the Syrian Accountability Act (Aoun contributed to adding the 'Lebanon Sovereignty Restoration' element to the law), he ceased to criticise the Syrian regime. Aoun believed that the conflict with Syria terminated after its troops left Lebanon. Most importantly, unlike other March 14 leaders, Aoun refused to see Lahoud removed from the presidency through political protest (Pakradouni 2009; Raful 2015).

For Hezbollah, which had expressed interest in Aoun even before 2006, the memorandum symbolised its first attempt to break the political siege imposed by March 14. The memorandum contributed to the policy of widening its political ties in Lebanon, which Hezbollah started in 1992. 'The understanding with the FPM', observed a careful student of Hezbollah, 'shielded the resistance with a Lebanese (particularly Christian) *social safety net* by preventing its isolation domestically as it fights the [Israeli] aggression' (Balkiz 2006: 81; emphasis original).

But the memorandum alarmed many Sunnis. In Lebanese sectarian calculations, the agreement represented a threatening alliance between the majorities of the Christians and Shi'as. The Hariri-led March 14 stood determined against attempts to derail its strategy to dissociate Lebanon from Syria. March 14 believed the memorandum offered Hezbollah the 'cover' to preserve what was increasingly becoming the illegal possession of weapons. March 14 continued to mount its discursive attacks against the Syrian regime and called for Lahoud, who was facing international and Arab isolation, to resign. In a trip to Washington, Jumblatt demanded US help against Assad and Hezbollah, whom he portrayed as Iran's 'proxy' in Lebanon (quoted in Pakradouni 2009: 413, 429).

To reduce the tension and mitigate the deepening political gap, Nabih Berri, Hezbollah's close Shi'a ally, organised several rounds of 'national dialogues', which included representatives of all major competing groups. These round-table discussions aimed to tackle the main dividing issues, especially Hezbollah's weapons. Both March 14 and March 8 camps agreed that Lebanon needed a so-called National Defence Strategy, but both parties accused each other of not being serious about this intention (A. Fadlallah 2015; Costanian 2015; Fatfat 2015).

Wars and the Continuation of Socialisation

By August 2006, the political deadlock in Lebanon showed no signs of abating. Between 2006 and 2017, three wars, however, would exacerbate Lebanon's political divides and deepen Hezbollah's socialisation in Lebanon and the region. The first was the Hezbollah–Israel war, hitherto the longest (34 days) war in the Arab–Israeli conflict; second was the short civil war, which involved Hezbollah's use of violence against its internal rivals, shattering its promises of not using its weapons domestically; and third was Hezbollah's military intervention in Syria (and Iraq and Yemen), which will be analysed separately in the last section of this chapter.

The July 2006 war as a 'divine victory'

On 12 July 2006, Hezbollah crossed international borders, attacked an Israeli border patrol, killed three Israeli soldiers and abducted another two. It claimed that the attack, code-named 'The Honest Promise', was intended to kidnap Israeli soldiers and exchange them for the remaining Lebanese detainees (including the 'Dean of detainees' Samir al-Qantar) in Israeli jails. But what Hezbollah did not expect (as Nasrallah confessed after the war) was the level of Israeli response.

In the period 2000–6, Israel pursued a policy of containment – one of 'unviable accommodation and undesirable war' – in relation to its enemy (Aran 2012: 841). However, unlike the contained Israeli response to the kidnapping of soldiers in 2000 (see above), in 2006 Israel launched a comprehensive air, sea and land attack aimed at Hezbollah's military positions and supply routes, including weapons warehouses, bunkers, missile launchers and supply roads that linked the south, Beirut and Syria. In effect Israel hoped to cut Lebanon off from the rest of the world. It targeted the Lebanese social and economic infrastructure, including petrol stations, power stations, civil industrial plants, television stations, main roads, bridges, Lebanon's international airport, aid and relief convoys, seaports and Dahieh, where, as in previous wars, Israel assumed Hezbollah's leadership would be based (Balkiz 2006: 74; Bregman 2016: 288–9).

Israel's declared political goals included the release of its prisoners, the elimination of Hezbollah's rocket capability against Israel and the deployment of the Lebanese army in the south. As you can see, these political goals resonate with UN resolution 1559 and the March 14 platform. Like the 1993 and 1996 wars, but with a greater destructive impact, Israel's military campaign hoped to create a political wedge between Hezbollah and its socio-political base, to deepen the divide with March 14 rivals and, ultimately, to isolate Lebanon from Syria (Balkiz 2006: 74–5; Bregman 2016: 289). The 'Strategy of Destruction', as Balkiz describes it, involved the dropping of millions of kilograms of bombs on several predominantly Shi'a areas (such as Baalbek, Tyre and Nabatieh), but especially over Dahieh. Israel dropped leaflets on several Shi'a villages urging their residents to leave: 'This exodus, the Israelis assumed, would cause a humanitarian crisis' (Bregman 2016: 290) for the Lebanese government and stir (Shi'a) opposition to Hezbollah. The Israeli politico-military leadership was generally convinced that an aerial bombardment would realise its political goals. Hezbollah's military and political response, however, challenged this perception, and ultimately prevented Israel from achieving its aims.

The Lebanese government denounced Hezbollah's attack on Israel. A Saudi spokesman described Hezbollah's actions as 'adventurous', a position that was echoed in Amman and Cairo.[9] All Western countries condemned the attack. On 14 July, Nasrallah gave a short audio speech that was aired on Al-Manar and many other television stations. In the speech, perceived by many as a historic moment in *Harb Tamuz* (the July War, as it came to be known), Nasrallah told an attentive Israel: 'let it be an open war; let it be a war on every level: across to Haifa and, believe me, even beyond and beyond Haifa'. Nasrallah hoped to raise the morale of his supporters after the initial Israeli attacks. He evoked Hezbollah's religio-political identity, one which in the context of war with Israel resonated with many Arabs and Muslims: 'You have no idea who you [Israelis] are fighting: you are fighting the sons of Muhammad, of Ali, of al-Hassan, and al-Hussein, of the Prophet's *Ahl al-Bayt* [and] the Prophet's companions'. He called for 'patience and unity' in Lebanon. In defiance of Arab leaders, Nasrallah rebuked that: 'we in Hezbollah *are* adventurers; we have been adventurers since 1982' and have generated for Lebanese 'freedom, liberation, honour and dignity'. Towards the end of the speech, Nasrallah, a commander-in-chief, announced his 'first surprises': a shore-to-ship missile attack on the Israeli vessel INS *Hanit*, which he claimed was 'now burning and sinking with tens of Zionist Israeli troops'.[10]Actually, the attack on *Hanit*, 'one of the IDF's most capable and latest ships', caused major damage and led to the death of four sailors (Bregman 2016: 289–90).

Generally defensive, Hezbollah's strategy aimed to debilitate the Israeli war aims. Before 2006, Hezbollah did not possess the art of deterrence; secrecy over Hezbollah's military capabilities, which is born out of the movement's guerrilla warfare, dominated Hezbollah's discourse. Whilst this secrecy may have contributed to Israel's miscalculations in the 2006 war and to Hezbollah's several military 'surprises', it did not deter Israel and thus could not have prevented the bloody war. The strike against *Hanit* was one such surprise. But Hezbollah had more surprises to disclose, which debilitated Israel's predominantly aerial campaign. Despite the Israeli leadership's promise of destroying Hezbollah's arsenal of missiles, Hezbollah continued to fire them at Israel. According to Israeli estimates, Hezbollah fired around 4,000 missiles and rockets in 2006 (compared to 639 in 1996) (Hezbollah claims it fired around 8,000 rockets.) (Bregman 2016: 298; Gabrielsen 2014: 266). Some Israeli sources claim that, thanks to its impressive intelligence, Israel managed to eliminate most of Hezbollah's long-range missile capabilities in the first phase of the war (Bregman 2016: 288). But Hezbollah sources question this, arguing that the first Israeli military strikes were based on false information and that missiles continued to be fired until the last day, 13 August (H. Fadlallah 2015: 185; Balkiz 2006: 86).

The firing of rockets continued on a daily but varying pace that aimed to deceive the Israeli government: for example, on 1 August only 4 missiles were fired, but on the following day 230 were fired (for the detailed figures, see Bregman 2016: 297). This strategy, Hezbollah believed, aimed to inflict economic and psychological pressure on the Israeli population, weakening its morale, and to sow political mistrust in the government and the IDF. The inability of Israel to eliminate Hezbollah's missile capability also affected its political position, obliging the Israeli government to moderate its political demands in the ongoing diplomatic negotiations.

Israel's aerial campaign had failed to subdue Hezbollah or to realise any of the war's aims after one week of the war. This led the divided Israeli government to consider partial and swift ground infiltrations to target Hezbollah. The operation was code-named 'Webs of Steel' (Bregman 2016: 293), in a clear defiance of Nasrallah's description of Israel as a 'spider-web' in his 2000 speech (see previous chapter). However, thanks to its anti-tank guided missiles (AT-14 Kornet), surface-to-air missiles and improvised explosive devices, Hezbollah managed to block several Israeli incursions. For example, in the battle of Wadi al-Hujeir, which lasted for 30 hours, Hezbollah struck around 20 Merkava-4 tanks leading to the deaths of 30 Israeli soldiers (Bregman 2016: 293; Balkiz 2006: 85–6; Gabrielsen 2014: 276–7; H. Fadlallah 2015: 185).[11]

At a social level, and to avoid politico-sectarian clashes between the internally displaced Shi'a and their (Christian, Druze and Sunni) hosts, Nasrallah urged his supporters to respect their hosts' customs and to abstain from any political provocations (Saouli 2011: 936). Moreover, Hezbollah mobilised its civil associations to offer aid relief to the displaced and began to survey the losses in properties; within a few days from the start of the war, the Shura Council met to discuss post-war reconstruction and compensation schemes. Here, Hezbollah aimed to contain the potential rage of its supporters and to thwart Israel's aims of sowing a divide between Hezbollah and its support base (H. Fadlallah 2015: 180).

On the political level, Hezbollah's instigation of the 2006 war deepened the divide between March 8 and March 14. It raised a pertinent question that March 14 had championed: who holds the decision for war and peace, Hezbollah or the government? March 14 condemned Hezbollah's actions and blamed it for the consequent destruction. Hezbollah, on the other hand, believed that Israel's war was part of a broader political strategy to eliminate Hezbollah, weaken Syria and subdue Iran. The US position reinforced Hezbollah's narrative. During the war, Condoleezza Rice, US Secretary of State, announced that 'it is unacceptable to have a situation where the decision of a terrorist group can drag an entire country, even an entire region, into violence'. She insisted that there should not be a return to the 'status quo' and that 1559 should be implemented. The war, she hoped, would be 'the birth pangs of new Middle East' ('Secretary Rice Holds a News Conference' 2006). It became clear by 28 July (the eighteenth day of the war) that the US was offering the political and diplomatic shield for Israel to carry the military campaign to realise its political goals. But Hezbollah's military survival and its continued ability to fire rockets at Israel (on this day, Hezbollah fired 111 rockets), as in the 1993 and 1996 wars, led to a political stalemate.

Moreover, the scenes of destruction, displaced people and killing of Lebanese innocent civilians began not only to arouse international public outrage but also to drastically turn the tide against Israel. In the early hours of the morning of 30 July, an Israeli air strike hit a three-storey building killing and injuring more than fifty civilians (including seventeen children) who were hiding in the basement in the village of Qana (Bregman 2016: 295); the bloody attack came to be known in Lebanon as the 'Second Qana Massacre'.

These scenes began to shake public and official opinions. Political demonstrations in many parts of the Arab world (including Egypt, Jordan, Kuwait, Morocco, Iraq, Yemen, Syria) expressed strong support for Hezbollah. On 20 July, a major demonstration took place in al-Azhar University (the bastion of Sunni-Islamic learning) in support of Nasrallah and the resistance against Israel. With time, even Hezbollah's rivals in Lebanon and the Arab world were condemning Israel's war, claiming that it was targeting Lebanon, its people and its infrastructure. Hosni Mubarak, former president of Egypt, acknowledged that Israel had 'crossed all red lines' and sent a delegation to Beirut to express solidarity.[12]

Israel faced two options: either mobilise troops for a large-scale invasion (an option that the Israeli leadership had hitherto resisted) or seek a political solution to the deadlock. The latter option won (Bregman 2016: 293–305). On 11 August, the Security Council unanimously adopted resolution 1701 calling for the cessation of 'hostilities'.[13] The following day the devastating war came to an end, having caused the deaths of more than 1,200 mostly civilian Lebanese, a third of which were children; the displacement of around one million citizens, mostly from south Lebanon; and massive destruction. Hezbollah lost around 100 fighters. Israel lost 120 soldiers and 38 civilians (Balkiz 2006: 75–6).

The July War constituted a turning point in Hezbollah's socialisation. Its mere survival against one of the world's most powerful armies and its ability to prevent Israel from realising its political goals led it to declare a 'divine victory' against its Zionist enemy. Despite the destruction it caused, which led many of Hezbollah's critics and rivals to announce the APM's failure, the war deepened Hezbollah's belief in its religio-political doctrine and war-making against Israel. In many ways, the war had adverse effects on Israel. Israel's destructive strategy, which hoped to punish Hezbollah's social base and Lebanon for their accommodation of the armed resistance, deepened people's admiration of and attachment to Hezbollah. On 12 August, just hours after the ceasefire, all displaced people, despite the Lebanese government's urge for caution, defiantly returned to their destroyed villages, towns and cities. For many Shi'as (and Lebanese), Hezbollah bravely stood against Israel and prevented it from occupying their territory; Nasrallah, whose pictures featured in most Shi'a homes and shops, was reinforced as a national hero.

The war contributed to uniting the Shi'as behind Hezbollah and, in a twist of irony for Israel, consolidated and developed Hezbollah's quest to establish the Resistance Society. Dahieh, which traditionally was perceived as the poor, underdeveloped and inferior periphery of Beirut, became the symbol of courage, resistance and honour – not least, in the eyes of its residents.

But the consolidation of a social base required more than the winning of Shi'a hearts. At the end of the war, Nasrallah announced a massive post-war reconstruction scheme. He promised every displaced family (around 15,000 in total) a temporary furnished accommodation and a monthly salary until their homes and other properties were rebuilt. This announcement came as a relief for the army of displaced, many of whom had lost all or most of what they owned: the flat and business in Dahieh and house in their southern village. The Jihad for Construction (JFC) (see Chapter 3) was tasked with post-war reconstruction. According to the association, the war demolished around 1,231 buildings, including 30,000 residential units. It was crucial, according to a JFC report, to work on two levels: first accommodate all the displaced families by offering the financial means to rent and furnish flats; and second to reconstruct or renovate the demolished buildings. In every village, town or city, Hezbollah's teams surveyed the demolished properties. To the surprise of distressed property owners, Hezbollah offered cash-handouts. Right after the war, Hezbollah swiftly activated its civil units to start removing the rubble from the war-ravaged areas. *The Guardian*'s correspondent observed how on the morning of 16 August 'Hezbollah's hardened fighters are swapping their missile launchers for spades, brooms and briefcases of cash' (Walsh 2006).

But Hezbollah's post-war behaviour should not have come as a surprise: the socio-economic policies adopted by Hezbollah were a continuation of its strategy to buttress the society of resistance – the continuation of war in socio-economic means, which we have examined in previous chapters. Yet, the 34-day war did expose Hezbollah, its resistance and conduct in a new light. For many Lebanese, especially the Christian supporters of Hezbollah's new ally, Michel Aoun, this was a movement that was willing and able to defend Lebanon against its mighty enemy; it was able to swiftly return the displaced to their homes; and it was able to compensate them for their losses (Raful 2015). Nasrallah's description of his fighters during the war as 'the immortal cedar on our mountains, and the humble spikes of wheat in our homes' and 'as mighty as Lebanon's mountains' (see Chapter 2) struck a chord with many Lebanese nationalists. The culture of resistance, which Hezbollah had been promoting since its birth, was finally finding a home outside Hezbollah's social base.[14] In the 'Festival of Victory', on 22 September, the orange flags of the FMP, among other flags, were present in the large crowd which came to celebrate victory.

Hezbollah's resistance and performance in the 2006 war had a strong and positive impact in the Arab world too ('Arab Neighbours Thinking Ahead' 2006). As Balkiz observes, Hezbollah's resistance in the 2006 war

> [l]iberated the Arabs from the barrier of fear that prevented them from expressing their grievances in the face of ruling regimes that demonises anyone that disagrees with them . . . [it] liberated them from the illusions of peace [with Israel] . . . it liberated them from the weighty feelings of inferiority . . . the resistance told them that 'the army that cannot not be defeated [Israel] was disgraced in the smallest Arab country'. (Balkiz 2006: 98–9)

To the chagrin of many Arab regimes, whose political strategy sought negotiations and settlement with Israel, the culture of resistance was making a revival in the Arab world.

The July 2006 war, several Israeli scholars agree, contributed to the erosion of Israel's deterrence policy. After all, Israel failed to realise its war goals, which triggered a national inquiry (The Winograd Commission) to draw lessons from the war. But make no mistake, despite Israel's failure to realise its goals or most of them, the amount of destruction and high levels of deaths the July War caused in Lebanon has deterred Hezbollah from instigating similar attacks against Israel; with the exception of a few contained incidents, since 2006 the Lebanese–Israeli border has been calm. Contributing to this outcome is also Israel's fear, which is born out of its wars with Hezbollah (1993, 1996, 2006), that should it start a war with Hezbollah, it will have no control over its length or outcome. This has established what has commonly been called a 'balance of fear'.

In Lebanon, Hezbollah's construction of a 'divine victory' did not resonate with the armed movement's rivals. The 2006 war sharpened the security paradoxes that interlocked Lebanon's contending rivals. For March

14, Hezbollah's instigation of the war and the socio-economic costs that Lebanon incurred as a result, highlighted and reinforced its own narrative: after all, *one* faction managed to take the whole country to a devastating war. The presence of an armed movement, March 14 emphasised, cannot coexist with the state. The 2006 war demonstrated that Hezbollah is a 'state within a state'; it is part of and serves a regional (Syria–Iranian) alliance. According to Fatfat (2015), in the National Dialogue discussions, Nasrallah promised not to cross the blue line (Lebanese border with Israel), but then betrayed his promise in August 2006.

Tensions between Hezbollah and March 14 deepened during, and continued after, the war. Prime Minister Siniora viewed the war as an 'entry' to 'solve' the problem of Hezbollah's possession of weapons. Armed with UNSC resolution 1701, Siniora insisted on two conditions: that Hezbollah voluntarily surrender its weapons to the Lebanese army; and, second, that the Lebanese army be allowed to deploy in the south with the freedom to confiscate the weapons. Hezbollah rejected both conditions, but it is clear from Fadlallah's narrative that the armed movement was walking a tightrope during the war: on the one hand, it was trying to de-escalate the tensions with March 14 and, on the other hand, it did not want to make any concessions on the strategic goal of maintaining the weapons (H. Fadlallah 2015: 186–90).[15] However, eager to end the war, Hezbollah accepted 1701 (with some reservations), including the deployment of the Lebanese army (which the UN resolution 1701 calls for and which March 8 had always refused to commit to).[16]

The May 2008 attack: transforming threats into opportunities

The post-war period, 2006–8, eroded whatever trust existed between Lebanon's political camps. Hezbollah became more vocal and critical about the role March 14 played in the war, accusing them of seeking to crush the resistance. The 2006 war increased Hezbollah's sense of vulnerability. Fadlallah notes that the political conditions Siniora imposed on Hezbollah contributed to the lengthening of the war and, thus, to the increase in destruction and casualties (H. Fadlallah 2015: 186–7). March 14, on the other hand, interpreted the war as an opportunity for Iran and Syria to increase their leverage in relation to the West; that Hezbollah transformed

Lebanon into a battlefield for regional rivalries, and that Hezbollah, a proxy of Iran, in effect has no authority over its actions. According to Fatfat (2015), after 2006, there was no room for dialogue because we 'were accused of treason'. Drawing on the 1701 resolution, March 14 continued to call for the disarmament of Hezbollah. Political pressure and the threat of withholding legitimacy and legality (March 14 continued to hold the majority in parliament and the government) over Hezbollah's weapons remained the most effective card March 14 possessed in the face of the popular Hezbollah. March 14, like its adversaries, also possessed the power of sectarian mobilisation.

But legitimacy is open for interpretation in a deeply divided society such as Lebanon's. Empowered militarily and politically, Hezbollah's behaviour in the post-2006 war continued to centre on protecting its resistance and maintaining its legality and legitimacy. Having prevented Israel (and the US) from altering the balance of power in Lebanon, Hezbollah wanted to foil March 14's attempts to isolate the movement politically. Once again, Hezbollah exercised restraint, and utilised all political, institutional and legal means to contain its rivals. Starting with the 'Victory Speech', Nasrallah emphasised that the 2006 victory was not for one party or sect, but a 'national' one. He emphasised that the fate of the Lebanese was to 'coexist'. To solve the 'issue of the resistance' (Hezbollah's weapons), Lebanon needed, he argued, a 'strong, capable and just state'.[17] Hezbollah's goal was not only to be part of the government, but also to shape the country's strategic vision. In reaction to March 14's norm of 'Free, Sovereign, Independent state', Hezbollah formulated the 'Army, Resistance and People' equation. The slogan, which would be adopted by many of its allies, including the FPM, would realise Hezbollah's principal goal: to preserve, legalise and legitimate the resistance. But this also served another of Hezbollah's strategic goals: to weaken Western political influence in Lebanon.

In addition to the conflict over Hezbollah's weapons, March 8 and March 14 clashed over the legalisation of the international tribunal for the Hariri assassination. March 14 welcomed the international tribunal as a supplement to the weak and politically laden Lebanese judiciary, as a punishment for the assassins of Hariri and as a deterrent for future political assassinations. March 8, especially Hezbollah, perceived the tribunal as an American–Israeli tool to punish Syria and Hezbollah and to sow political divides in Lebanon. After failing to gain sufficient time to consider the legal basis of the international tribunal, in November 2006, March 8 ministers (five Shi'as and one Christian) resigned from the government, declaring it unconstitutional. Hezbollah, hoping to weaken Siniora's government, called the FMP to join the government. On the other hand, Berri refused to hold parliamentary sessions to discuss and ratify the agreement to institutionalise the tribunal. March 14 believed Hezbollah was complicit in the assassination of Hariri and wanted to derail the establishment of the tribunal, and requested the UN to establish the tribunal without Lebanon's consent.

The political deadlock was gradually eroding the power of and trust in institutions shifting the struggle to the street. Convinced that they represented the majority of the Lebanese, if not its parliamentary majority, March 8 and FMP staged a large demonstration, demanding the formation of a new 'national unity' government that included FMP. The demonstration turned into an 18-month sit-in in the centre of Beirut, surrounding the government headquarters where Siniora was based. Whilst Hezbollah and its allies framed the sit-in as a democratic 'peaceful, civil and civilised' demonstration (Nasrallah quoted in Saouli 2011; Raful 2015), March 14 considered it an 'invasion of Beirut' by Hezbollah, which, emboldened by the outcome of the 2006 war, was now trying to control Lebanon and invite back Syrian influence (Fatfat 2015; Costanian 2015).

With each step March 14 or 8 was taking to buttress its own security, it was provoking a sense of insecurity in the other, intensifying the overall tension. The more powerful Hezbollah was entrapped in the image it wanted to represent as a national, non-sectarian movement that would not exploit its military force in domestic struggles. On the other hand, it wanted to sustain pressure and extract political concessions from its rivals. It continued to exercise restraint in the use of violence. As clashes between supporters of the two camps were sporadically taking place in different areas, Nasrallah declared during an *Ashura* speech in January 2007, that 'even if you [March 14] shoot 1,000 of us, we will not shoot back'. The BBC correspondent observed that the commemoration of *Ashura* that year 'carried a message of restraint'. When clashes broke out between Sunni and Shi'a students in the Beirut Arab University, and threatened to disperse to other areas, Nasrallah issued a *fatwa* urging his supporters 'to exercise self-restraint and withdraw from the streets' (Saouli 2011: 937).

However, on 5 May 2008, after more than 18 months of political paralysis, the Lebanese government reluctantly made two decisions that led Hezbollah, for the first time since 1990, to use violence against its rivals. First the government dismissed Beirut's head of security due to his close ties to Hezbollah. And, second, it outlawed Hezbollah's telecommunications network.[18] According to March 14, the secret fibre-optic network, which the government found in April 2008 (sharing the information with Saudi Arabia and the US), was 'illegal' and through it Hezbollah and Iran hoped to control Lebanon: the telecommunications network, which 'bypasses Syria', argued Marwan Hamade of March 14, is a 'strategic victory for Iran' (Bazzi 2015). Fatfat (2015) adds that this network had spread to Christian areas of Lebanon.

For Hezbollah, these decisions amounted to a 'declaration of war'. In a long-televised press conference, Nasrallah asked the government to rescind the decisions. He threatened that when the government 'seize our weapons for the benefit of the enemy, then this is not an internal war; it is a war on the front'. Nasrallah believed that March 14 crossed the 'red lines' and that Hezbollah would have to cross them. Fearing that his next step would turn many (Sunni) Arabs against him, Nasrallah urged the Arab world to 'understand' the armed movement's position (Saouli 2011: 938–9).

Heavily armed and disciplined, in a matter of hours Hezbollah and its allies (Amal, the National Social Syrian Party (NSSP)) controlled west Beirut, routed pro-government militants (many of whom fled) and blocked all major (including the airport) roads in the capital. Fearing a division on a sectarian basis, the Lebanese army took a neutral stand. Hezbollah and its allied armed groups attacked the Future Television station, the mouthpiece of FM, drawing it off the air, and burned the offices of the Future newspaper (Worth and Bakri 2008). Whilst Hariri and Jumblatt were hiding in their fortified compounds and protected by the Lebanese army, properties and homes of some March 14 MPs and supporters were attacked and looted.[19] The violent clashes were turning into a sectarian confrontation and by 11 May violence spread to Druze areas of Mount Lebanon where Hezbollah confronted stiff resistance from Walid Jumblatt's fighters.

Hezbollah's swift military takeover of the capital was clearly plotted in advance.[20] Although Hezbollah's use of its weapons internally was triggered by the government's orders on 5 May, and although Hezbollah believes it was 'obliged' to take these measures, the military action was determined by both short- and long-term strategic motivations. Hezbollah transformed a developing strategic threat (March 14 attempts to isolate and delegitimise the armed movement) into a strategic opportunity to expand its influence in Lebanon.[21] On the short term, Hezbollah moved from a defensive to an offensive position: the military ambush broke the political stalemate and obliged March 14 to surrender to political negotiations, an outcome which political protests and pressures had failed to realise. Hezbollah also freed itself from the socio-political constraint (sectarian and political divisions in Lebanon) that prevented it from using its weapons internally; this constraint now ceased to be an asset that could be used by its rivals to blackmail the Shi'a armed movement. Hezbollah MP, Nawaf al-Moussawi, argued that 'we [Hezbollah] have promoted national and Islamic unity to buttress the resistance; however, if we had to choose between domestic unity and the resistance, the priority will be for the latter' (quoted in Saouli 2011: 939). Violence and the threat of its use now became a Hezbollah *asset* in its domestic rivalries. In long-term strategic calculations, Hezbollah established itself as Lebanon's most powerful actor. It stood to guarantee that neither the government nor any other political actor could threaten its status as an armed political movement or to steer Lebanon to the orbit of its regional or international enemies. Hezbollah gradually filled the politico-military vacuum the Syrian withdrawal left.

But, despite all of that, Hezbollah neither toppled the existing regime (some of Hezbollah's allies perceived this as an opportunity to lay the foundations for a new political system), nor made demands on behalf of its Shi'a community. Hezbollah's military offensive, rather, paved the way for the signing of the Doha Agreement in 2008, when Lebanese political factions decided to elect a new president (former military chief Michel Sleiman), to vote on a new electoral law, and to form a national unity government. Indeed, a national 'unity' government was formed by PM Fouad Siniora. Hezbollah's choice not to monopolise power in Lebanon was dictated by strategic motivations. A total political control would generate grave costs: it would alienate the vast majority of Lebanese Sunnis and Druze, and a significant segment of Lebanon's Christians; it would exacerbate sectarian divisions and increase Lebanon's vulnerability to external intervention and, possibly, war; a government controlled by Hezbollah would not earn regional and international recognition; last, but not least, this would require Hezbollah to govern, a condition that the party, focused on war-making with Israel, had consciously sought to avoid. Lebanon's consociationalism offered a better safety net for Hezbollah than the unknowns of political hegemony.

Nevertheless, Hezbollah's realist approach had its limits. Hezbollah constructed its military offensive as a brief 'surgical operation' or, according to Nasrallah, a 'great day (7 May)' that 'saved' Lebanon from a civil war. But Hezbollah had no control over the interpretations of its political rivals in Lebanon and the Arab world. The move, after all, reinforced Hezbollah's rivals' narrative that the armed movement wanted to 'control' Lebanon and that when push came to shove Hezbollah's weapons would be used for domestic purposes. After the military attack, Sheikh Mohammed Qabbani, Lebanon's (Sunni) Mufti, contended that Hezbollah transformed from a 'resistance movement into an armed force to occupy Beirut'. He called upon the Arab and Muslim worlds to come to the aid of Lebanon's Sunnis (*Al-Akhbar* 2008). Since the 'occupation of Beirut', Hezbollah, in the eyes of March 14, became a 'militia'. In the war of words, the 'resistance', which Hezbollah symbolised for a long time, became one of Lebanon's most contentious labels. While Hezbollah's politico-military power was expanding, its hope of preserving the 'culture of resistance' was eroding outside the confines of its own political base and alliances. Hezbollah's use of violence, as we shall see below, offered the basis for other groups – allies or rivals – to seek the possession of weapons and deepened the Sunni–Shi'a divide, which Hezbollah was trying to avoid.

After the May 2008 attack, in the period 2008–11, Hezbollah resumed its strategy of exercising restraint in the use of violence, despite the political polarisation and institutional paralysis. It is no exaggeration to argue that Lebanon in the period 2005–15 was living a war that was short of the use weapons – despite their occasional use: institutions were stalled; society was divided according to the March 8 and 14 lines; sectarianism reached unprecedented levels; the media was mobilised in endless political debates; the economy was stagnant; there was an increase in crimes and corruption; there was a fragmented foreign policy; last, but not least, there developed a total erosion of social values. It was a light form of state collapse. The security of Lebanon was hanging on the shared goal of preventing a total war similar to the one that had ravaged the country in 1975–90. Hezbollah had an interest in maintaining the calm, despite everything else. One example is in the movement's response to Hariri's international tribunal. In 2009, after four years of accusing Syria, a *Der Spiegel* report alleged that Hezbollah was behind the assassination (Follath 2009). Given its vision of the international system and law (see previous chapter), Hezbollah could have simply demonised the tribunal as an imperialist tool, which it did, but the armed movement chose also to engage with legal and normative debates to delegitimise the tribunal. In a series of press conferences and talks, Nasrallah and Hezbollah MPs argued that the tribunal challenged Lebanon's sovereignty, that it was implicated in corruption and that it lacked the legal standards to investigate and make judgments. He expressed his surprise that the investigation did not consider the possibility of an Israeli role in the Hariri assassination (Saouli 2011; Abboud and Muller 2013). He then went as far as to present what he considered as 'strong indicators' of Israel's involvement in the assassination of Hariri. Hezbollah sought to make the legal and normative case to delegitimise the tribunal and to contest March 14's own justification. Though this resonated with Hezbollah's supporters, in the eyes of its rivals Hezbollah was now not only possibly implicated in the murder, but also trying to block all attempts to disclose the 'truth' of the assassination of the beloved leader (Fatfat 2015; Costanian 2015).

It is ironic, but not alien to security paradoxes, that in trying to contain and isolate Hezbollah, in trying to realise its own strategy, March 14 provoked the armed movement and contributed to its growth and expansion in Lebanon. Qassem argues that, in the wake of the 2008 military offensive, Hezbollah was in the position of 'defence: they were preparing to attack us.'[22] Abd al-Halim Fadlallah (2015) adds that it is the 'policies of the other [March 14] that led Hezbollah to grow and expand in Lebanon after 2005'. On the other hand, as Hezbollah was trying to secure itself, it deepened the fears of March 14, and provoked its mobilisation. As Fatfat (2015) argues, their 'plan is to dominate; our discourse is due to our fear of them using their weapons in assassination attempts, in the siege of the government headquarters, [as] in 7 May . . . we are scared; we are in the position of fear.' 'Would it have been possible to try to contain Hezbollah after the Syrian withdrawal?' I dared to suggest to a March 14 member. 'Contain?!' he retorted, 'we now want Hezbollah to contain us!' 'March 14 is on the defensive!' (Constanian 2015).

The Ironies of International Socialisation

If the period 2004–11 saw Hezbollah expanding its role and influence in Lebanon, 2011–17 witnessed the armed political movement's increasing regional role. External expansion was triggered by the political uprisings that shook various Arab regimes, including Syria's, and consequently Hezbollah's controversial decision to intervene militarily in Syria, and other Arab countries.

The war in Syria (2011–17): strategic threats and opportunities

The Arab revolts of 2011–14 surprised ruling regimes and scholars. For several decades, authoritarian Arab regimes appeared stable; scholars focused on regime maintenance (Hinnebusch 2017). The 2011 uprisings were initially spontaneous popular revolts that amalgamated various political and social segments over the goal of regime change. In 2011, uprisings in Tunisia and Egypt toppled former presidents Zine El Abidine Ben Ali and Hosni Mubarak, respectively, before the rage diffused to other Arab countries (Libya, Bahrain, Syria, Yemen, Iraq). Galvanised by the fall of the two US-allied presidents, Hezbollah greeted the uprisings as 'national liberation' revolutions against despotic regimes. But in March 2011 the uprisings reached Syria and threatened to topple Assad's regime. The initially peaceful uprising against Assad's authoritarian regime represented a strategic opportunity for the enemies of the Resistance Alliance, including Lebanon's March 14. The uprising, the US and its regional allies gambled, would topple Assad's regime, sever Syria's strategic ties to Hezbollah, Iran and Palestinian armed movements (particularly Hamas and Islamic Jihad) and steer it to the US-led regional alliance. For the US and Saudi Arabia, the fall of Assad would cut Iran's strategic depth and isolate it in the region. For the resurgent Turkey and ambitious Qatar, it was an opportunity to bring about a Muslim Brotherhood regime in tune with Turkey's AKP regional designs (Saouli 2014b).

Given Syria's critical role in the Resistance Alliance and its geopolitical location (see previous chapter), the prospect of its fall to Hezbollah's enemies constituted an existential threat – the second strategic 'threat' highlighted by Qassem. As early as March 2012, Iran's Imam Khamenei claimed that 'the Islamic Republic will defend Syria because of its support for the resistance front against the Zionist regime' ('Iran Opposes any Foreign Intervention in Syria' 2012). But Hezbollah also reasoned that, in the worst-case scenario, Syria could turn into a collapsed state that provided a sanctuary for armed movements, such as al-Qaida, which would endanger not only Syria's location in the Resistance Axis, but also Lebanon's stability and territorial integrity (Nasrallah quoted in H. Fadlallah 2015: 152–3). Regime change in Syria would also empower Hezbollah's Lebanese rivals placing the armed political movement under immense political pressure that would expose it to Israel (Saouli 2014c).

It is these strategic calculations that determined Hezbollah's stand towards and later military intervention in Syria. It is also these considerations that would *deepen* Hezbollah's socialisation in regional politics. Just as Hezbollah advanced to fill the security vacuum the Syrian regime left in Lebanon, its military intervention in Syria aimed to appropriate the gaps left by the faltering regime in Syria. The period October 2011–May 2013 raised speculation about Hezbollah's military role in Syria. Initially it claimed that its intervention in Syria was limited to defend 'Lebanese villages' on the Lebanon–Syria border. Later on, Hezbollah claimed that its presence in Damascus served to protect Shi'a shrines, particularly the Sayyidah Zaynab mausoleum. By the end of 2012, Hezbollah hinted there was a greater involvement against what it depicted as the '*takfiri*' threat in Syria: among others, Islamist jihadists and al-Qaida-affiliated groups (Al-Mayadeen 2012). *Takfiris* refers to Islamic jihadist groups that delineate religious and political opponents as *kafirs* (unbelievers), enabling their persecution.

However, on 25 May 2013, Hezbollah clearly announced its motivations and goals in Syria. In that year, Hezbollah commemorated the 'Resistance and Liberation Day' in Machghara, a small town in the western Beqaa district. Hezbollah's choice of location and date signified the movement's new orientation: looking eastward to Syria. Beqaa, which three decades earlier formed the springboard for Hezbollah's armed resistance against Israel and its socialisation in Lebanon, now formed the passage to Hezbollah's military intervention in Syria, and the region. Speaking on the occasion, Nasrallah offered a justification to what would become Hezbollah's most controversial decision ('Hassan Nasrallah, 25 May 2013' n.d.):

> We are celebrating this occasion as the Lebanese and as peoples of this region are facing several threats and dangers, most important of which are: the permanent threat that is represented by Israel and its plans and second the changes taking place in Syria, meaning in our neighbourhood, at the doors of our cities, villages and homes and the salience of *takfiri* groups in the [Syrian] arena . . . The most prominent force in the armed [Syrian] opposition is the *takfiri* groups funded and armed by Western and regional states . . . Now we cannot talk anymore about a people rebelling against a regime . . . We believe that the control of these groups over territories in Syria and especially ones that are adjacent to the Lebanese borders constitutes a major threat to Lebanon and to the Lebanese.
>
> Syria has become an arena for the imposition of an American strategy in the region; [the] American strategy is an Israeli strategy.
>
> To be clear, Syria is the bulwark and supporter of the Resistance. The Resistance cannot stand idle as its rear-guard [strategic depth] is exposed or its bulwark is broken . . . foolish is the one who stands idle as he sees death, siege and conspiracy encroaching . . . If Syria falls to the Americans, Israelis and *takfiris*, and America's proxies in the region . . . the Resistance will be encircled and Israel will enter Lebanon to impose its wishes . . . If Syria falls, Palestine will be lost, the resistance in Palestine will be lost; Gaza, the West Bank and the Holy Jerusalem will be lost. There are two sides [in the regional rivalry]; Hezbollah cannot side with the US, Israel or the . . . *takfiris*.

Nasrallah's speech reinforced Hezbollah's religio-political identity, its strategic choices and interdependence with Syria and Iran – the main elements of its socialisation process. The speech confronted Hezbollah's supporters and allies with the emerging geopolitical realities the armed political movement faced: either accept regime change in Syria, which would subdue Hezbollah and 'destroy all the achievements and sacrifices [of past years]'; or fight for survival. This was 'the culture of the resistance', which Nasrallah contended, his critics did not understand. Regional rivalries in and over Syria, he would acknowledge several years later, have 'sucked' Hezbollah into 'the Syrian crisis' (Al-Manar 5 March 2016).

These justifications were important to mobilise Hezbollah's social base.

But additionally, the Islamist movement activated its religio-political identity. By 2013, the Shi'a community was beginning to adapt to the scene of dead Hezbollah fighters returning, not from south Lebanon as they had been attuned to, but from what was framed as the 'sacred jihad' in Syria, or elsewhere. Protecting Shi'a shrines in Syria and Iraq and fighting the 'killers of Imam Hussein' (read extreme Islamist jihadists), who, Hezbollah alleged, were in alliance with the US and Israel, formed the main slogans that mobilised many Lebanese Shi'as. In one *Ashura* speech, Ibrahim Amin al-Sayyid contended that Hezbollah was now fighting 'Yazid . . . [who] is back in Nineveh [referring to the fall of Mosul to ISIS]' (Al-Manar 31 October 2014). The slogans of *Labayki ya Zaynab* (at your service O Zaynab!) and 'Zaynab shall not be enslaved again' (referring to the first enslavement of Zaynab, see Chapter 2) now were crafted on the fighters' uniforms and displayed in Dahieh and other Shi'a areas of Lebanon. Testimonies and stories of Hezbollah's fighters reveal how the 'sacred jihad' in Syria was 'similar' to the battle of Karbala. The fighters felt 'connected' to Imam Hussein and to Sayyidah Zaynab. According to one story, Imam Hussein cautioned a fighter in a dream the he would be slaughtered but that the Imam would be there to guide him to the afterlife. Another story narrates that Sayyidah Zaynab informed a fighter of the date and time of his death, which then materialised, and invited him to her dining table.[23]

Hezbollah's military intervention in Syria (and other engagements in Iraq or Yemen) had a religio-political meaning. In addition to the strategic threats these wars posed, the war presented a threat to *Wilayat al-Faqih*, represented in the Islamic Republic. Hezbollah fighters, believing to be the 'soldiers of the *Mahdi*', were also fighting for the survival of the *wilayah*, and in consequence the Islamic Republic. One fighter (Ali Abu Ta'am), who was killed in 2014 in Qalamoun, Syria, addressed the awaited *Mahdi*, saying: 'My leader, the waiting has prolonged. My patience is eroding: when is the relief [*faraj*]? How I wished to see you . . . We are your soldiers, fighting your causes and sacrificing for you.'

But there were other reasons that contributed to garner support for Hezbollah's military intervention: Shi'a (and Christian) communal fears. The sectarian discourse of jihadist groups, such as Jabhat al-Nusra (al-Qaida's affiliate in Syria) and the 'Islamic State' – who perceive and treat Shi'as as 'infidels' and *rawafid* (or rejectionists) – and the horrendous violence they inflicted on minorities and political opponents in Syria and Iraq, pushed many members of targeted groups to support Hezbollah and Assad. When Nasrallah announced that the battle in Syria was 'existential' in nature, many attributed this not only to the survival of the Resistance Alliance, but also to the mere survival of various minority groups. According to Abd al-Halim Fadlallah (2015), history would not forgive Hezbollah if it stood watching the 'radical and dangerous balance of power' shifting to the enemy or to the *takfiris*, who would threaten the sectarian, ethnic and cultural pluralism of the region. In many ways these fears dovetailed with the Syrian regime's narrative, which is a common regime technique of survival in other Arab dictatorships: 'me or the terrorists' (Saouli 2015). Hezbollah's discourse by 2013 focused on the '*takfiris*' and 'terrorists'. As Nasrallah noted in his speech, 'now we cannot talk about a people rebelling against a regime', a narrative, which as we shall see shortly, ignited fierce criticism of Hezbollah.

The war against the so-called Islamic State, which rival parties used as justification to join the war in Syria, was one that would consolidate Hezbollah's other motivations for its intervention. The intervention was gradual and dictated by the changing military balance on the ground. The weaker the regime and the higher the threat of its fall became, the more Hezbollah stepped in to fill the void and to offer the necessary backing. Hezbollah offered manpower, military advisers, trainers for pro-regime militias and, crucially for wars in urban areas, reconnaissance, sniper fire and light infantry. Hezbollah's experience in guerrilla warfare supplemented the regime's conventional army (Sullivan 2014: 9). Along with Iran, Hezbollah also played a key role in the training of the National Defence Forces (NDF), a pro-regime militia, which is predominantly formed of Alawite and regime loyalists. The founding of the militia served to supplement the Syrian army, which was 'weakened, by years of fighting, defections, and rebel infiltrations', with manpower (Sullivan 2014: 14; Hamade 2014: 253).

Although media reports indicated that Hezbollah intervened as early as October 2011 and had fighters killed in Syria as the regime was repressing the revolts and fighting the Free Syrian Army (FSA), it has denied these claims (Sullivan 2014: 11). Initially, Hezbollah sent fighters to Damascus to protect Shi'a shrines and contribute to safe-guarding the capital. However, it was in the battle of Qusayr that Hezbollah publicly acknowledged its military intervention in Syria. Located in central Syria and adjacent to the Lebanese border, the strategic town of Qusayr connects Damascus to Syria's coastal areas and to the northern cities of Homs and Aleppo. It fell into rebel hands in mid-2012 and threatened to cut Damascus from the rest of the country. Opposition groups were using the town to smuggle weapons and fighters through the predominantly Sunni north of Lebanon. For Hezbollah, the fall of Qusayr and other border areas also threatened to isolate Lebanon from Syria, thus endangering Hezbollah's own lines of communication: Beirut–Damascus–Tehran. Additionally, the control of rebel groups – particularly jihadist groups – threatened Hermel, Hezbollah's strategic town in northern Lebanon. In April 2013, Hezbollah, the Syrian army and pro-regime forces began to isolate Qusayr by occupying surrounding areas in the south and north. Then by mid-May, as the Syrian army was hitting the town by air strikes and artillery, Hezbollah led a ground unit of 1,200–1,700 fighters who attacked Qusayr overcoming fierce resistance. By 3 June 2013, Qusayr fell back to regime forces. In the battle Hezbollah lost around 200 fighters (Sullivan 2014: 14–16; Hamade 2014, 229–54; Chulov 2013).

The battle of Qusayr formed a strategic shift in the war of Syria, gradually turning the tide in favour of the regime. After Qusayr, the regime advanced to regain lost territories in Homs, Aleppo and Damascus. Hezbollah played key roles in these battles (Sullivan 2014: 17) where regime forces and its allied militias would encircle areas controlled by the rebels, hit them by air strikes and artillery and then commit a ground attack. In Damascus, Hezbollah, and other Shi'a militias from Iraq and Afghanistan, fought to defend the Sayyidah Zaynab shrine in south-eastern Damascus. The area strategically ties Damascus city centre (where the Presidential Palace is located) to Damascus International Airport. It is also located between western Ghouta and eastern Ghouta. The regime, with strong participation from Hezbollah, has attempted to regain control of eastern Ghouta, which has been under siege since 2013. On 21 August 2013, it was believed that the regime targeted eastern Ghouta with chemical weapons, killing hundreds of civilians, mostly children (McKernan 2017).

In late 2013, Hezbollah and the regime targeted the mountainous

Qalamoun area, which ties Damascus to Homs. As with Qusayr, Qalamoun threatened Hezbollah's stronghold in the Beqaa region. Since mid-2012, opposition groups have controlled the area and used it as a zone to transit weapons to and from Arsal, a Sunni town in Beqaa. Hezbollah led the ground offensive in Qalamoun accompanied by regime air strikes and bombardments. By March 2014, Qalamoun and Yabroud, a stronghold of al-Qaida affiliates, fell to Hezbollah and regime forces (Hamade 2014: 265–6; Sullivan 2014: 20–1).

Hezbollah's military intervention in Syria had a strong impact on the war, contributing to maintaining Assad's regime in the war-torn country. By 2013, it was estimated that Hezbollah had a force between 3,000 and 5,000 (Sullivan 2014: 22). However, as the war progressed and as Hezbollah's role therein deepened, Hezbollah must have deployed more troops. By 2017, according to unofficial estimates (Hezbollah has not disclosed its losses in Syria), Hezbollah had lost around 1,800 fighters.[24] This is a huge loss compared to the losses Hezbollah incurred in its war with Israel in 1982–2000 (see above). But the figure remains much lower than the estimated losses of the Syrian army and its paramilitary forces, which in 2014 stood at 50,000 (Sullivan 2014: 26).

By 2016, Hezbollah's strategic goal of keeping Assad's regime intact was realised. Its military intervention was only one component of this outcome. The bloody Syrian war, which pitted Russia, Iran, the Syrian regime, Hezbollah and Iraqi Shi'a militias against Turkey, Qatar, Saudi Arabia and the US, transformed Syria from a regional actor in 2010 to a battlefield in 2012–17 (Saouli 2014b; Lawson 2014). In one of its manifestations the war reflected the Iranian–Saudi rivalry which heightened the sectarian divide in the Middle East and beyond. By 2017, the Russian-led alliance had the upper hand. Divisions within the Syrian opposition and the absence of a clear political platform, regional rivalries for control of the opposition, the emergence of the 'Islamic State' in Iraq and Syria, and Russia's military intervention in 2015 all contributed to the prevailing of Assad and his allies. The Iran-led alliance appeared more coherent, with clear objectives. Russia's military intervention, which was enabled by President Barack Obama's cautious and ambivalent attitude towards the Syrian war, supplemented Iran's goals in Syria. Justified by its fight against 'IS' terrorism, the Russian military intervention helped Assad consolidate his gains and to reassert control over main cities, such as Aleppo, which fell in December 2016 (Quinn 2016).[25]

Beyond its military battles against the Syrian opposition, Hezbollah has sought to transform its presence in the collapsed state into an opportunity to fight Israel. As early as 2013, Nasrallah expressed his willingness to support a 'popular resistance' against Israel in Syria. Hezbollah and Iran wanted, in addition to south Lebanon, another base from which to fight their Zionist enemy. Hezbollah dispatched several exploratory missions to the area surrounding the Golan Heights. Playing a key role in these missions was Samir al-Qantar, who was freed in 2008, after a 30-year detainment in Israel. In Qassem's words, al-Qantar wanted to 'open new horizons' for Hezbollah.[26] Israel, on the other hand, wanted to thwart these aims. Since the start of the war in Syria it has been targeting what it claims are Hezbollah military sites and convoys; the aim has been to stop Iran from developing a base in Syria (Beaumont 2017). In January 2015, an Israeli air strike targeted a Hezbollah convoy in the province of Quneitra, near the occupied Golan, killing among others the 20-year-old Jihad Mughniyah, the son of the late Imad Mughnieh (Malm 2015). In December 2015, al-Qantar was killed when a suspected Israeli air strike hit his compound in the outskirts of Damascus.

Ethical and political quandaries

However, Hezbollah's military intervention in support of Assad's authoritarian regime, which brutally repressed its opponents, raised ethical questions: how could a movement that claims to be struggling for freedom against occupation and oppression and one which had celebrated the national uprisings in Tunisia, Libya, Egypt or Bahrain, support another equally authoritarian regime? Hezbollah's former supporters in the Arab world began to accuse it of 'hypocrisy' and ethical bankruptcy: how can Hezbollah betray the Syrian people who admired it, supported its resistance and accommodated its refugees during the 2006 war? (See Introduction.)[27] Addressing this ethical gap became a crucial element in Hezbollah's discourse and justification for its military intervention in Syria. Its conversationalist in-chief, Nasrallah, played a key role in this effort. His appearances increased since 2012. For example, excluding the interviews given to television stations and newspapers, Nasrallah delivered 27 speeches in 2012, the year Hezbollah began to intervene in Syria. In 2015, he delivered 29 speeches, almost a speech every fortnight.[28] All speeches were transmitted live via Al-Manar and other (allied) Lebanese stations. Following Nasrallah's speeches, Al-Manar invited commentators – several of whom can be more accurately described as informal speakers of Hezbollah – to highlight the points he made and to reinforce his message among his supporters.

Nasrallah has attempted to connect Hezbollah's strategic goals to what Ned Lebow (2003: 16) calls 'a language of justice'. His speeches aimed to narrow the gap between political goals and ethical values, as Wajeeh Kanso observes (Kanso 2013). For example, in 2012, he contended that Hezbollah's stance on Arab regimes stood on two fundamentals: a regime's willingness to reform (to address popular demands) and its stance towards Israel. Nasrallah believed that Assad, who enacted some 'reforms' in the wake of the Syrian uprising, satisfied both criteria. When in July 2012 four high-ranking Syrian officers were killed in an attack in Damascus, Nasrallah's condolences described them as 'martyr leaders who [were] comrades in-arms in the struggle against the Israeli enemy'. Most of the weapons that Hezbollah employed in the July 2006 war, he added, came from Syria (quoted in Saouli 2013: 41).

By intervening in Syria, Hezbollah was making an indispensable Niebuhrian tragic choice: sacrificing one value (freedom of the oppressed) for a perceived higher value (survival of the Resistance Alliance). The language used to justify the military intervention is ironic for a movement that has fought for liberation. After Nasrallah's speech in 2013, Hezbollah and its allies (politicians and commentators) began to use the discourse of the powerful which Hezbollah had for many years detested and fallen victim to. The military intervention in Syria, they justified, is for 'defensive' purposes; it is a 'pre-emptive war' against 'terrorists'; better fight the enemy on its own turf before it comes closer to home.[29] Hezbollah was now waging its own 'war on terrorism'.

It was on this basis that Nasrallah announced in 2015 that Hezbollah 'will be where it is necessary to be'. Survival and the realisation of goals in the anarchic regional order has no limits, ethical or otherwise. Hassan Fadlallah, Hezbollah's MP and the movement's biographer, laid the politico-intellectual rationale for Hezbollah's external role. He claimed that Hezbollah has managed to strengthen the Lebanese state by establishing the 'Army, People and

Resistance' formula. 'The Resistance', to the chagrin of his Lebanese rivals, is 'stronger than the state [army]' and can now 'perform a role [or influence] outside the national boundaries'. The quest for 'national security and interest', he adventurously suggested, 'transcends boundaries' (H. Fadlallah 2015: 218–22). Hezbollah's 'resistance' has outgrown Lebanon.

But is the 'resistance' a means or an end? For Sheikh Jaradi (2015), 'it is possible for the means to gain its sacredness from the end it is generating'. 'From a doctrinal perspective', he indicates, 'the preservation [fighting outside Lebanon] of what was achieved [liberating the land] is not less sacred than the initial achievement'. Put in less philosophical terms, and in tune with this book's argument (see Chapter 2), is Abu Rida's (2012: 582) assertion that 'the ideology of the "resistance" in the discourse of Hezbollah has been both a means and an end' in the realisation of Hezbollah's goals.

Hezbollah's views and behaviour challenge all previous interpretations of the 'Lebanonisation' of Hezbollah, if that meant Hezbollah's giving up of its universalist ideology. They also challenge suggestions that Hezbollah is now conditioned by international norms of sovereignty and nationhood (Dionigi 2014). External threats have offered Hezbollah an opportunity to realise its broader religio-political goals: weakening of US (and Western) influence in the region, transforming divided states (like Syria, Iraq and Yemen) into sites of influence and, ultimately, reconfiguring regional power to fight Israel. By 2017, Hezbollah appeared to be more than a political party or armed resistance in Lebanon: it was exposed as a member of a religio-political network of armed organisations coordinated by Iran's Islamic Revolutionary Guards in Syria, Yemen and Iraq (Farhi 2017; McInnes 2015; Ehteshami 2014; Filkins 2013).

But Hezbollah's military support of Assad and its interventions in Iraq or Yemen – in theoretical parlance Hezbollah's deeper socialisation in the anarchical order – had a negative impact on the movement in Lebanon and the Arab world. The military intervention in Syria exacerbated sectarian and political division within Lebanon, which started in 2004 (you can also argue that these same divisions – the absence of a Lebanese unity – motivated Hezbollah to enter Syria to minimise its domestic vulnerability). The intervention deepened the Sunni–Shi'a divide. By supporting Assad and Iran, Hezbollah's foes reaffirmed their narrative of Hezbollah as a sectarian movement that is determined to preserve and deepen Iranian infiltration of the Arab world in the hope of creating a 'Shi'a' or 'Persian' crescent, tying Tehran, Baghdad, Damascus and Beirut. Hezbollah's religio-political and sectarian slogans, its coordination and alliance with Shi'a militias from Iraq and Afghanistan and its support of the 'Alawite' regime in Syria all reaffirmed the March 14 political narrative (Fatfat 2015; Costanian 2015).[30]

In Lebanon (and Iraq) many spoke of Sunni 'marginalisation' and 'repression' by a Shi'a alliance in Iraq, Syria and Lebanon. In the eyes of Sunni Salafi groups, FM is weak, does not represent the Sunnis and is unable to confront Hezbollah. Hezbollah's ascendancy in Lebanon and its contribution to the repression of what they perceive as a Sunni revolt against Assad, galvanised Lebanon's Salafis. Amidst the increasing sectarian polarisation in Lebanon and the region, one Salafi leader threatened to issue a *fatwa* calling upon all Sunnis to defect from the Lebanese army. Another, Sheikh Ahmed al-Assir, called for a rebellion against Hezbollah adopting both political and violent means in expressing what he perceived as Sunni grievances. For several months in 2013, al-Assir blocked some roads in Sidon. He mounted a revolt against Hezbollah:

> The Iranian agenda is dominating our country . . . the Iranian agenda is killing us . . . Our men are being imprisoned by the military intelligence, which is loyal to Hezbollah and Iran . . . they killed Rafic Hariri . . . and humiliatingly brought down his son . . . In May 7 [2008] and its aftermath . . . they placed the government headquarters under siege (quoted in Saouli 2016: 55).

In emulation of their Shi'a rival, many Sunnis Islamists were now aspiring to adopt Hezbollah's model. In 2013, al-Assir established his own 'security quarter', protected by armed men, which included a mosque where he preached to his followers. March 14 exploited the rise of these Islamist factions to contain Hezbollah. But it also had to make sure these groups did not threaten its own influence in the Sunni community. It attempted to show that Hezbollah's Shi'a extremism is generating an equivalent in the Sunni community. Speaking from Tripoli, were many Salafis operate, March 14 announced that: 'We reject some Shi'a hardliners who have come from Tehran through transnational [ideology of] *Wilayat al-Faqih*, which has repressed, excommunicated, bombed and killed' (quoted in Saouli 2016: 58). Fatfat and other Hezbollah critics contend that 'Hezbollah has a repressive discourse; I call it *Takfiri*, for it considers any rival as an [external] collaborator or treacherous' (Fatfat 2015).

For one Salafi figure, the fall of Qusayr to Hezbollah forces and the battle against al-Assir placed many Sunnis 'in a state of emergency to stop Farsi-Crusader invasion' (quoted in Saouli 2016: 57). In the period July to December 2013, Dahieh and Hezbollah would be the target of terrorist attacks by Islamist jihadists hoping to bring the battle to Hezbollah's own turf and to punish it for its military intervention in Syria. Four decades after Hezbollah's improvisation of the suicide attack, its own enemies – now Islamist Sunni jihadists – would use the same tactic against the Shi'a stronghold. In one of the attacks, on 15 August, a suicide bomber exploded his car in a busy area in Dahieh, killing 22 innocent lives and injuring more than 200; an unknown 'Battalion of Aysha' (the wife of the Prophet who Shi'a believe hated Imam Ali) claimed responsibility for the attack against the 'Iranian colony'. On 19 November, two suicide bombers targeted the Iranian embassy in Beirut, killing 22 people, including the Iranian Cultural Attaché, and injuring 140 others. Eager to deepen the Sunni–Shi'a divide in Lebanon, al-Qaida's Abdallah Azzam Brigades claimed responsibility for the 'double martyrdom operation carried out by two heroic Sunnis of Lebanon' (Saouli 2016: 57–8).

Like all violent acts, these attacks against Hezbollah in Lebanon generated different political interpretations. For Hezbollah, the attacks reinforced its own narrative that the threat coming from Syria is from *takfiris*, who are the product of an Israeli–American–Saudi plot to fight the Resistance Alliance and to kill Shi'as. Fighting the *takfiris* in Syria, Iraq, Yemen or 'where necessary' is both a national as well as a religio-political duty. 'Ethically, Hezbollah will be responsible for its silence' or if it stood still as these groups developed, contends Abd al-Halim Fadlallah (2015).

For Hezbollah's critics, the attacks are a result of the Shi'a movement's sectarianism, its military intervention in Syria and the silence the movement, its media outlets and army of commentators showed in relation to Assad's bloody repression. Hezbollah, they assert, has debunked all claims that it is a liberation movement fighting for Lebanon; the Shi'a movement is a proxy of Iran that recognises no borders and works to realise Iranian aspirations in the Arab world. In Syria, Hezbollah has become an 'occupying power' (Fatfat 2015; FutureTV 2015; Kilo 2016; Costanian 2015).

By 2016, the Syria war had cost the lives of around half a million people and displaced more than 40 per cent of the Syrian population (Black 2016).[31] Hezbollah's critics capitalised on these developments to delegitimise the Islamist movement or to reshape their strategy. Okab Saqr, a Shi'a member of the FM (himself accused of supporting the Syrian opposition), contended that Hezbollah 'believes that there is no Syrian people, only terrorists'. He argued that Hezbollah's military intervention has flared the Sunni–Shi'a sectarian war and led to the 'killing of innocent rebels': 'Can you sleep at night, Sayyid [Nasrallah], when [Syrian] children are being slaughtered?' Saqr asked (FutureTV 2015).

In a video posted on Facebook in 2013, Moaz al-Khatib, a member of the Syrian opposition, urged Nasrallah to withdraw his troops from Syria to avoid a 'Sunni–Shi'a *fitna*':

> The blood of your [Lebanese] fighters should not be spilt against the oppressed people in Syria . . . Is the madhhab [school] of *Ahl al-Bayt*, peace be upon them, to support virtue/right, as I know it, or to stand with an oppressive regime? All the people of Syria embody the tragedy of Imam Hussein, the oppressed and repressed martyr.[32]

Without question, Hezbollah's military intervention in Syria posed serious ethical questions for the movement. For Sayyid Ali Fadlallah (2015), son of the late M. H. Fadlallah, who still maintains his father's distance from various political groups, argues that the Shi'as always stand with the oppressed: 'we are for justice and against oppression where it takes place. We support Assad's backing of the resistance; however, we do not support him when he drops barrel bombs or when he kills with no due or when he insults [innocent] people.' Reflecting on Hezbollah's considerations, however, Fadlallah, argues that 'if the Russia–Iran alliance wins, then this is a triumph for the Resistance Axis which is against Israeli oppression or injustice; they [the Resistance camp] believe to be working [also] on an ethical basis.'

Likewise, Hezbollah's military intervention in Syria formed an opportunity for its regional foes to delegitimise and fight the Shi'a movement. In

2012, Hamas, allured by the prospects of the Muslim Brotherhood reaching power in various Arab states (Syria, Egypt, Tunisia, Yemen) and concerned about its own legitimacy as a Sunni-Islamist party, gradually abandoned the Resistance Alliance (Saouli 2013). It asked Hezbollah to withdraw from Syria. Hamas's withdrawal, moreover, exposed the Resistance Alliance as a Shi'a axis. Frustrated by Hezbollah's support of Assad's regime and its intervention in other Arab countries, upon a Saudi proposal, the Gulf Cooperation Council and then the Arab League designated Hezbollah as a terrorist organisation in March 2016 (Iraq and Lebanon voted against the decision) (Sinclair 2016). Arabsat and Nilesat, Saudi and Egyptian satellite companies, respectively, suspended Al-Manar's transmission because it was 'provoking sectarian strife' (An-Nahar 2016). These decisions were enabled by Hezbollah's loss of public support and by the mobilisation against the Shi'a movement in many Arab countries.

These decisions came after more than two years of Saudi–Hezbollah tensions. In December 2013, Nasrallah accused Saudi Arabia of orchestrating the suicide attacks against it in Lebanon. In the period 2014–17, Nasrallah waged an unprecedented campaign against the Saudi monarchy, accusing it of supervising al-Qaida and 'IS'. Saudi's Wahhabi religious thought, he claimed, formed the basis for the jihadi-Salafism that is destroying the Arab world (Saouli 2016: 58). In Hezbollah parades and ceremonies, its supporters now chanted: 'Death to the Sauds'.

Tension between Hezbollah and Saudi Arabia was one manifestation of the regional rivalry between the Kingdom and Iran in the divided societies of Lebanon, Syria, Iraq or Yemen. The fall of Mosul to 'IS' in 2014 and the threat this posed to Iraq's predominantly Shi'a rule, offered Iran and Hezbollah the opportunity to transfer weapons, knowledge and fighters, and, ultimately, to reshape the balance of power in their favour (*Al-Akhbar* 2017). Fearing that 'IS' could extend its reach to Baghdad and Shi'a regions of Iraq, Ayatollah Sistani, Iraq's prominent Shi'a cleric, issued a *fatwa* to resist IS giving birth to the Hashd al-Sha'bi (Popular Mobilisation Forces) – a Shi'a umbrella group including Badr, Asa'ib Ahl al-Haq and Kata'ib Hezbollah (Haddad 2016). By defeating 'IS', which occupied a large territory that covered most of western Iraq and eastern Syria, the Iran-led coalition hoped to break the strategic boundary dividing Iraq and Syria that served to block the Islamic Republic's strategic reach in the region. US (and allied) airpower contributed to the fall of IS in Iraq in 2017. However, all this served the troops and militias actually fighting on the ground: Iran, the Syrian regime, the Hashd, Hezbollah and other Shi'a militias. The meeting of Iraqi and Syrian forces in the Abu Kamal border region in late 2017 reflected a strategic transformation in the Middle East: the carving of a Tehran–Baghdad–Damascus–Beirut land route. The scene of Qasem Soleimani, the Qud's Force Commander (a unit of the Islamic Revolutionary Guards, which reports directly to Imam Khamenei) (McInnes 2015), in different battlefields in Syria and Iraq was a testimony of Iran's increasing influence.[33] These advances led Nasrallah to announce 'victory' against IS and their backers in Syria (and the region). Hezbollah's allies hailed the strategic depth that now tied all members of the Resistance Alliance. In a future war with Israel, Nasrallah threatened, 'hundreds of thousands of fighters from all over the Arab and Islamic world [would] participate – from Iraq, Yemen, Iran, Afghanistan and Pakistan' (Reuters 2017).

But the realities on the ground in Syria are more complex. It was not only Nasrallah who declared victory in the most penetrated country of the region. In addition to an Iranian salient presence, by 2017, Syria was host to several Russian, Turkish and US military bases, which manifested the various actors' spheres of influence in the war-torn country. The strategic corridor that ties Tehran–Damascus–Beirut is cordoned by US air and military bases in southeast and northeast Syria (controlled by the opposition and the Kurdish armed groups, respectively) (Ammer 2017; O'Connor 2017; Reuters 2016).

As in Syria and Iraq, the gradual rise of the Houthis, who renamed as Ansar Allah, and their controlling of Sana'a in September 2014, offered Iran and Hezbollah another opportunity to extend their strategic regional reach; in this case, to inflict pressure on Saudi Arabia from the southern tip of the Arab Peninsula. Saudi Arabia accused Iran and Hezbollah of transferring weapons and military expertise to Ansar Allah. A video, transmitted by Saudi Arabia's Al Arabiya satellite television, showed Hezbollah operatives plotting and training Yemenis to plant bombs in the Saudi kingdom.[34] In 2015, Saudi Arabia led a coalition of forces to wage a war on Yemen. As Iran and Hezbollah intervened in Syria to prevent the fall of Assad, in Yemen, Saudi Arabia stepped in to preserve the power of its ally, President Abdrabbuh

Mansur, and to prevent the Houthis from becoming 'another Hezbollah' (Arab News 2017).

An exposition of Hezbollah's increasing regional role goes beyond the scope of this book and deserves a more focused treatment. But Hezbollah's interventions, a deepening of the Islamist movement's socialisation in the region, transformed it in the eyes of supporters into a de facto 'regional force' and in the eyes of its enemies into an 'Iranian thorn in the Arab world'. This socialisation exposed many political and ethical inconsistencies. Like other rival powers in the region, Hezbollah was calling upon its enemies to withdraw from Syria, Iraq or Yemen, whilst it was guilty of intervening in these same territories. How can Hezbollah ask Saudi Arabia to stop its military intervention in support of its allies in the poverty-ridden country, when it has stepped in to support its own allies in Syria? Hezbollah's support of Ansar Allah and the Yemeni people against the bloody Saudi war (by 2017 the war in Yemen cost the lives of 10,000), on the other hand, contradicted the movement's silence toward Assad's repressive campaign in Syria.

In November 2016, Hezbollah published pictures of a military parade, including a convoy of tanks, that it organised in the Syrian town of Qusayr. It was not clear whether the parade aimed to flex Hezbollah's muscles, presumably to deter enemies, or whether it was a sign of a developing hubris. But it was a salient departure from Hezbollah's more restrained attributes; in the beginning of its intervention in Syria, Hezbollah used to attribute most of the 'victories' to the Syrian army. These scenes provoked anger. One Arab daily observed 'a strange phenomenon': Hezbollah's 'pre-emptive activities' to secure Lebanon and Shi'a shrines resembles Israel's principle of securing Israel 'which the occupying army used for most of its military operations in Lebanon'. The emphasis on its military force and 'arrogance' led Hezbollah to 'lose its credibility, turning it into an occupying sectarian power'. Like Israel, the editorial continued, Hezbollah and its supporters have utilised the discourse of past oppression and narratives of marginalisation and repression in history to justify the actions of the present (al-Quds al-Arabi 2016).

But survival, a prerequisite to the realisation of other goals, in the anarchical order of the Middle East may have coerced and conformed Hezbollah to actions that make its behaviour similar to other actors in the system.

Survival trumps all other considerations. One Hezbollah official straddles the delicate balance between the movement's interests and popular legitimacy:

> As a party, we don't stake out our position based on whether people will like them or not. We have a clear vision and constant principles. When we stood against the American occupation in Iraq, the Shiites of Iraq blamed us and were opposed to us . . . It is true that having a strong popular base is important for us, but we won't achieve it at any price. Popularity and support fluctuate. (quoted in International Crisis Group 2012)

Notes

1. Two years later Hezbollah exchanged the abducted Israelis (Elhanan Tannenbaum and the bodies of the three Israeli soldiers) for 345 Lebanese and Palestinian detainees and 59 bodies of Hezbollah soldiers.
2. According to Karim Pakradouni, a veteran Lebanese politician and former leader of the Phalange, a woman asked Hariri if he supported the opposition and he replied that: 'this was the million dollar question!' He went on to add, 'I am not in government, so logically I am in the opposition; but the question is which opposition? I am an ally of Jumblatt and it is no secret that I have a disagreement with Syria, but Syria is a friend [of Lebanon] and will look for the best relations with her' (quoted in Pakradouni 2009: 352).
3. Several allies of Syria joined the demonstration, including: Amal, SSNP, Ba'ath Party and supporters of various leaders such as Suleiman Frangieh, Talal Arslan, Omar Karami and others.
4. All quotes from Nasrallah's March 8 speech are available at <https://www.mediarelations-lb.org/article.php?id=3064&cid=94#.WyplWBJKigQ> (last accessed 20 June 2018).
5. See <https://www.youtube.com/watch?v=9732c3ZBGTk> (last accessed 22 June 2017).
6. See <https://www.youtube.com/watch?v=hDCQuOXsm-w> (last accessed 22 June 2017).
7. These included Jamil Al Sayyed, Head of the General Security; Ali Al Hajj, Head of Internal Security; Raymond Azar, General Head of the Army's General Intelligence; and Mustafa Hamdan, Chief of the Republican Guard.
8. The new parliament had three major blocks: Hariri and Jumblatt's block with 72 MPs, Michel Aoun's block of 21 MPs and an opposition (mainly Shi'a) block of Hezbollah and Amal with 35 MPs (Pakradouni 2009: 392).

9. See <http://assafir.com/Article/341/437385> (last accessed 20 June 2018).
10. The speech is available at <https://www.youtube.com/watch?v=-S5A7Ml37q0> (last accessed 16 October 17).
11. See also the report on the Al Mayadeen website regarding this battle: <http://www.almayadeen.net/reports/803525> (last accessed 18 October 2017).
12. For these and other detailed information on the 2006 War, see *As-Safir*'s 'The Days of the July War', <http://assafir.com/Channel/341> (last accessed 20 October 2017). See also Achcar and Warschawski 2007.
13. For details of the negotiations (at the UN, in Israel and in Lebanon) leading to this outcome see Bregman 2016 (295–306); H. Fadlallah 2015 (182–94).
14. According to Pierre Raful, General Coordinator of the FMP, 'Hezbollah are a good and patriotic people; they are strong believers and are ready to sacrifice their life for their beliefs'. Instructed by Aoun, in the beginning of the war, the FMP established an 'Emergency Committee' to work for the accommodation and relief of the displaced people. For Raful, the Lebanese army, devoid of quality weapons, cannot defend Lebanon on its own: Lebanon can be protected by 'the army, the people and the resistance' (Raful 2015).
15. As Hezbollah was making achievements on the ground, Hezbollah's main representative in the government, Muhammad Fneish, was instructed by his leadership to deliver a strong message: that March 14 is a party to the war against the resistance and Hezbollah will deal with March 14 'on that basis'.
16. One article (8) clearly calls for disarmament of armed groups: 'full implementation of the relevant provisions of the Taif Accords, and of resolutions 1559 (2004) and 1680 (2006), that require the disarmament of all armed groups in Lebanon, so that, pursuant to the Lebanese cabinet decision of 27 July 2006, there will be no weapons or authority in Lebanon other than that of the Lebanese State' ('Security Council 1701 (2006)' n.d.).
17. For the speech, see <https://www.mediarelations-lb.org/article.php?id=3684&cid=164#.WyprKxJKigQ> (last accessed 20 June 2018).
18. Fatfat, a minister at the time, contends that Prime Minister Siniora was against making these decisions, but Walid Jumblatt threatened to resign from the government if it did not make these decisions (Fatfat 2015).
19. According to Fatfat, Hezbollah and Amal attacked his office and the home of another Future MP, Ammar Houri, which was looted. Fatfat believes it was Amal fighters who looted the flat, but Hezbollah was happy for 'the anarchy to take place; they did not want to do this directly'.
20. Naim Qassem argues that Hezbollah was 'prepared' for such a possibility;

see <https://www.youtube.com/watch?v=HtNk2pdQsxQ> (last accessed 28 October 2017).

21. Both Hezbollah and the Future Movement believe that Hezbollah exploited an opportunity. Fadlallah (2015) believes that March 14's actions presented this opportunity for Hezbollah. Fatfat argues that March 14 offered Hezbollah the opportunity to dominate. Hezbollah, he contends, 'was not afraid, Hezbollah was waiting for the opportune time to strike' (Fatfat 2015).
22. See <https://www.youtube.com/watch?v=HtNk2pdQsxQ> (last accessed 28 October 17).
23. See the episode on 'Sacred Defence and the Spirit of Karbala' in the programme *Habet Misk* on Al-Manar: <http://mail.almanar.com.lb/programs/pdetails.php?did=1090351&pid=3647&eid=166956&wid=4497> (last accessed 20 June 2018).
24. A source close to Hezbollah estimated that since the 2006 war Hezbollah has lost 2,000 fighters. We know that in 2006 Hezbollah lost around 200 fighters, leaving the figure of 1,800 for the Syria war since 2011. This must also include Hezbollah's losses in Iraq and Yemen, <http://al-akhbar.com/node/279576> (last accessed 3 July 2017).
25. This brief analysis does not do justice to the protracted Syrian war (2011–17). For a deeper and extensive analysis of the causes and consequences of the war, see Phillips 2018; Hinnebusch and Imady 2018.
26. On Samir al-Qantar and his involvement in Syria, see the Al Mayadeen documentary 'al-Qantar', <https://www.youtube.com/watch?v=c9ihvaweGAg> (last accessed 20 December 2017).
27. Hezbollah enjoyed a lot of support in Syria prior to the war. In a visit to Syria in the summer of 2010, I observed the pictures of Nasrallah in many shops and streets of Damascus. Most of these were raised during and after the July 2006 war.
28. For the list of Nasrallah's speeches, see the archive on Hezbollah's media relations unit website: <https://www.mediarelations-lb.org/catdetails.php?catidval=84&catid=94> (last accessed 20 June 2018).
29. See the television interviews of Hassan Fadlallah on Orange TV (25 June 2013) and Nawaf al-Moussawi on Lebanese Broadcasting Corporation (5 July 2013). See also Nasrallah's interview with Al Mayadeen on 21 March 2016.
30. For Ahmad Fatfat (2015), 'Hezbollah intervened in Syria based on an Iranian decision. In our view, Iran uses Lebanon's Shi'as to protect Bashar Assad: no more no less'.

31. The Syrian regime is accused of committing most of the violence. According to the Syrian Network for Human Rights, the Syrian regime dropped around 13,000 barrel bombs in 2016 alone. See <http://sn4hr.org/blog/2017/01/09/30900/> (last accessed 18 December 2017). See also the Human Rights Watch 2017 report at <https://www.hrw.org/world-report/2017/country-chapters/syria> (last accessed 20 June 2018).
32. For the video, see <https://www.alhurra.com/a/khatib-asks-nasrallah-to-pull-party-members-out-of-syria/222648.html> (last accessed 24 October 2017).
33. On Qassem Suleimani's regional role, see Filkins 2013.
34. Available at <https://www.youtube.com/watch?v=2NmLhAzRj8o> (last accessed 12 December 2017). See also <https://www.foreignaffairs.com/articles/2016-03-31/houthi-hezbollah> (last accessed 20 June 2018).

Conclusion

Socialisation and Hezbollah

Going through this book, you would have noticed that Hezbollah has come a long way. It developed from a loose, scattered organisation that was searching for space in Lebanon's overcrowded political landscape to become the Middle East's most powerful armed political movement. At 36, it might still be young, at least compared to its ageing Lebanese counterparts. In its 36-year journey, Hezbollah has gone through various phases, a process I chose to call socialisation. Or, to be more precise, purposeful socialisation: the participation of political actors in a society with the aim of integrating in, preserving or reforming existing power structures. I demonstrated that Hezbollah is a product of an amalgam of socio-political conditions: a war-torn and externally penetrated Lebanon; an aggrieved and politically ambitious Shi'a community; a humiliating Israeli invasion of Beirut; a revolutionary set of ideals; an Islamic Revolution that offered hope to young Shi'a-Lebanese men that hoped to be the party of God.

But I also showed that Hezbollah hoped to remake the context that produced it. Carrying a set of ideals and strategic goals that distinguished it as the *Islamic Revolution in Lebanon*, Hezbollah embarked on a journey to reconfigure Lebanon's and the region's politics. It made itself known to the world in the Open Letter in 1985, which I argued continues to be the blueprint of Hezbollah's religio-political doctrine and strategic goals. Hezbollah then socialised in a society which was politically hesitant to accommodate it. Socialisation, I also proposed, involves participants' exposure to and interaction with existing political actors, institutions and social norms. Through careful religio-political mobilisation, external patronage and lots of blood,

Hezbollah carved for itself a space in Lebanon of the tumultuous 1980s. Hezbollah's embryonic phase in the 1980s, I have found, offers the pattern for its long-term socialisation: the armed political movement's constant attempts to overcome socio-political constraints and to capitalise on emerging opportunities to realise its religio-political goals. Hezbollah, I found, was neither attempting to establish an Islamic state in Lebanon; nor, and more importantly, was it able to do so. Hezbollah was struggling to create the conducive political conditions to realise another goal: war-making with Israel and the West in Lebanon and the region.

Hezbollah, this book has found, is in many ways a product of war-making: it makes war, and war makes it what it is and what it will become. War-making with a powerful state, Israel, has shaped Hezbollah's socialisation process, in both Lebanon and the region, transforming it into one of the most vigilant, disciplined, politically sophisticated and military powerful organisations in the world. Rivalry with Israel has transformed Hezbollah into a state-like organisation, albeit one that cannot gain recognition due to its location in another recognised state – Lebanon. To understand Hezbollah's war-making with Israel, one can tweak Imam Ali's saying (which many Muslims reiterate) on friendship, 'Tell me who you befriend, I tell you who you are' into 'Tell me who you fight, I tell you who you are'.

But I have also found that understanding Hezbollah, its identity and goal requires a closer look at the movement's religio-political doctrine: the set of beliefs that make and motivate Hezbollah. These I argued are not only instruments that Hezbollah utilises, they are at the heart of Hezbollah's being. Religio-political doctrine offers the frame for Hezbollah's strategic goals; the material to mobilise, recruit and indoctrinate fighters and members; and the ideals to establish a socio-political base – the Resistance Society. I have shown that religio-political doctrine forms the cement that keeps Hezbollah intact, disciplined, committed and, ultimately, hopeful; in Hezbollah's mind, jihad against evil generates either *shahadah* or victory! A win–win situation! Religio-political doctrine is at the bulwark of Hezbollah's war-making efforts.

Socialising in Lebanese politics in times of war and peace exposed Hezbollah to Lebanese formal and informal norms and to a complex *nizam siyasi* (political order), one that has shaped and disciplined the armed political movement. In the 1990s, the *Islamic Resistance in Lebanon* exploited available opportunities – Syrian political control and relative political stability – to continue its armed resistance and to widen its socio-political support. Quietly, it buttressed and expanded its socio-political base by a careful diffusion of religio-political doctrine – an Islamisation from below – the promotion of the culture of resistance, and the provision of social welfare. The Islamist movement re-presented its political image; it adopted Lebanese norms of coexistence, equal representation, consociationalism and the Republic's flag. Hezbollah's survival in several wars – 1993 and 1996 – and Israel's withdrawal in 2000, the first of its kind, I found, reinforced Hezbollah's religio-political doctrine and political orientation, earning the party unprecedented respect in Lebanon and the Arab world.

But I also suggested that socialisation, despite an actor's best intentions, leads to unintended outcomes that shape and affect the participants' worldviews, reputation and political behaviour. For a movement that once (wrongly) believed that it was 'above politics' – religiously committed and too focused on war-making with Israel to be embroiled in petty and corrupt politics – Hezbollah's socialisation in Lebanon and the region must have formed a shock to the party's understanding of itself and its mission. It is ironic for Hezbollah, which believes in Islamic unity, to have entered into a bloody conflict with its Shi'a brothers in Amal; then Syria, with which it shared political goals; and then Lebanese rivals against whom it promised not to raise arms. But Hezbollah was seeking survival and attempting to realise its goals within orders not of its own choosing, and ones that have brought it to the heart of Lebanese politics, both shaping and being shaped by them.

Gradually, Hezbollah began to conform to the dictates of what I constructed in this book as the anarchical orders of Lebanon and the region. Whilst its revolutionary ideals continued to enlighten the movement, its behaviour was gradually resembling the enemies it fights against. Hezbollah's socialisation in the divided society has offered, as I have shown, both a sanctuary and a springboard for the Islamist movement. This socialisation has both enabled and interlocked Hezbollah. The strategic necessity of keeping Lebanon stable, to minimise the armed political movement's vulnerability towards Israel, led Hezbollah to buttress its communal power, deepening the sectarian divide which the movement initially 'abhorred'. Moreover, to avoid risking crucial political alliances that reproduce stability and offer legitimacy to the armed movement, Hezbollah has turned a blind eye towards sectarian apportionment and corruption. Although itself a product and victim of state weakness, Hezbollah with time became another Lebanese political faction whose actions perpetrated state weakness.

Likewise, to thwart threats and to capitalise on emerging opportunities, Hezbollah became embroiled in regional politics. Its regional role, you could argue after reading this book, is in tune with the movement's ideals and mission as a transnational movement. But what this book has found is that, despite its revolutionary ideals and goals that seek to reconfigure the international regional order, Hezbollah has with time conformed to the dictates of the system. War-making has required the amassing of material (weapons, training) and ideological (mobilisation, diffusion) power to protect itself and to compete with and deter enemies. This I have found has intellectual origins that are primarily found in the works and deeds of Imam Khomeini and Ayatollah M. H. Fadlallah. But this is equally borne from constant preparation for war and occasional bloody confrontations with Israel – the stuff of war-making. Both have shaped Hezbollah's perception of the international system as a self-help, unforgiving and lawless order. With time, the socio-political and military power Hezbollah amassed required preservation, and consequently the deterrence of perceived threats. The ties it has established with its main regional allies – Iran and the Syrian regime – with time became ones of interdependence, interlocking the actors in a constant quest for survival. Hezbollah justified its military intervention in Syria and interference in Iraq and Yemen (and other Arab countries) as pre-emptive actions to deter terrorists, and to protect and promote its national and/or religio-political goals. It championed the rights and sacrifices of the Yemeni and Bahraini peoples; but remained silent on the sacrifices and rights of the Syrian people. Its critics and enemies, you should not be surprised, began to use the discourse Hezbollah once employed against its perceived oppressors. They accused the armed political movement of occupation, double standards and hypocrisy. I explained and depicted this outcome as one of the tragic ironies of socialisation. In 2009, a veteran Lebanese journalist welcomed Hezbollah to the 'political Lebanese club' (Salman 2015). By 2017, we can welcome Hezbollah to the international political club of states and armed political movements. But regardless, Hezbollah believes all these memberships are political avenues to realise its strategic goals.

Socialising into the Future: Opportunities, Constraints

What does the future hold for Hezbollah? I do not believe that good social science should be in the business of speculating about the future of political actors. But good social science can reflect on the history, context, genesis, motivations and socialisation of political actors to assess how past trajectories can inform a better reading of the present and the future; to understand possible opportunities and limitations for the actors' realisation of goals; and to highlight potential tensions in future trajectories.

In Lebanon, Hezbollah has established itself as the country's most powerful political force, *al-dabit al-amni wa al-siyasi* (the political and security regulator of the system), as some describe the movement. But this generates tensions for the armed political movement. It is not an exaggeration to argue that Hezbollah's power and influence will mean that Lebanon – the state, society and political forces – will have to adapt to Hezbollah, not the other way around. This will place Hezbollah under heavy responsibilities, ones that it has attempted to avoid. Despite its power, Hezbollah's possession of weapons will continue to generate tensions with other forces and raise key, and still unresolved, questions, which Hezbollah will have to answer. Who – the Lebanese government or Hezbollah – will decide how the weapons that Hezbollah has amassed will be used and for what purpose? Will this be shaped by a national defence strategy? Who will define the main parameters of this strategy? (Qassir 2015) Moreover, would Hezbollah, which has regional and religio-political commitments that transcend Lebanon, commit to such a strategy? Hezbollah's intervention in Syria and the region and its persistent discourse on the 'liberation of Jerusalem' indicate that Hezbollah's potential commitment to such a *national* strategy will be unlikely; such a commitment would limit Hezbollah's military capacity and curb its ability to realise its religio-political goals. Or if it does commit, if and when an external threat emerges, Hezbollah will act, with or without, the Lebanese government's blessing. Hezbollah's weapons and armed status is determined not by internal Lebanese considerations, but by geopolitical determinants, of which the Iranian strategy in the Middle East is key. The Islamist movement is not really 'accountable to Lebanon'; its weapons now have a 'regional value' (Pakradouni 2015).

Hezbollah has attempted to reconcile its national and strategic religio-political commitments. But this has not come without its discontents. On the one hand, to gain domestic legitimacy and legal cover for its armed status, Hezbollah has attempted to fuse its armed resistance with the state and society in the formula: 'Army, People, Resistance'. But, on the other hand, this has implicated the Lebanese government and people in Hezbollah's regional agenda and interventions in other countries. Hezbollah's rivals and enemies – be they Saudi Arabia, Israel or the US – have held the Lebanese government responsible for Hezbollah's actions. To limit the costs on the country, Hezbollah has attempted to detach itself from the government, which contradicted its domestic strategy. Will Hezbollah be able to maintain a balance between its domestic and regional commitments? An increasing pressure on Hezbollah will intensify this tension.

Also, would these weapons be used internally? What would stop Hezbollah from employing its military power to extract political concessions? Again, if the past decades offer any hints, then it is very likely that Hezbollah will not use its weapons internally, unless these are threatened. At the moment, and after the 2008 Hezbollah offensive, no political actor has the capability or interest to confront Hezbollah militarily. Hezbollah's rivals, particularly the FM, will resort to political pressure and mobilisation. They will be very cautious not to provoke Hezbollah, not least to avoid pushing the powerful Shi'a movement to a situation where it could seek to alter the political and constitutional order in Lebanon. Hezbollah, which will continue to face external pressure, will not want to confront its rivals. For now.

But this brings us to another related domestic factor: social and economic spheres. Part of Hezbollah's conformism to Lebanon's system involved its silence to corruption and *muhasasah* (allotment of state positions on sectarian and political bases). Hezbollah's strategic goals and commitments to domestic allies have incapacitated the Islamist movement's ability to promote a socio-economic agenda. Alliances with Amal, which is crucial to maintain stability in the Shi'a community, and FPM, which is crucial as a Christian cover for the legitimacy of Hezbollah's armed resistance, have kept Hezbollah silent on the deeply entrenched corruption growing in Lebanon since the end of the war (Leenders 2012; Wakim 1998). Corruption has meant that the Lebanese state has been unable, even twenty-five years after the end of the war, to deliver basic social goods such as electricity, clean water and fair justice, or to collect garbage (Saouli 2015). Disastrous economic policies since 1992 and political paralysis from 2005 to 2016 have generated a colossal debt (US$70 billion, 140 per cent of GDP), an increase in crimes, diffusion of weapons and food scandals, revealing the erosion of state power and ethical social standards. It is no wonder that, as a result of a garbage collection crisis, massive demonstrations erupted in 2015 and informed the Lebanese political class that 'You Stink' (Saouli 2015). Hezbollah, which for long attempted to remain at the peripheries of this class, began to become a target of critics. One critic claimed that as long as you are a supporter of the 'resistance', then you have a 'free rein'. Some point out that some members of the Lebanese Resistance Brigade (see Chapter 3) and Hezbollah have exploited their political and military prowess for economic gain. Others highlight the increasing saliency of and opposition to corruption within Hezbollah.[1] Will Hezbollah be able to maintain a balance between its strategic goals and Lebanon's intensifying social and economic conditions? It is clear that Hezbollah, which has, like its Lebanese peers, secured a loyal socio-political base, whom it offers jobs, security and a doctrine for the afterlife, is avoiding embroilment in any form of economic management. The costs of direct governance would be high and it is unlikely that Hezbollah will be able to advance its plan in the divisive political setting in Lebanon. The enabling conditions for reform are not present, it argues (A. H. Fadlallah 2015). But can the increasing number of *mahrumin* (oppressed) understand these constraints? The rise of socio-economic tensions has even led Hezbollah's close allies to urge the movement to turn an eye to domestic socio-economic affairs.[2]

Having secured, for the medium to long term, a strong position in Lebanon, Hezbollah will continue to use it as a springboard to advance its and Iran's strategy in the region. The divided societies of the region, where significant Shi'a populations exist, such as Iraq, Yemen, Syria, will continue to offer opportunities for Hezbollah and Iran. The Resistance Alliance's much celebrated Tehran–Baghdad–Damascus–Beirut land route, which Iran and its allies have painstakingly drawn in the region, will continue to form a sphere of influence that Hezbollah on one end and Tehran on the other will attempt to preserve. The route will be used to deter or maybe fight Israel in the struggle to liberate Palestine. US President Donald Trump's reckless decision to recognise Jerusalem as Israel's capital might revive the Resistance Alliance's narrative that armed struggle is the only means to liberate Palestine. Nasrallah told an angry demonstration in Dahieh that with the defeat of 'IS' in Syria and Iraq, the alliance can now turn its attention to Palestine.

But the Tehran–Beirut connection might be mired by constraints. Iran's support of armed political movements in each of these countries will face, like Hezbollah in Lebanon, domestic obstacles. In Syria, Iran has a sphere of influence, but this sphere is shared by Russia, which has its own strategies and ones which might not suit the ideals of the Resistance Alliance. To weaken Iran and Hezbollah, Russia might strengthen Assad, who, in dire need to re-establish his power in Syria and to elevate his status in the Resistance Alliance, will welcome Russia's strategy. But Syria is home to other spheres of influence – Turkey, US – which will also constrain Iran's strategy in the country. The battle in and over Syria will be determined by Russian and American understanding or rivalry. In Iraq, the quest to rebuild the country and to increase foreign investment might require strong ties with the US, Saudi Arabia, Turkey, which might weaken Iran's attempts to influence the policy of the country. Attempts to institutionalise the Hashed might dilute Iran's influence on this armed group; in the absence of a threat from IS or al-Qaida-affiliated groups, Ayatollah Sistani might *nationalise* Iraqi foreign policy, away from Iranian strategies.

Last, but not least, is Iran: the spring of Islamic Revolution. The biggest challenge to Hezbollah's strategy and survival remains in Iran. As long as the Islamic Republic exists and is able to project power externally, Hezbollah will benefit. However, if the Islamic Republic is under threat, if the Islamist regime falls – say due to cracks in the regime, a popular rebellion or external military attack – Hezbollah's regional role will contract.

These areas will continue to be spheres of contestations between Iran and its rivals in the Middle East, offering opportunities but also limitations for Hezbollah's regional role. These opportunities/threats will determine Hezbollah's war-making with Israel. War-making with Israel will continue to form the cornerstone of Hezbollah's conduct in Lebanon and the region, not least because of the enmity and the geographical proximity that ties the two actors. Developments in the region – namely, the contraction or expansion of Iranian influence – will determine the possibilities of another war between Israel and Hezbollah. Although both actors prefer not to engage in a new round of violence, and although the balance of power curbs such a possibility, both parties hope that one day they will eradicate their enemy. The next war, if it is to happen, might be long, bloody and regional.

Finally, if the findings of this book are accurate, then they demonstrate that Hezbollah does not mask its religio-political doctrine, for without it Hezbollah is stripped of any identity or meaning. Religio-political doctrine is the framework that guides Hezbollah's behaviour and the one that identifies its ideals and motivations. On the other hand, Hezbollah's behaviour does not simply mirror political developments. Hezbollah's long-term actvity, as this book has repeatedly claimed, reveals that the Islamist movement seeks to overcome socio-political constraints, which sometimes require pragmatism; but it also capitalises on emerging opportunities to advance and realise its goals. The book found that Hezbollah is particularly apt at transforming threats into opportunities, whether in Lebanon or the region. The ebb and flow of Middle East geopolitics will determine Hezbollah's capacity to expand or contract its influence in the region and Lebanon. But, regardless of the uncertainties of the regional political tide, Hezbollah's last, and only, sanctuary will remain Lebanon.

A Last Word on Theory

Finally, what are the main theoretical and scholarly implications of this study? This study has drawn on the rich intellectual tradition of Historical Sociology (HS). HS locates actors (such as Hezbollah) within their context; it attempts to understand the genesis of actors, their motivations and the constraints and opportunities they face as they try to realise their goals. It takes history seriously to show how actors socialise over time in contexts not of their own choosing. This socialisation places actors in *relation* to others, events and goals. It reveals both the intended goals of actors and the unintended outcomes they may generate.

HS frees the researcher from some dichotomies that have impeded the systematic study of social and political actors, events and contexts – including those of Hezbollah. These dichotomies include 'identity versus interest', 'ideology versus context', 'domestic versus international', 'actor versus structure' or the common dichotomy in the study of Hezbollah (and other Islamist groups), 'violence versus politics'. This book showed that the study of socialisation offers an important research framework to interrogate how these factors – not dichotomies – *configure* to explain trajectories of political actors. The empirical analysis of the study revealed how, first, by analytically isolating these factors (religio-political doctrine (ideals), actor (Hezbollah), anarchical orders (contexts)) and, second, by connecting them, we are able to understand and explain the trajectory of political actors – in this case Hezbollah.

HS offers a rewarding and enriching framework for the examination of the causes and consequences of socialisation of political actors, like Hezbollah. Hezbollah, Lebanon and the Middle East, on the other hand, offer a fertile ground for the construction, development or refutation of theory. Historical Sociology may be the path for a fruitful socialisation of 'Middle East Studies' in the Social Sciences.

Notes

1. See <http://janoubia.com/2017/10/04/%D8%A8%D9%8A%D8%A7%D9%86-%D8%A8%D8%A5%D8%B3%D9%85-%D8%B4%D9%87%D8%AF%D8%A7%D8%A1-%D8%A7%D9%84%D8%AF%D9%81%D8%A7%D8%B9-%D8%A7%D9%84%D9%85%D9%82%D8%AF%D8%B3-%D9%8A%D8%B7%D8%A7%D9%84%D8%A8/> (last accessed 26 March 2018).
2. See Ibrahim al-Amin, 'Has the time not come to re-evaluate the domestic policy?', <https://al-akhbar.com/Politics/237745> (last accessed 25 March 2018).

Appendix

The Imamate line of succession according to Shi'a-Islam

Names of Twelve Shi'a Imams	Year (in AD)
Ali	600–661
Hassan	625–669
Hussein	626–680
Ali Zayn al-Abidin	659–714
Muhammad al-Baqir	676–731
Ja'far al-Sadiq	702–765
Musa al-Kazim	745–799
Ali al-Rida	765–818
Muhammad al-Jawad	811–835
Ali al-Hadi	828–868
Imam Hassan al-Askari	846–874
Imam Muhammad al-Mahdi	869–living in the occultation

Sources and Bibliography

List of Interviewees

Aballan, Hassan (2015), Amal Movement
Amin, Ali (2013), journalist
Atrissi, Talal, Dr (2013), academic
Costanian, Albert (2015), Phalange Party
Fadlallah, Abd al-Halim, Dr (2015), Hezbollah member and head of its Institute for Consultative Studies
Fadlallah, Ali Sayyid (2015), religious scholar, and son of Ayatollah M. H. Fadlallah
Fatfat, Ahmad, Dr (2015), Future Movement and MP
Hanna, Elias, General (2015), former army general and academic
Jaradi, Shafik, Sheikh (2015), head of Hezbollah's Ma'arif Institute for Religious and Philosophical Studies
Kanso, Wajeeh, Dr (2013), writer and academic
Mouzahem, Haytham, Dr (2013), writer and academic
Pakradouni, Karim (2015), politician and writer
Qassir, Qassem (2015), writer on Islamic movements
Qatisha, Wehbe (2015), Lebanese Forces Party
Raful, Pierre (2015), Free Patriotic Movement
Salman, Talal (2015), journalist and owner of the former *As-Safir*
al-Sayed, Radwan, Dr (2013), Future Movement and academic

Consulted Sample of Hezbollah Fighters' Testaments

The sample is drawn from the Al-Manar's programme *Ahya'a 'inda Rabihim* (Alive with God) and from testaments posted via YouTube. The programme episodes can be found via Al-Manar's website: <http://mail.almanar.com.lb/programs/edarhive.php?pid=3019&page=3> (last accessed 20 June 2018).

Khalid Ali Abdallah
Ali Muhammad Achmar
Hassan Amad Akil
Hassan Ahmad A'lawiya
Asaad Muhammad al-Atat
Rani Adnan Bazi
Mohammad Ja'far Dagher
Qassem Ezzeddine
Hussein Mustafa al-Gouni
Hussam Mohammad Ha'lal
Fares Hassan Hawi
Has'san Muhammad Hijazi
Na'ame Muhammad Hseiki
Yussuf Abd al-Rahim al-Jawhari
Ali Jammal Jeshi
Ibrahim Khalil Khalaf
Husam Abd al-Hadi al-Mussawi
Hadi Hassan Nasrallah
Muhammad Ali Nasreddine
Hassan Ahmad Nasser
Khodor Obeid
Adnan Musa Rida
Tahseen Ali Sharifa
Ahmad Ibrahim al-Sharqawi
Hussein Mohammad Shbeib
Muhammad Ahmad Srur
Ali Ahmad Abu Ta'am
Haidar Ali Tarhini
Muhammad Ali Wehbe
Al-Mahdi Mohammad Hussein Yaghi
Has'san Muhammad Zahreddine
Mustafa Ali Zalzali
Tayseer Muhammad Zeineddine

Primary and Secondary Bibliography

Aballan, Hassan (2015), interview with the author.

Abboud, Samer N., and Benjamin J. Muller (2012), *Rethinking Hizballah*, Farnham: Ashgate.

Abboud, Samer N., and Benjamin J. Muller (2013), 'Geopolitics, Insecurity and Neocolonial Exceptionalism: A Critical Appraisal of the UN Special Tribunal for Lebanon', *Security Dialogue* 44 (5–6):467–84.

Abisaab, Rula Jurdi (2006), 'The Cleric as Organic Intellectual: Revolutionary Shi'ism in the Lebanese Hawzas', in H. E. Chehabi (ed.), *Distant Relations: Iran and Lebanon in the Last 500 Years*, London: I. B. Tauris, pp. 231–58.

Abisaab, Rula Jurdi (2014), *The Shi'ites of Lebanon: Modernism, Communism, and Hizbullah's Islamists*, Syracuse: Syracuse University Press.

Aboudi, Sami, and Omar Fahmy (2017), 'Powerful Saudi Prince Sees No Chance for Dialogue with Iran', *Reuters*, 2 May 2017, <http://www.reuters.com/article/us-saudi-prince-iran-idUSKBN17Y1FK> (last accessed 21 June 2018).

Abrams, Philip (1982), *Historical Sociology*, London: Open Books.

Abrantes, Pedro (2013), 'Opening the Black Box of Socialization: Emotions, Practices and (Biographical) Identities', *International Journal of Sociology and Anthropology* 5 (9):391–401.

Abu-Rabi, Ibrahim M. (1995), *Intellectual Origins of Islamic Resurgence in the Modern Arab World*, Albany: State University of New York Press.

Abu Rida, Hussein (2012), *al-Tarbiyah al-hizbiyyah al-Islamiyyah: Hizbullah namuzajan* [Islamic partisan education: Hezbollah as example], Beirut: Dar Al-Ameer.

Achcar, Gilbert, and Michel Warschawski (2007), *The 33-Day War: Israel's War on Hezbollah in Lebanon and its Consequences*, Boulder, CO: Paradigm Publishers.

Ahzab Lubnan: Hizb Allah [Parties of Lebanon: Hezbollah] (2003), Beirut: Sabbah Media Corporation.

Alagha, Joseph Elie (2006), *The Shifts in Hizbullah's Ideology: Religious Ideology, Political Ideology, and Political Program*, Amsterdam: Amsterdam University Press.

Alagha, Joseph Elie (2010), 'Wilayat Al-Faqih and Hizbullah's Relations with Iran', *Journal of Arabic and Islamic Studies* 10 (1):24–44.

Alagha, Joseph Elie (2011), *Hizbullah's Documents: From the 1985 Open Letter to the 2009 Manifesto*, Amsterdam: Amsterdam University Press.

Al-Akhbar (2008), '7 May 2008: Smaller than a War and Larger than a Popular Protest', 8 May 2008, <http://www.al-akhbar.com/node/117958> (last accessed 21 June 2018).

Al-Akhbar (2014), 'Bayna Tamuzayn [Between two Julys]', 14 August 2014.

Al-Akhbar (2017), newspaper, 18 August 2017.

Alderson, Kai (2001), 'Making Sense of State Socialization', *Review of International Studies* 27 (3):415–33.

Alexander, Jeffrey C. (2006), 'Cultural Pragmatics: Social Performance between Ritual and Strategy', in Jeffrey C. Alexander, Bernhard Giesen and Jason L. Mast (eds), *Social Performance: Symbolic Action, Cultural Pragmatics, and Ritual*, Cambridge: Cambridge University Press, pp. 29–90.

Allam, Abeer (2013), 'Sunni Clerics in Accord over Hizbollah in Syria', *Financial Times*, 6 June 2013, <http://www.ft.com/cms/s/0/2f77648e-cec7-11e2-8e16-00144feab7de.html#axzz3u83xrxtj> (last accessed 21 June 2018).

Allana, Alia (2017), 'How War Created the Cholera Epidemic in Yemen', *The New York Times*, 12 November 2017, <https://www.nytimes.com/2017/11/12/opinion/cholera-war-yemen.html> (last accessed 21 June 2018).

Al-Manar Television (2014), Ibrahim Amin al-Sayyid speech, 31 October 2014.

Al-Manar Television (2016), Nasrallah interview, 5 March 2016.

Al-Mayadeen Television (2012), Nasrallah interview, September 2012.

Almuhager, Gaafar (1992), *al-Ta'asis li al-tarikh al-Shi'a fi Lubnan wa Suriya* [Foundations to the history of Shi'as in Lebanon and Syria], Beirut: Dar Al Malak.

Almuhager, Gaafar (1994), *al-Ta'sis li tarikh al-Shi'a (2): sitat fuqaha' abtal* [Foundation of Shi'a history (2): six heroes and jurisprudents], Beirut: Lebanese Higher Islamic Shi'a Council.

al-Quds al-Arabi (2016), 'Hizb Allah: min harakat muqawamah ila jaysh ihtilal [Hezbollah: from a resistance movement to an occupying army]', *Al-Quds Newspaper*, 16 November 2016, <http://www.alquds.co.uk/?p=631485> (last accessed 21 June 2018).

al-Sayed, Radwan (2013), interview with the author.

al-Sayyid, Ibrahim Amin (2008), *Ala difaf al-furat*, Beirut: Dar Al maaref Alhikmiah.

Amin, Ali (2013), interview with the author.

Amin, Ibrahim (2014), 'An ya'ish al-yaqin [To live certainty]', *Al-Akhbar*, 14 August 2014.

Ammer, Abida (2017), 'The Aborted Revolution: Has Assad's Moment of Announcing Victory Arrived? ', <http://midan.aljazeera.net/reality/politics/2017/12/13/الثورة-المنتكسة-هل-اقتربت-لحظة-إعلان-انتصار-الأسد> (last accessed 21 June 2018).

An-Nahar (2016), 'Arab Satellite Drops Hezbollah's Al Manar TV', *An-Nahar*, 6 April 2016, <http://en.annahar.com/article/348102-hezbollahs-al-manar-goes-off-air-in-lebair-in-lebanon-after-arab-satellite-drops> (last accessed 21 June 2018).

'Arab Neighbours Thinking Ahead' (2006), *The Economist*, 24 August 2006, <http://www.economist.com/node/7843340> (last accessed 21 June 2018).

Arab News (2017), 'Saudi Crown Prince Says Houthis "Must Not Become Another Hezbollah"', *Arab News*, 26 October 2017, <http://www.arabnews.com/node/1183801/saudi-arabia> (last accessed 21 June 2018).

Aran, Amnon (2012), 'Containment and Territorial Transnational Actors: Israel, Hezbollah and Hamas', *International Affairs* 88 (4):835–55.

As-Safir (2006a), newspaper, 8 February 2006.

As-Safir (2006b), newspaper, 3 March 2006.

Atrissi, Talal (2012), 'Ashura': ihya' al-taghyir [Ashura: reviving change]', in *al-Shi'a fi Lubnan: min al-tahmish ila al-musharakah al-fi'liyyah* [Shi'as of Lebanon: from marginalisation to active participation], Beirut: Dar Al maaref Alhikmiah, pp. 331–61.

Atrissi, Talal (2013), interview with the author.

Azani, Eitan (2011), *Hezbollah: The Story of the Party of God: From Revolution to Institutionalization*, 2nd reprint edition, Basingstoke: Palgrave Macmillan.

Badran, Tony (2009), 'Hezbollah's Agenda in Lebanon', *Current Trends in Islamist Ideology* 8:52–67.

Balkiz, Abdel Ilah (2006), *Hizb Allah min al-tahrir ila al-radi (1982–2006)* [Hezbollah: from liberation to deterrence (1982–2006)], Beirut: Centre for Arab Unity Studies.

Baradat, Leon P. (1997), *Political Ideologies: Their Origins and Impact*, 6th edition, Toronto: Prentice-Hall International, Inc.

Barnett, Michael N. (1998), *Dialogues in Arab Politics: Negotiations in Regional Order*, New York: Columbia University Press.

Barnett, Michael N., and Jack S. Levy (1991), 'Domestic Sources of Alliances and Alignments: The Case of Egypt, 1962–73', *International Organization* 45 (3):369–95.

Bazzi, Mohamad (2015), 'Lebanon and the Start of Iran and Saudi Arabia's Proxy War', *The New Yorker*, 26 May 2015, <https://www.newyorker.com/news/news-desk/lebanon-and-the-start-of-iran-and-saudi-arabias-proxy-war> (last accessed 21 June 2018).

Beaumont, Peter (2017), 'Israeli Jets Attack Anti-Aircraft Battery in Syria in Retaliatory Strike', *The Guardian*, 16 October 2017, <http://www.theguardian.com/world/2017/oct/16/israeli-jets-attack-anti-aircraft-battery-in-syria-in-retaliatory-strike> (last accessed 21 June 2018).

Berti, Benedetta (2013), *Armed Political Organizations: From Conflict to Integration*, Baltimore: Johns Hopkins University Press.

Betts, Richard K. (2000), 'Is Strategy an Illusion?' *International Security* 25 (2):5–50.

Black, Ian (2016), 'Report on Syria Conflict Finds 11.5% of Population Killed or Injured', *The Guardian*, 11 February 2016, <http://www.theguardian.com/world/2016/feb/11/report-on-syria-conflict-finds-115-of-population-killed-or-injured> (last accessed 21 June 2018).

Booth, Ken, and Nicholas Wheeler (2007), *Security Dilemma: Fear, Cooperation, and Trust in World Politics*, 1st edition, New York: Palgrave Macmillan.

Bregman, Ahron (2016), *Israel's Wars: A History Since 1947*, 4th edition, New York: Routledge.

Brewer, Marilynn B. (1991), 'The Social Self: On Being the Same and Different at the Same Time', *Personality and Social Psychology Bulletin* 17 (5):475–82.

Brown, Leon Carl (1984), *International Politics and the Middle East: Old Rules, Dangerous Game*, Princeton: Princeton University Press.

Brynen, Rex (1990), *Sanctuary and Survival: The PLO in Lebanon*, Boulder, CO: Westview Press Inc.

Bull, Hedley (2012), *The Anarchical Society: A Study of Order in World Politics*, 4th edition, Basingstoke: Palgrave Macmillan.

Cammett, Melani (2014), *Compassionate Communalism: Welfare and Sectarianism in Lebanon*, Ithaca: Cornell University Press.

Chehabi, H. E. (2006a), 'The Anti-Shah Opposition and Lebanon', in H. E. Chehabi (ed.), *Distant Relations: Iran and Lebanon in the Last 500 Years*, Oxford: The Centre for Lebanese Studies, pp. 180–98.

Chehabi, H. E. (2006b), 'Iran and Lebanon in the Revolutionary Decade', in H. E. Chehabi (ed.), *Distant Relations: Iran and Lebanon in the Last 500 Years*, Oxford: The Centre for Lebanese Studies, pp. 201–30.

Chulov, Martin (2013), 'Syrian Town of Qusair Falls to Hezbollah in Breakthrough for Assad', *The Guardian*, 5 June 2013, <http://www.theguardian.com/world/2013/jun/05/syria-army-seizes-qusair> (last accessed 21 June 2018).

Cole, Juan R. I. (ed.) (2009), *Shi'ism and Social Protest*, New Haven: Yale University Press.

Costanian, Albert (2015), interview with the author.

Dabashi, Hamid (2012), *Shi'ism: A Religion of Protest*, reprint edition, Cambridge, MA: Harvard University Press.

Darwich, May (2016), 'Ideational and Material Forces in Threat Perception: The Divergent Cases of Syria and Saudi Arabia during the Iran–Iraq War (1980–1988)', *Journal of Global Security Studies* 1 (2):142–56.

DeVore, Marc R. (2012), 'Exploring the Iran-Hezbollah Relationship: A Case Study of How State Sponsorship Affects Terrorist Group Decision-Making', *Perspectives on Terrorism* 6 (4–5):85–107.

DeVore, Marc R., and Armin B. Stähli (2015), 'Explaining Hezbollah's Effectiveness: Internal and External Determinants of the Rise of Violent Non-State Actors', *Terrorism and Political Violence* 27 (2):331–57.

Dionigi, Filippo (2014), *Hezbollah, Islamist Politics, and International Society*, New York: Palgrave Macmillan

Ehteshami, Anoushiravan (2014), 'The Foreign Policy of Iran', in Raymond Hinnebusch and Anoushiravan Ehteshami (eds), *The Foreign Policies of Middle East States*, 2nd edition, Boulder, CO: Lynne Rienner Publishers, pp. 261–88.

Ehteshami, Anoushiravan, and Raymond A. Hinnebusch (2014), *Syria and Iran: Middle Powers in a Penetrated Regional System*, New York: Routledge.

Elias, Norbert (1984), *What is Sociology?*, New York: Columbia University Press.

Elias, Norbert (2000), *The Civilizing Process*, 2nd edition, Oxford: Wiley-Blackwell.

Elias, Norbert (2001), *Society of Individuals*, ed. Michael Schroter, tr. Edmund Jephtcott, New York: Continuum.

El-Khazen, Farid (1997), *The Breakdown of the State in Lebanon*, London: I. B. Tauris.

Elsässer, Sebastian (2007), 'Between Ideology and Pragmatism: Fathī Yakan's Theory of Islamic Activism', *Die Welt Des Islams* 47 (3):376–402.

Engel, Eliot (2003), 'H.R.1828 - 108th Congress (2003-2004): Syria Accountability and Lebanese Sovereignty Restoration Act of 2003', 12 December 2003, <https://www.congress.gov/bill/108th-congress/house-bill/1828> (last accessed 21 June 2018).

Erskine, Toni, and Ned Lebow (eds) (2012), *Tragedy and International Relations*, Basingstoke: Palgrave Macmillan.

Fadlallah, Abd al-Halim (2015), interview with the author.

Fadlallah, Ali (2015), interview with the author.

Fadlallah, Hassan (1994), *al-Khiyar al-akhar: Hizb Allah, al-sirah al-dhatiyyah wa al-mawqif* [The alternative option: Hezbollah, biography and stand], Beirut: Dar Alhadi.

Fadlallah, Hassan (2009), *Harb al-iradat* [The war of wills], Beirut: Dar Alhadi.

Fadlallah, Hassan (2015), *Hizb Allah wa al-dawlah fi Lubnan: al-ru'yah w al-massar* [Hezbollah and the state in Lebanon: vision and path], Beirut: All Prints Distributors & Publishers s.a.l.

Fadlallah, Mohammad Hussein (2003), *al-Islam wa mantiq al-quwwah* [Islam and the logic of power], Beirut: Dar Al Malak.

Fadlallah, Mohammad Hussein (2004), *Min ajl al-Islam* [For Islam], Beirut: Dar Al Malak.

Fakhoury, Tamirace (2015), 'Lebanon's Perilous Balancing Act', *Current History* 114 (776):349–54.

Farhi, Farideh (2017), 'Iranian Power Projection Strategy and Goals', Middle East Program, Washington, DC: Center for Strategic and International Studies, <https://www.csis.org/analysis/iranian-power-projection-strategy-and-goals> (last accessed 21 June 2018).

Fatfat, Ahmad (2015), interview with the author.

Fawn, Rick, and Raymond A. Hinnebusch, (eds) (2006), *The Iraq War: Causes and Consequences*, Boulder, CO: Lynne Rienner Publishers.

Filkins, Dexter (2013), 'The Shadow Commander', *The New Yorker*, 23 September 2013, <https://www.newyorker.com/magazine/2013/09/30/the-shadow-commander> (last accessed 21 June 2018).

Fillieule, Olivier (2013), 'Political Socialization and Social Movements', in David Snow, Donatella della Porta, Bert Klandermans, and Doug McAdam (eds),

The Wiley-Blackwell Encyclopedia of Social and Political Movements, Oxford: Blackwell, pp. 968–74.

Finnemore, Martha, and Kathryn Sikkink (1998), 'International Norm Dynamics and Political Change', *International Organization* 52 (4):887–917.

Fisk, Robert (2001), *Pity the Nation: Lebanon at War*, updated edition, Oxford: Oxford University Press.

Fletcher, Jonathan (1997), *Violence and Civilization: An Introduction to the Work of Norbert Elias*, Cambridge: Polity.

Flockhart, Trine (2006), '"Complex Socialization": A Framework for the Study of State Socialization', *European Journal of International Relations* 12 (1): 89–118.

Follath, Erich (2009), 'Breakthrough in Tribunal Investigation: New Evidence Points to Hezbollah in Hariri Murder', *Spiegel Online*, 23 May 2009, <http://www.spiegel.de/international/world/breakthrough-in-tribunal-investigation-new-evidence-points-to-hezbollah-in-hariri-murder-a-626412.html> (last accessed 21 June 2018).

FutureTV (2015), *Inter-Views* – حلقة خاصة مع النائب عقاب صقر, <https://www.youtube.com/watch?v=72lNsxeOuW0> (last accessed 21 June 2018).

Gabrielsen, Iver (2014), 'The Evolution of Hezbollah's Strategy and Military Performance, 1982–2006', *Small Wars & Insurgencies* 25 (2):257–83.

Gerth, Hans, and C. Wright Mills (eds) (1974), *From Max Weber: Essays in Sociology*, London: Routledge & Kegan Paul Ltd.

Gleis, Joshua L., and Benedetta Berti (2012), *Hezbollah and Hamas: A Comparative Study*, Baltimore: Johns Hopkins University Press.

Goldenberg, Suzanne Goldenberg (2000), 'Chaos and Humiliation as Israel Pulls out of Lebanon', *The Guardian*, 24 May 2000, <https://www.theguardian.com/world/2000/may/24/israelandthepalestinians.lebanon> (last accessed 21 June 2018).

Goodarzi, Jubin M. (2009), *Syria and Iran: Diplomatic Alliance and Power Politics in the Middle East*, London: I. B. Tauris.

Haddad, Fanar (2016), 'Shia-Centric State Building and Sunni Rejection in Post-2003 Iraq', Carnegie Endowment for International Peace, 7 January 2016, <http://carnegieendowment.org/2016/01/07/shia-centric-state-building-and-sunni-rejection-in-post-2003-iraq-pub-62408> (last accessed 21 June 2018).

Halliday, Fred (2011), *The Middle East in International Relations: Power, Politics and Ideology*, Cambridge: Cambridge University Press.

Hamade, Nidal (2014), *Ma'rakat Qadesh al-thalithah: asrar harb al-Qusayr* [The third battle of Qadesh: secrets of the Qusayr battle], Paris: Nidal Hamade Printing and Publishing.

Hamzeh, Ahmad Nizar (1993), 'Lebanon's Hizbullah: From Islamic Revolution to Parliamentary Accommodation', *Third World Quarterly* 14 (2):321–37.

Hamzeh, Ahmad Nizar (2004), *In the Path of Hizbullah*, Syracuse: Syracuse University Press.

Harb, Mona, and Reinoud Leenders (2005), 'Know Thy Enemy: Hizbullah, "Terrorism" and the Politics of Perception', *Third World Quarterly* 26 (1): 173–97.

Harik, Judith Palmer (2005), *Hezbollah: The Changing Face of Terrorism*, London: I. B. Tauris.

Hassan, Abed (2006), *Iqtarab al-zuhur* [The appearance is approximating], Beirut: Dar Al Mahaja Al Baydaa.

'Hassan Nasrallah, 25 May 2013' (n.d.), <https://www.youtube.com/watch?v=SDk0q5lKmn4> (last accessed 15 December 2015).

'Hassan Nasrallah, Speech 25 July 2015' (n.d.), <http://www.almanar.com.lb/adetails.php?eid=546203&frid=61&cid=61&fromval=1&seccatid=191> (last accessed 15 December 2015).

Hinnebusch, Raymond (2015), *The International Politics of the Middle East*, Manchester: Manchester University Press.

Hinnebusch, Raymond (ed.) (2017), *After the Arab Uprisings: Between Democratization, Counter-Revolution and State Failure*, Oxford: Routledge.

Hinnebusch, Raymond, and Omar Imady (eds) (2018), *The Syrian Uprising: Domestic Origins and Early Trajectories*, Oxford: Routledge.

Hizb Allah: al-wathiqah al-siyasiyyah [Hezbollah: political document] (2009), Beirut: Hezbollah Media Relations.

Ibn Abi Talib, Ali (2003), *Nahj al-balaghah* [The path/approach of eloquence], ed. Muhammad Abdo, 4 vols, Beirut: Dar Al-Balagha.

International Crisis Group (2012), 'A Precarious Balancing Act: Lebanon and the Syrian Conflict', Brussels.

'Iran Opposes any Foreign Intervention in Syria' (2012), The Office of the Supreme Leader, 30 March 2012, <http://www.leader.ir/en/content/9293/Iran-opposes-any-foreign-intervention-in-Syria> (last accessed 21 June 2018).

Jabar, Faleh A. (2003), *The Shi'ite Movement in Iraq*, London: Saqi Books.

Jaber, Hala (1997), *Hezbollah: Born with a Vengeance*, New York: Columbia University Press.

Jaradi, Shafik (2014), *Wa'i al-muqawamah wa qiyamiha* [The consciousness of the resistance and its values], Beirut: Dar Al maaref Alhikmiah.

Jaradi, Shafik (2015), interview with the author.

Kalyvas, Stathis N. (2000), 'Commitment Problems in Emerging Democracies: The Case of Religious Parties', *Comparative Politics* 32 (4):379–98.

Kanso, Wajeeh (2013), interview with the author.

Khalaf, Samir (2004), *Civil and Uncivil Violence in Lebanon: A History of the Internationalization of Communal Conflict*, New York: Columbia University Press.

Khashan, Hilal (2013), 'Hezbollah's Plans for Lebanon', *Middle East Quarterly* 20 (3), <http://www.meforum.org/3534/hezbollah-lebanon?keepThis=true&TB_iframe=true&height=450&width=600&caption=Middle+East+Forum+%3A%3A+Writings> (last accessed 21 June 2018).

Khatib, Lina (2011), 'Hizbullah's Political Strategy', *Survival* 53 (2):61–76.

Khomeini, Imam (n.d.), *Governance of the Jurist (Velayat-e Faqeeh): Islamic Government*, tr. Hamid Algar, Tehran: The Institute for the Compilation and Publication of Imam Khomeini's Works.

Khoury, Jack, and Reuters (2017), 'Nasrallah Admits: Hezbollah Smuggled Advanced Arms into Gaza', *Haaretz*, 20 November 2017, <https://www.haaretz.com/middle-east-news/nasrallah-admits-hezbollah-smuggled-advanced-arms-into-gaza-1.5467043> (last accessed 21 June 2018).

Kilo, Michel (2016), 'To Nasrallah: You Turned Yourself into an Enemy of the Syrian People', *The New Arab*, 23 June 2016, <https://www.alaraby.co.uk/opinion/2016/6/22/%D8%B1%D8%B3%D8%A7%D9%84%D8%A9-%D8%A5%D9%84%D9%89-%D8%AD%D8%B3%D9%86-%D9%86%D8%B5%D8%B1-%D8%A7%D9%84%D9%84%D9%87-1> (last accessed 21 June 2018).

Klein, Olivier, Russell Spears, and Stephen Reicher (2007), 'Social Identity Performance: Extending the Strategic Side of SIDE', *Personality and Social Psychology Review: An Official Journal of the Society for Personality and Social Psychology, Inc* 11 (1):28–45.

Knio, Karim (2013), 'Structure, Agency and Hezbollah: A Morphogenetic View', *Third World Quarterly* 34 (5):856–72.

Kostagiannis, Konstantinos (2014), 'Hans Morgenthau and the Tragedy of the Nation-State', *The International History Review* 36 (3):513–29.

Kourani, Mohammad (2012), 'Harakat al-muqawamah 'ind Shi'a fi Jabal Lubnan [Shi'a Resistance Movements in Mount Lebanon]', in *al-Shi'a fi Lubnan:*

min al-Tahmish ila al-musharakah al-fi'liyyah [Shi'as of Lebanon: From Marginalisation to Active Participation], Beirut: Dar Al maaref Alhikmiah, pp. 97–146.

Kramer, Martin (1990), 'The Moral Logic of Hizballah', in Walter Reich (ed.), *Origins of Terrorism: Psychologies, Ideologies, Theologies, States of Mind*, New York: Cambridge University Press, pp. 131–57.

Krieken, Robert van (1998), *Norbert Elias*. London: Routledge.

Lawson, Fred H. (2014), 'Syria's Mutating Civil War and its Impact on Turkey, Iraq and Iran', *International Affairs* 90 (6):1351–65, <https://doi.org/10.1111/1468-2346.12173>.

Lebow, Richard Ned (2003), *The Tragic Vision of Politics: Ethics, Interests and Orders*, New York: Cambridge University Press.

Leenders, Reinoud (2012), *Spoils of Truce*, Ithaca: Cornell University Press.

Levi, Margaret (1997), 'A Model, a Method, and a Map: Rational Choice in Comparative and Historical Analysis', in Mark I. Lichbach and Alan S. Zuckerman (eds), *Comparative Politics: Rationality, Culture, and Structure*, Cambridge: Cambridge University Press, pp. 19–41.

Levitt, Matthew (2013), *Hezbollah: The Global Footprint of Lebanon's Party of God*, London: C. Hurst & Co. Publishers Ltd.

Lieberman, Elli (2012), *Reconceptualizing Deterrence: Nudging Toward Rationality in Middle Eastern Rivalries*, 1st edition, Oxford: Routledge.

Long, Theodore E., and Jeffrey K. Hadden (1985), 'A Reconception of Socialization', *Sociological Theory* 3 (1):39–49.

Luckmann, Thomas, and Peter L. Berger (1991), *The Social Construction of Reality: A Treatise in the Sociology of Knowledge*, Harmondsworth: Penguin.

Malm, Sara (2015), 'Israeli Strike on Syrian Golan Heights "Kills Son of Top Military Commander and Five Other Fighters from Lebanese Shiite Militant Groups"', *Mail Online*, 18 January 2015, <http://www.dailymail.co.uk/news/article-2915635/Israel-kills-son-Hezbollahs-late-military-chief-Syria-Hezbollah-sources.html> (last accessed 21 June 2018).

Marx, Karl (1963), *The Eighteenth Brumaire of Louise Bonnaparte*, New York: International Publishers.

McInnes, J. Matthew (2015), 'Iran's Strategic Thinking: Origins and Evolution', Washington, DC: American Enterprise Institute.

McKernan, Bethan (2017), 'Ghouta Chemical Attack: Four Years Later, the World Looks on as Syria's People Continue to be Gassed', *The Independent*, 20 August 2017, <http://www.independent.co.uk/news/world/middle-east/ghouta-chem-

ical-attack-syria-assad-anniversary-no-justice-for-survivors-a7903506.html> (last accessed 21 June 2018).

Mearsheimer, John (2014), *The Tragedy of Great Power Politics*, New York: W. W. Norton & Company.

Mennell, Stephen, and Johan Goudsblom (1997), *The Norbert Elias Reader*, Oxford: John Wiley & Sons.

Mithaq harakat Amal [Amal movement charter] (n.d.), Amal Movement.

Morrison, Kenneth (1995), *Marx, Durkheim, Weber: Formations of Modern Social Thought: Foundations of Modern Social Thought*, 1st edition, London: Sage Publishing Ltd.

Mustafa, Amin (2003), *al-Muqawamah fi Lubnan* [Resistance in Lebanon] *1948–2000*, Beirut: Dar Alhadi.

Nasrallah, Hassan (2006), 'Mawqi' al-muqawamah al-Islamiyyah fi Lubnan: radd al-Sayyid Hassan Nasrallah 'ala risalat al-mujahidin' [Sayyid Hassan Nasrallah's response to the address of the *mujahidin*], <http://www.moqawama.org/essaydetails.php?eid=7814&cid=319> (last accessed 21 June 2018).

Nasrallah, Hassan (2017), 'al-Nass al-kamil li kalimat samahat al-amin al-'amm li Hizb Allah li al-Sayyid Hassan Nasrallah fi al-ihtifal bi dhikra al-sannawiyyah al-ula li al-qa'id al-jihadi al-kabir Hajj Mustafa Badr al-Din (Dhul Fiqar)' [Text of the speech of the Secretary General Sayyid Hassan Nasrallah on the first anniversary of Hajj Mustafa Badr al-Din], Manar TV, 11 May 2017, <http://www.almanar.com.lb/2016166> (last accessed 21 June 2018).

Newman, Andrew (2013), *Twelver Shi'ism: Unity and Diversity in the Life of Islam*, Edinburgh: Edinburgh University Press.

Niebuhr, Reinhold (1952), *The Irony of American History*, Chicago: University of Chicago Press.

Niemi, Richard G., and Mary A. Hepburn (1995), 'The Rebirth of Political Socialization', *Perspectives on Political Science* 24 (1):7–16.

Nofel, Mamdouh (2006), *Magdousheh: The Story of the War against the Refugee Camps in Lebanon*, Ramallah: Muwatin.

Norton, Augustus Richard (1987), *Amal and the Shi'a: Struggle for the Soul of Lebanon*, Austin: University of Texas Press.

Norton, Augustus Richard (2007), 'The Role of Hezbollah in Lebanese Domestic Politics', *The International Spectator* 42 (4):475–91.

Norton, Augustus Richard (2014), *Hezbollah: A Short History:* Princeton: Princeton University Press.

O'Connor, Tom (2017), 'US, Russia and Iran are Battling to Build Bases in Syria as ISIS Falls', *Newsweek*, 18 July 2017, <http://www.newsweek.com/us-russia-iran-battle-isis-build-bases-syria-637998> (last accessed 21 June 2018).

Paipais, Vassilios (2013), 'Necessary Fiction: Realism's Tragic Theology', *International Politics* 50 (6):846–62.

Pakradouni, Karim (2009), *Sadma wa sumud: 'ahd Emil Lahoud, 1998–2007* [Shock and resilience: the Emil Lahoud Tenure, 1998–2007], Beirut: All Prints Distributors & Publishers s.a.l.

Pakradouni, Karim (2015), interview with the author.

Phillips, Christopher (2018), *The Battle for Syria: International Rivalry in the New Middle East*, reprint edition, New Haven: Yale University Press.

Pierson, Paul (2004), *Politics in Time: History, Institutions, and Social Analysis*, Princeton: Princeton University Press.

Posen, Barry R. (1993), 'The Security Dilemma and Ethnic Conflict', *Survival* 35 (1):27–47.

Qassem, Naim (2008a), *Hizb Allah: al-manhaj . . . al-tagrubah . . . al-mustaqbal* [Hezbollah: doctrine, history and the future], Beirut: Dar Alhadi.

Qassem, Naim (2008b), *Mujtama' al-muqawamah: iradat al-shahadah wa sina'at al-intisar* [The Resistance Society: the will of martyrdom and the creation of triumph], Beirut: Dar Al maaref Alhikmiah.

Qassem, Naim (2010a), *al-Mahdi al-Mukhallis* [The Mahdi, the Saviour], 4th edition, Beirut: Dar almahaja al-baidaa.

Qassem, Naim (2010b), *Ashura*, Beirut: Dar almahaja al-baidaa.

Qassir, Qassem (2015), interview with the author.

Qatisha, Webbe (2015), interview with the author.

Qazzi, Fayez (2013), *Hizb Allah: aqni'ah Lubnaniyyah li wilayah Iraniyyah, dirasah watha'iqiyyah* [Hezbollah: Lebanese masks for Iranian guardianship, a documentary study], Beirut: Riad El-Rayyes Books S.A.R.L.

Quinn, Ben (2016), 'Russia's Military Action in Syria – Timeline', *The Guardian*, 14 March 2016, <http://www.theguardian.com/world/2016/mar/14/russias-military-action-in-syria-timeline> (last accessed 21 June 2018).

Rafizadeh, Majid (2016), 'In First, Hezbollah Confirms all Financial Support Comes from Iran', Al Arabiya Network, <https://english.alarabiya.net/en/2016/06/25/In-first-Hezbollah-s-Nasrallah-confirms-all-financial-support-comes-from-Iran.html> (last accessed 30 June 2018).

Raful, Pierre (2015), interview with the author.

Ranstorp, Magnus, and C. B. E. Waite (2003), *Hizb'allah in Lebanon: The Politics of the Western Hostage Crisis*, New York: Palgrave USA.

Reicher, Stephen (2004), 'The Context of Social Identity: Domination, Resistance, and Change', *Political Psychology* 25 (6):921–45.

Reuters (2016), 'US Builds Two Air Bases in Kurdish-Controlled North Syria: Kurdish Report', 6 March 2016, <https://www.reuters.com/article/us-mideast-crisis-syria-usa-base/u-s-builds-two-air-bases-in-kurdish-controlled-north-syria-kurdish-report-idUSKCN0W80R7> (last accessed 21 June 2018).

Reuters (2017), 'Hezbollah Says Future Israel War Could Draw Fighters from Iran, Iraq, Elsewhere', 23 June 2017, <https://www.reuters.com/article/us-mideast-crisis-hezbollah/hezbollah-says-future-war-with-israel-could-draw-fighters-from-across-region-idUSKBN19E1X4> (last accessed 21 June 2018).

Rose, Gregory (1983), 'Velayet-e Faqih and the Recovery of Islamic Identity in the Thought of Ayatollah Khomeini', in Nikki R. Keddie (ed.), *Religion and Politics in Iran: Shi'ism from Quietism to Revolution*, New Haven: Yale University Press, pp. 166–90.

Rotberg, Robert I. (ed.) (2003), *State Failure and State Weakness in a Time of Terror*, Washington, DC: Brookings Institution Press.

Saade, Bashir (2016), *Hizbullah and the Politics of Remembrance: Writing the Lebanese Nation*, Cambridge Middle East Studies, Cambridge: Cambridge University Press.

Saad-Ghorayeb, Amal (2002), *Hizbu'llah: Politics and Religion*, London: Pluto Press.

Sadiki, Larbi (2010), 'Reframing Resistance and Democracy: Narratives from Hamas and Hizbullah', *Democratization* 17 (2):350–76.

Sadiki, Larbi (2011), 'Hezbollah's Hypocritical Resistance', *The New York Times*, 13 December 2011, <http://www.nytimes.com/2011/12/13/opinion/hezbollahs-hypocritical-resistance.html> (last accessed 21 June 2018).

Saffieddine, Hashem (2007), 'Murtakazat fi thaqafat Hizb Allah [Hizbullah's cultural foundations]', in *al-Intisar al-muqawamah: hawiyat al-intisar wa tada'iyyatahu al-istratighiyyah* [The victory of the resistance: the identity of victory and its strategic implications], Beirut: Islamic Centre for Theoretical Studies, pp. 41–62.

Salman, Talal (2015), interview with the author.

Saouli, Adham (2003), 'Lebanon's Hizbullah: The Quest for Survival', *World Affairs* 166 (2):71–80.

Saouli, Adham (2006), 'Stability under Late State Formation: The Case of Lebanon', *Cambridge Review of International Affairs* 19 (4):701–17.

Saouli, Adham (2011), 'Hizbullah in the Civilising Process: Anarchy, Self-Restraint and Violence', *Third World Quarterly* 32 (5):925–42.

Saouli, Adham (2012), *The Arab State: Dilemmas of Late Formation*, London and New York: Routledge.

Saouli, Adham (2013), 'Hizbullah, Hamas, and the Arab Uprisings: Structures, Threats, and Opportunities', *Orient* 54 (2):37–44.

Saouli, Adham (2014a), 'Intellectuals and Political Power in Social Movements: The Parallel Paths of Fadlallah and Hizbullah', *British Journal of Middle Eastern Studies* 41 (1):97–116.

Saouli, Adham (2014b), 'Syria's Predicament: State (de-)Formation and International Rivalries', *Sharaka* (10):1–15, <http://www.iai.it/en/pubblicazioni/syrias-predicament>.

Saouli, Adham (2014c), 'The Foreign Policy of Iraq and Lebanon', in Raymond Hinnebusch and Anoushiravan Ehteshami (eds), *The Foreign Policies of Middle East States*, 2nd edition, Boulder, CO: Lynne Rienner Publihers, pp. 105–32.

Saouli, Adham (2015), 'Performing the Egyptian Revolution: Origins of Collective Restraint Action in the Midan', *Political Studies* 63 (4):730–46.

Saouli, Adham (2016), 'Lebanon's Salafis: Opportunities and Constraints in a Divided Society', in Francesco Cavatorta and Fabio Merone (eds), *Salafism after the Arab Awakening: Contending with People's Power*, London: C. Hurst & Co. Publishers Ltd, pp. 43–60.

Schiff, Ze'ev, and Ehud Ya'ari (1985), *Israel's Lebanon War*, New York: Touchstone.

Schulze, Kirsten E. (2008), *The Arab–Israeli Conflict*, 2nd edition, London: Routledge.

Schwedler, Jillian (2011), 'Can Islamists Become Moderates? Rethinking the Inclusion-Moderation Hypothesis', *World Politics* 63 (2):347–76, <https://doi.org/10.1017/S0043887111000050>.

'Secretary Rice Holds a News Conference' (2006), *Washington Post*, 21 July 2006, <http://www.washingtonpost.com/wp-dyn/content/article/2006/07/21/AR2006072100889.html> (last accessed 21 June 2018).

'Security Council 1701 (2006)' (n.d.), United Nations, <https://www.un.org/press/en/2006/sc8808.doc.htm> (last accessed 23 October 2017).

Shaheen, Kareem (2017), 'Yemen Death Toll Has Reached 10,000, UN Says', *The Guardian*, 16 January 2017, <http://www.theguardian.com/world/2017/jan/16/yemen-war-death-toll-has-reached-10000-un-says> (last accessed 21 June 2018).

Sharara, Wadah (2007), *Dawlat Hizb Allah: Lubnan Mujtama'an Islamiyyan* [The state of Hezbollah: Lebanon as an Islamic society], 5th edition, Beirut: Dar Alnahar.

Siklawi, Rami (2012), 'The Dynamics of the Amal Movement in Lebanon 1975–90', *Arab Studies Quarterly* 34 (1):4–26.

Siklawi, Rami (2014), 'The Social and Political Identities of the Shi'i Community in Lebanon', *Arab Studies Quarterly* 36 (4): 278.

Sinclair, Harriet (2016), 'Arab League Designates Hezbollah as a Terrorist Organisation, Increasing Regional Tensions', *The Independent*, 12 March 2016, <http://www.independent.co.uk/news/world/middle-east/arab-league-designates-hezbollah-as-terrorist-organisation-increasing-regional-tensions-a6927591.html> (last accessed 21 June 2018).

Skocpol, Theda (1984), *Vision and Method in Historical Sociology*, Cambridge: Cambridge University Press.

Slackman, Michael (2009), 'Egypt Accuses Hezbollah of Plotting Attacks and Arms Smuggling to Gaza', *The New York Times*, 13 April 2009, <https://www.nytimes.com/2009/04/14/world/middleeast/14egypt.html> (last accessed 21 June 2018).

Smith, Dennis (1992), *The Rise of Historical Sociology*, Philadelphia: Temple University Press.

Smith, Dennis (2001), *Norbert Elias and Modern Social Theory*, London: Thousand Oaks.

Snow, David A., Sarah A. Saoule, and Hanspeter Kriesi (2004), 'Mapping the Terrain', in David A. Snow, Sarah A. Saoule, and Hanspeter Kriesi (eds), *The Blackwell Companion to Social Movements*, Oxford, Blackwell Publishing, pp. 3–16.

Sullivan, Marisa (2014), 'Hezbollah in Syria', Middle East Security Report 19, Washington, DC: Institute for the Study of War.

'Syria Claims to Have Captured Rebel Stronghold on Lebanese Border' (2014), *The Guardian*, 16 March 2014, <https://www.theguardian.com/world/2014/mar/16/syria-rebel-stronghold-lebanese-border-yabroud> (last accessed 21 June 2018).

Tarrow, Sidney (2012), *Strangers at the Gates: Movements and States in Contentious Politics*, Cambridge: Cambridge University Press.

'Text of Israel-Lebanon Cease-Fire Understanding' (n.d.), Jewish Virtual Library, <http://www.jewishvirtuallibrary.org/text-of-israel-lebanon-cease-fire-understanding> (last accessed 8 June 2017).

Tezcür, Günes Murat (2010), 'The Moderation Theory Revisited: The Case of Islamic Political Actors', *Party Politics* 16 (1):69–88, <https://doi.org/10.1177/1354068809339536>.

Thies, Cameron G. (2012), 'International Socialization Processes vs. Israeli National Role Conceptions: Can Role Theory Integrate IR Theory and Foreign Policy Analysis?', *Foreign Policy Analysis* 8 (1):25–46, <https://doi.org/10.1111/j.1743-8594.2011.00170.x>.

Tilly, Charles (1985), 'War Making and State Making as Organized Crime', in Peter Evans, Dietrich Reuschemeyer, and Theda Skocpol (eds), *Bringing the State Back In*, Cambridge: Cambridge University Press, pp. 169–87.

Tilly, Charles (2006), *Regimes and Repertoires*, Chicago: University of Chicago Press.

Valbjørn, Morten, and André Bank (2012), 'The New Arab Cold War: Rediscovering the Arab Dimension of Middle East Regional Politics', *Review of International Studies* 38 (1):3–24, <https://doi.org/10.1017/S0260210511000283>.

Van Dam, Nikolaos (2011), *The Struggle for Power in Syria: Politics and Society under Asad and the Ba'th Party*, 4th edition, London: I. B. Tauris.

Volpi, Frederic (2010), *Political Islam Observed*, London: C. Hurst & Co. Publishers Ltd.

Walsh, Declan (2006), 'After 34 Days of War, Hizbullah Turns its Attention to Rebuilding Southern Lebanon', *The Guardian*, 17 August 2006, <http://www.theguardian.com/world/2006/aug/17/syria.israelandthepalestinians1> (last accessed 21 June 2018).

Walt, Stephen M. (1990), *Origins of Alliance*, Ithaca: Cornell University Press.

Waltz, Kenneth (1979), *Theory of International Politics*, 1st edition, Long Grove, IL: Waveland Press Inc.

Watt, W. Montgomery (1983), 'The Significance of the Early Stages of Imami Shi'ism', in Nikki R. Keddie (ed.), *Religion and Politics in Iran: Shi'ism from Quietism to Revolution*, New Haven: Yale University Press, pp. 21–32.

Weber, Max (1978), *Economy and Society: An Outline of Interpretive Sociology*, ed. Guenther Roth and Claus Wittich, Berkeley: University of California Press.

Wendt, Alexander (1999), *Social Theory of International Politics*, Cambridge: Cambridge University Press.

Wiegand, Krista E. (2010), *Bombs and Ballots*, Burlington, VT: Ashgate.

Wood, Graeme (2015), 'What ISIS Really Wants', *The Atlantic*, March 2015, <https://www.theatlantic.com/magazine/archive/2015/03/what-isis-really-wants/384980/> (last accessed 21 June 2018).

Worth, Robert F., and Nada Bakri (2008), 'Hezbollah Seizes Swath of Beirut from U.S.-Backed Lebanon Government', *The New York Times*, 10 May 2008, <https://www.nytimes.com/2008/05/10/world/middleeast/10lebanon.html> (last accessed 21 June 2018).

Ynetnews (n.d.), 'Operation Accountability (1993)', <http://www.ynetnews.com/articles/0,7340,L-3284732,00.html> (last accessed 31 May 2017).

Zartman, William I. (ed.) (1995), *Collapsed States: The Disintegration and Restoration of Legitimate Authority*, Boulder, CO: Lynne Rienner Publishers.

Index